Exploring Alaska's
KENAI FJORDS

Culturally modified spruce tree (CMT) at Nuka Island.

Exploring Alaska's
KENAI FJORDS

A Coastal Guide to the
Kenai Peninsula Outer Coast

DAVID WM. MILLER

Wilderness Images
wildernessimage.com

Cover photo: Tree-crowned islet, Harris Bay.

Photographs & Maps © 2017 by David Wm. Miller, unless otherwise credited.

Published by Wilderness Images (wildernessimage.com)

This publication is designed to provide accurate and authoritative information in regard to the subject matter covered. It is sold with the understanding that the publisher is not engaged in rendering professional services. If professional advice or other expert assistance is required, the services of a competent professional person should be sought.

Miller, David Wm.
    Exploring Alaska's Kenai Fjords / by David Wm. Miller
    Bibliography:p.
    Includes index.
    ISBN 978-0-9613954-4-5
        1. Alaska—Kenai Peninsula—Kenai Fjords—Guidebooks. 2. Description and travel—Kenai Peninsula—Alaska—Guidebooks. 3. Outdoor recreation—Boating—Alaska—Guidebooks. I. Title.

Library of Congress control # 2016918615

First Edition: 2004
Second Edition: 2017

Printed in the United States of America.

This book is dedicated to
my beloved wife Anne

To the reader,

Great efforts have been made to make the information in this book as accurate as possible. Over time, however, coastal conditions change, especially along the Kenai Fjords. The material covered in this guide-book should be viewed akin to other local knowledge and be tempered by the situation, weather, sea, and tidal conditions. This book offers tips to assist in trip planning and to provide general background information on the coastal waters from Port Bainbridge to Port Chatham, Alaska. It is intended for the ocean-experienced, small boat and sea kayak operator as a supplement to the U.S. Coast Pilot #9 and NOAA marine charts. The observations, suggestions, or opinions in this book do not supersede recommendations by the U. S. Coast Pilot, NOAA marine charts, or common sense. Activities suggested in the pages of this book have inherent risks and are not applicable in all situations. Small craft operators are responsible for using safe, sound judgment, especially when traveling in and around island passages, exposed bodies of open water, stream mouths, tidal lagoons, glacial moraines and lakes, and in tidewater glacial fjords with drifting ice. Be sure to file a float plan with a friend or harbormaster before your departure.

Ogive Glacier sits at tidewater, Northwestern Fjord.

Contents

PREFACE xi
- How to Use this Book xiii
- Map List xv
- Map Legend xvi

PART 1   INTRODUCTION TO THE KENAI FJORDS 1

CHAPTER 1 TOURING RESURRECTION BAY BY ROAD
- Tourist Information 3
- Kenai Fjords National Park Visitor Center 3
- Exit Glacier 4
- Alaska SeaLife Center 5
- Lowell Point 5
- 4th of July Creek Waterfront Area 6

CHAPTER 2 KENAI FJORDS LAND OWNERSHIP
- Kenai Fjords National Park 9
- Alaska Maritime National Wildlife Refuge Lands 11
- Port Graham Corporation Lands 11
- English Bay Corporation Lands 11
- State of Alaska Lands 11
- Other Private property 13

CHAPTER 3 KEY VESSEL DESTINATIONS
- Resurrection Bay 15
- Heading Eastward 17
- Heading Westward 18

CHAPTER 4 KAYAK DESTINATIONS
- Resurrection Bay..25
- Day Harbor..27
- Kenai Fjords National Park 29
- Kachemak Bay State Park............................30
- Glacial Basins and Tidewater Glaciers 30
- Tidal Lagoons and Glacial Lakes................32

CHAPTER 5 WILDLIFE IN THE FJORDS
- Marine Birds..35
- Marine Mammals..36
- Vessel Guidelines for Viewing Marine Mammals........38
- Land Mammals.. 43
- Bear Tips for Campers and Hikers 45

PART II   HISTORY OF THE KENAI FJORDS....................49
CHAPTER 6 BIRTH OF THE FJORDS
- Origin of the Kenai Peninsula.......................51
- Sculpting the Kenai Fjords...........................52
- The Fjord Environment.................................54
- Habitats and Plant Communities.................56
- Wind in the Fjords 57

CHAPTER 7 THE SUGPIAQ PEOPLE
- Early Dwellers of the Kenai Fjords 59
- Culturally Modified Trees 61
- Disease and Social Change........................62

CHAPTER 8 RUSSIAN FUR TRADERS
- A Foreign Invasion 65
- Alexander Baranov.......................................67
- James Shields and the Building the *Phoenix* 69

CHAPTER 9 CHARTING THE FJORDS
- Early Marine Surveys 73
- Notable Maritime Disasters on the North Gulf Coast...76

PART III   MARINE GUIDE TO THE KENAI FJORDS.......79
CHAPTER 10 RESURRECTION BAY
- Overview 81
- Lowell Point to Aialik Cape..........................83
- Fourth of July Creek Area to Cape Resurrection 96
- Resurrection Bay Islands 103

SECTION 1 EASTWARD FROM RESURRECTION BAY...........111

CHAPTER 11 DAY HARBOR
- Cape Resurrection to Fault Point 113

CHAPTER 12 CHUGACH COAST
- Fault Point to Cape Puget 127

CHAPTER 13 PORT BAINBRIDGE
- Cape Puget to Elrington Point.................................. 139

SECTION 2 WESTWARD FROM RESURRECTION BAY...........151

CHAPTER 14 AIALIK BAY
- Aialik Cape to Aligo Point....................................... 153

CHAPTER 15 CHISWELL AND HARBOR ISLANDS
- Circumnavigating the Islands................................... 175

CHAPTER 16 HARRIS BAY
- Aligo Point to Surok Point 181

CHAPTER 17 NORTHWESTERN FJORD
- Northwest Passage to Northwestern Glacier 193

CHAPTER 18 MCCARTY PENINSULA
- Surok Point to Harrington Point 205

CHAPTER 19 PYE ISLANDS
- Exploring Ragged, Rabbit, and Outer Islands 219

CHAPTER 20 NUKA BAY
- Harrington Point to Yalik Point 227

CHAPTER 21 NUKA ISLAND AND NUKA PASSAGE
- Islet Basin to Tonsina Bay 239

CHAPTER 22 PORT DICK
- Gore Point to Qikutulig Bay.....................................255

CHAPTER 23 ROCKY BAY AND PORT CHATHAM
- Rocky Bay to Port Chatham 263

APPENDICES
- Birds of the Kenai Peninsula 274
- Marine Mammals of the Kenai Fjords.......................278
- Selected Plants of the Kenai Fjords 279

BIBLIOGRAPHY...285

PHOTO LIST...289

INDEX 293

North Point of Taz Basin, Granite Island.

Preface

Though mostly uninhabited, the 800 nautical mile long Kenai Fjords seacoast enjoys the reputation of being one of Alaska's premier tourist attractions. Its magnificent natural setting, abundant marine life, calving tidewater glaciers, world-class fishing, and stunning tourist destinations, such as the Kenai Fjords National Park and Chiswell Islands, meld with an oceanic mystique to forge an unforgettable maritime adventure.

An essential part of the Kenai Fjords' appeal is the ambiance created by its powerful seascapes, most notably the Eldorado Narrows, Harding Gateway, Aialik Peninsula, Granite Island, Thunder Bay, and the Pye and Chugach islands. Another striking feature, Northwestern Fjord is among the finest and most spectacular example of raw, glacial landscapes on the Kenai Peninsula. The Kenai Fjords further boast an extensive collection of majestic bays, coves, and rarely visited beaches.

For most of the last century, hundreds of miles of pristine shoreline remained a mystery to all but a few local seal hunters, prospectors, commercial fishers, and a handful of charter vessels that poked their noses into the region. Today, with the help of seaworthy boats and kayaks, in addition to a growing tourist infrastructure, these out-of-reach places are being rediscovered.

Public attention to the Kenai Fjords began growing when the newly designated Kenai Fjords National Park (1980) aroused curiosity from local

Natoa Island in the Harbor Island group.

Alaskans. However, not until the disastrous *Exxon Valdez* oil spill (1989) and its extensive response and clean-up activities did public attention focus on the region. Since then, significant amounts of historical, archaeological, geological, and biological research has been shedding new light on the area. As the Kenai Fjords slowly gives up its secrets, dramatic physical transformations continue to occur daily.

Change characterizes an ongoing theme, as glaciers continue their dramatic retreat, which began more than a century ago. This deglaciation process annually reveals new portions of seacoast never before seen. Presently, the Harding and Sargent icefields cover more than 2,000 square miles of the Kenai Peninsula. Approximately 57 glaciers including nine tidewater glaciers flow from these massive icefields.

For visitors, accessing the Kenai Fjords has never been easier. In the past, the outer coast was extremely challenging and expensive to visit, especially if you did not own a boat, kayak, or plane. Today, the roadless and remote wilderness areas of the Kenai Fjords offer a rare maritime adventure, as witnessed by tens of thousands of summer visitors that depart on wildlife tour vessels and return with vivid tales of marine mammal encounters, and a profound awareness of the region's awesome physical beauty. A raft of commercial outfitters, wildlife viewing vessels, water taxis, charter fishing boats, and kayak rental services have dramatically improved accessibility into the fjords for people with diverse interests and abilities.

Granite headwall at Abra Cove, Aialik Bay.

How to use this book

Part I comprises five introductory chapters with a selection of special maritime destinations for recreational boaters and kayakers. These destinations outline the most popular locations along the Kenai Fjords seacoast. A contributing chapter highlights the more abundant species of wildlife.

Part II looks at the history of the Kenai Fjords beginning with the physical forces shaping the region. It also introduces the indigenous Sugpiaq, early dwellers on this seacoast, and Russian fur traders and explorers who charted the coast and recorded their observations.

Part III includes thirteen chapters with a series of regional maps and tips to aid recreational boaters and touring kayakers. The maps in the book provide a quick overview of different coastal regions. Do not depend on the maps in this book for navigation, they are only intended for clarifying the text. In Seward, authorized NOAA map distributors include the Alaska Natural History Association, inside the Kenai Fjords National Park Visitor Center. Visit NOAA online for free electronic chart downloads.

Five NOAA charts cover the area described in this guide book:

- *#16702 Latouche Passage to Whale Bay* (includes Port Bainbridge)
- *#16683 Point Elrington to Cape Resurrection*
- *#16682 Cape Resurrection to Two Arm Bay*
- *#16681 Seal Rocks to Gore Point*
- *#16645 Gore Point to Anchor Point*

Besides a NOAA tide and tidal current table, another essential item for mariners to have on board is the *U. S. Coast Pilot #9, Cape Spencer to Beaufort Sea*. If you intend to explore the backcountry, I recommend a satellite phone and the appropriate topographical or GPS maps.

All references to compass directions in this book are based on true north. All water depth descriptions are fathoms, measured from a 0.0 foot tide or "mean lower low water," which is consistent with marine charts and tide tables. Distances over water, from point to point, are described in nautical miles (nm) or yards. Land distances are conveyed in statute miles and feet. Land height (rocks, islands, islets) is measured in feet above mean high water. The term 'spring tide' refers to the tide having the greatest rise and fall, occurring when the sun, moon, and earth are aligned. Neap tides are smaller tides, associated with quarter moons.

Flexible trip planning is essential. An isolated seacoast like the Kenai Fjords presents a host of logistic and weather related issues. Rigid time scheduling may be impossible to follow safely. There are no refueling stations or general stores on the Kenai Fjords coast, except in Seward.

Recreational boating and sea kayaking along the Kenai Fjords coast carries inherent risks and is primarily a summer activity. The most favorable ocean conditions typically occur between June and August. Rough sea conditions may interrupt small vessel activities for a week or longer, even in summer. During the months of October through March, persistent storms, rough seas, and freezing temperatures may prevail for extended periods of time preventing any small vessel travel.

This book is not intended to be an instructional manual on vessel or kayak seamanship. If you have any doubts about your abilities, you should consult a professional guiding service. It is presumed all vessel and kayak operators have rough water (ocean) experience and their crafts are seaworthy and comply with all State of Alaska and Coast Guard regulations before venturing into the fjords.

If you would like additional information about the Kenai Fjords coast, I recommend two excellent reference books: *A Stern and Rock-Bound Coast* by Linda Cook and Frank Norris, and *U.S. Coast Pilot # 9*. Another valuable marine reference which addresses nautical issues not discussed here is *Cruising Guide to Prince William Sound* by Jim and Nancy Lethcoe. The resources listed in the bibliography at the end of the book also may be helpful. If you wish to peruse a fine collection of books, magazines articles, and historical photo material on the Kenai Peninsula visit the Alaska Room of the Loussac Library in Anchorage, Alaska, and the Rasmuson Library on the campus of the University of Alaska, in Fairbanks.

Map List

- Map Legend XVI
- Major Embayments & Icefields XVIII
- Seward Area 2
- Kenai Fjords Ownership Lands... 8
- State Recreation Areas & Marine Parks 12
- Kenai Fjords Regional Map Overview 78
- Resurrection Bay...80
  - Upper Western Shore 86
  - Lower Eastern Shore 100
- Heading Eastward from Resurrection Bay 110
- Day Harbor 112
  - Bootleg Cove 118
  - Head of Day Harbor... 121
- Chugach Coast...126
  - Puget Bay 135
- Port Bainbridge 138
  - Upper Port Bainbridge 143
  - Eastern Elrington Island 148
- Heading Westward from Resurrection Bay...................................150
- Aialik Bay...152
  - Aialik Glacial Basin 159
  - Lower Western Shore 169
- Chiswell and Harbor Islands 174
- Harris Bay 180
  - Taz Basin 183
- Northwestern Fjord 192
  - Northwestern Passage 195
- McCarty Peninsula...204
  - Two Arm Bay 206
  - Thunder Bay and Black Bay 209
  - Lower McCarty Fjord 214
- Pye Islands 218
- Nuka Bay...226
  - Palisade Lagoon 231
  - Beauty Bay and Shelter Cove 234
- Nuka Island and Nuka Passage 238
  - Pete's Cove 244
  - Mike's and Berger Bay 248
  - Tonsina Bay 251
- Port Dick...254
  - Eastern Shore, Port Dick..257
- Rocky Bay and Port Chatham 262
  - Rocky Bay 265
  - Port Chatham 270

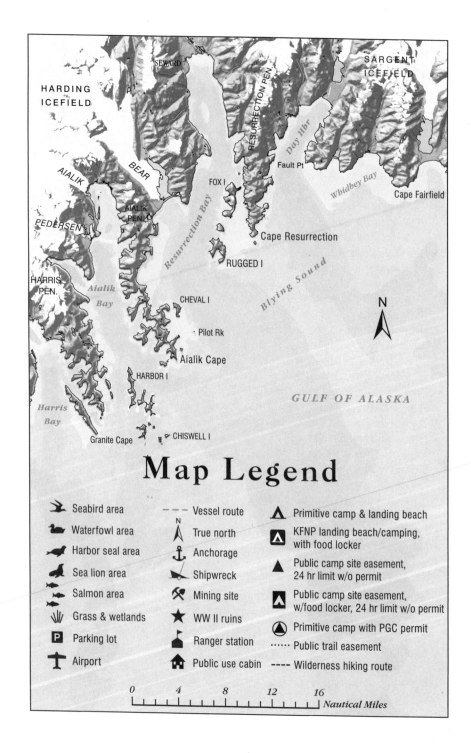

HARDING
ICEFIELD

SEWARD

RESURRECTION PEN.

SARGENT
ICEFIELD

Day Hbr

AIALIK

BEAR

Fault Pt

FOX I

Whidbey Bay

Cape Fairfield

PEDERSEN

AIALIK
PEN.

Resurrection Bay

Cape Resurrection

HARRIS
PEN.

Aialik
Bay

RUGGED I

Blying Sound

CHEVAL I

Pilot Rk

N

Aialik Cape

HARBOR I

GULF OF ALASKA

Harris
Bay

Granite Cape

CHISWELL I

Map Legend

Seabird area	--- Vessel route	Primitive camp & landing beach
Waterfowl area	True north	KFNP landing beach/camping, with food locker
Harbor seal area	Anchorage	Public camp site easement, 24 hr limit w/o permit
Sea lion area	Shipwreck	
Salmon area	Mining site	Public camp site easement, w/food locker, 24 hr limit w/o permit
Grass & wetlands	WW II ruins	Primitive camp with PGC permit
Parking lot	Ranger station	...... Public trail easement
Airport	Public use cabin	---- Wilderness hiking route

0   4   8   12   16
                              Nautical Miles

ACKNOWLEDGMENTS

I would especially like to thank the people who contributed their time and effort to improving this project. First, my wife Anne who is a wonderful sounding board, teacher, and critic. She dragged me through the rough parts, and unselfishly kept the household together during my extended forays on the coast. Anne, a marine biologist, also added some of her 40 years of local knowledge to the pages of this book, especially with Chapter 5 "Wildlife" and Chapter 6 "Birth of the Fjords". Only with her steadfast assistance did this project persevere. I also thank my sons Sean and Phelan for their participation and dedicated beachcombing abilities. A special thanks go to my editors Ami Wright and Sandy Wassilie for their skillful editing and insightful comments. Two important individuals Doug Capra and Jim Pfeiffenberger, from the Kenai Fjords National Park in Seward, worked overtime to enlighten me on historical material, natural resources, and land ownership issues within the Park. My gratitude further extends to Judy Kessler, Linda Cook, and Frank Norris from the National Park Service in Anchorage. They contributed their expertise and shared valuable resource material on the Kenai Fjords. A big thank you goes to Patricia Linville and Pam Hermann at the Seward public library for their assistance in reconnecting me to the library's wonderful Alaska book collection.

The marine material in this guidebook is the result of collecting bits and pieces of information, from repeated coastal excursions in a variety of weather conditions. It has been greatly influenced and illuminated by the people who work, play, and live along the Kenai Peninsula's outer coast including commercial and sport fishers, charter boat operators, deckhands, park rangers, sea kayakers, marine biologists, loggers, geologists, bush pilots, seal hunters, and homesteaders. A hardy thanks goes to my adventurous crew mates David Firth and Gary Graham who sometimes volunteered to spend extended periods of time on the coast when they could have stayed home, warm and dry. I'd also like to thank the following people who kindly shared a little of their outer coast knowledge, either through friendly conversations, their writings, or by relating personal accounts of their past and present activities: Harold Hardin, Keith Knighten, Martin Goresen, Austin Post, Fred Woelkers, Dean Kasischke, Aron Crowell, Clem Tillion, Marion Beck, Alan and Betty Manass, Jack Sinclair, Paul and Lynda Paquette, Dan and Marie Bair, Bob Linville, Matt Gray, Louis Garding, the Carvahlo brothers, Richard and Sue Schmidt, Katya Wessels, Ray and Tom Tressler, Steve and Mike Miller, Jon Andrews, Bonnie Herbold, Chrysanna Miller, John Davidson, Jack Pine, Thomas English, Jerry Theros, Gary Mingus and many others.

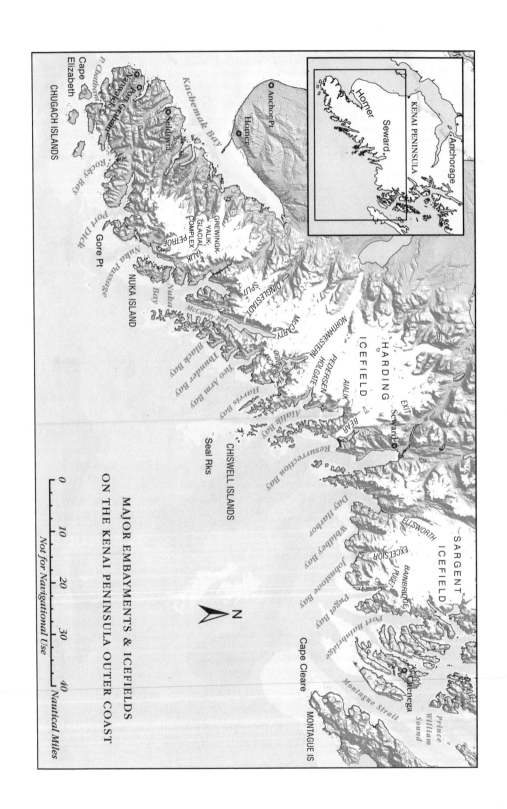

MAJOR EMBAYMENTS & ICEFIELDS
ON THE KENAI PENINSULA OUTER COAST

Not for Navigational Use

0   10   20   30   40
Nautical Miles

N

CHUGACH ISLANDS

Cape
Elizabeth

P. Chatham

Port Graham

Seldovia

Kachemak Bay

Anchor Pt

Homer

Homer

KENAI PENINSULA

Seward

Anchorage

Rocky Bay

Port Dick

Gore Pt

Nuka Passage

NUKA ISLAND

Nuka Bay

GREWINGK-
YALIK
GLACIAL
COMPLEX

PETROF

YALIK

Black Bay

Thunder Bay

Two Arm Bay

Harris Bay

McCarty Fjd

SPLIT

DINGLESTADT

McCARTY

NORTHWESTERN

PEDERSEN

HOLGATE

AIALIK

BEAR

Aialik Bay

Seal Rks

CHISWELL ISLANDS

Resurrection Bay

HARDING
ICEFIELD

EXIT

Seward

Day Harbor

Whidbey Bay

Johnstone Bay

Puget Bay

Port Bainbridge

ELLSWORTH

EXCELSIOR

PUGET

BAINBRIDGE

SARGENT
ICEFIELD

Cape Cleare

Chenega

Montague Strait

Prince
William
Sound

MONTAGUE IS

Part I

Introduction
to the
Kenai Fjords

Outwash beach at the head of Aialik Bay.

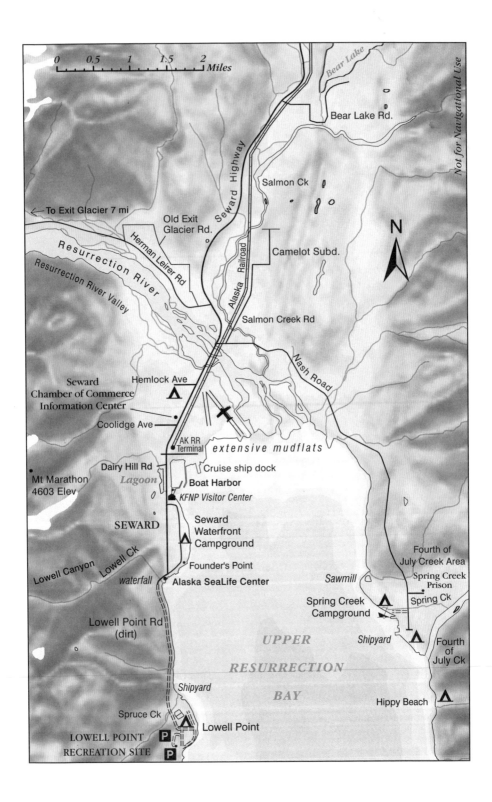

0   0.5   1   1.5   2   Miles

Bear Lake

Bear Lake Rd.

Salmon Ck

Seward Highway

← To Exit Glacier 7 mi

Old Exit Glacier Rd.

Herman Leirer Rd

Resurrection River

Resurrection River Valley

Camelot Subd.

Alaska Railroad

Salmon Creek Rd

N

Nash Road

Hemlock Ave

Seward
Chamber of Commerce
Information Center

Coolidge Ave

AK RR
Terminal

extensive mudflats

Dairy Hill Rd

Cruise ship dock

Lagoon

Boat Harbor

KFNP Visitor Center

Mt Marathon
4603 Elev

SEWARD

Seward
Waterfront
Campground

Lowell Canyon

Lowell Ck

Founder's Point

waterfall

Alaska SeaLife Center

Sawmill

Fourth of
July Creek Area

Spring Creek
Prison

Spring Ck

Spring Creek
Campground

Lowell Point Rd
(dirt)

Shipyard

UPPER

RESURRECTION

Fourth
of
July Ck

BAY

Shipyard

Spruce Ck

LOWELL POINT
RECREATION SITE

Lowell Point

Hippy Beach

P

P

1

Touring Resurrection Bay by Road

• TOURIST INFORMATION • KENAI FJORDS NATIONAL PARK VISITOR CENTER • EXIT GLACIER • ALASKA SEALIFE CENTER • LOWELL POINT • FOURTH OF JULY CREEK AREA

Seward, a picturesque town of 2,700 people has all the necessary amenities to whisk you comfortably and efficiently into the Kenai Fjords. Visitors may quickly find that negotiating the summer traffic around the Seward boat harbor is the most unnerving part of the adventure. The first challenge for curious visitors is to gather helpful information.

TOURIST INFORMATION

The Seward Chamber of Commerce (www.sewardak.org) is located on the Seward Highway, one-half mile north of the small boat harbor. I recommend that new visitors to Seward make the Chamber of Commerce building their first stop. The City of Seward takes tourism seriously and the Chamber of Commerce has knowledgeable people to help you sift through the reams of brochures that are continuously updated with information on lodging, camping areas, charter fishing services, wildlife cruises, car, kayak, and boat rentals, city maps, and everything else concerning tourism around Resurrection Bay.

THE KENAI FJORDS NATIONAL PARK VISITOR CENTER

The Kenai Fjords National Park (www.nps.gov/kefj) Visitor Center sits adjacent to the Seward Harbormaster building next to the boat harbor on Fourth Avenue. The visitor center offers wildlife exhibits, books, maps,

3

Resurrection River Valley and Exit Glacier.

and other publications, as well as film and slideshow presentations on local history, natural history, and the marine environment.

The only portion of the Kenai Fjords National Park accessible to visitors by road is the Exit Glacier area.

Exit Glacier

Exit Glacier lies 13 miles northwest of Seward. The glacier spills from the 5,000 foot high ramparts of the Harding Icefield onto the Resurrection River Valley floor. This land-based glacier is the only glacier in the Kenai Fjords National Park that is approachable by road. The Herman Leirer Road turnoff is located at mile 3.7 of the Seward Highway. The fully paved road follows along Resurrection River's eastern flank. The scenic 9-mile-long road has several parking areas with foot access to the river and its expansive gravel streambed. At the entrance to the Kenai Fjords National Park, a bridge crosses the Resurrection River and enters a staging area where the Park Service has established a ranger station, parking lot, restrooms, and a nature center. No fee is charged to visitors entering the park. A tent camping area is located one-quarter mile before the parking area at the end of the road.

Today, Exit Glacier continues its steady retreat from the Resurrection River Valley floor. Wooden signposts located along the road notify visitors where the glacier's terminus rested during the past two centuries.

Exit Glacier's name describes its convenient location for descending from the Harding Icefield. The National Park Service maintains a variety of wildlife and flora displays, an interpretive shelter, and a series of connected trails that loop around the recently deglaciated terrain and the silt-clouded creek flowing from the glacier's base. A paved, wheelchair-accessible path begins at the parking lot and reaches to within one-quarter mile of the ice terminus.

Serious hikers should consult a park ranger before tackling the strenuous 8.2-mile round-trip of the Harding Icefield Trail. The trail parallels the glacier's rocky northern flank. Be sure and pack plenty of water and check the bulletin board located near the parking lot for current trail and weather conditions. Daily wildlife observations and bear reports also are posted. In places, the Icefield Trail is steeply sloped with patches of crumbling rock. Hikers frequently see black bears and mountain goats. At the trail's end, near the 3,500 foot elevation, tired hikers are rewarded with a commanding view of the Harding Icefield and Resurrection River Valley. During periods of heavy rain, park rangers may close the Icefield Trail.

THE ALASKA SEALIFE CENTER

The Alaska SeaLife Center (www.alaskasealife.org) is located along the waterfront of downtown Seward, at milepost 0 of the Seward Highway. Established after the *Exxon Valdez* oil spill, it is dedicated to generating and sharing scientific knowledge to promote understanding and stewardship of Alaska's marine ecosystems. The SeaLife Center has a variety of marine mammals, seabirds, and fish displayed in underwater viewing habitats that reflect marine life along the Kenai Fjords coast and elsewhere in Alaska. The visitor center also offers behind-the-scene tours of ongoing research and wildlife rehabilitation activities.

LOWELL POINT

Lowell Point, two miles south of Seward, is well-equipped to serve visitors. Lowell Point Road is unpaved and usually bumpy. The Eads brothers first bulldozed a rough road along the steep shoreline between Seward and Lowell Point in 1961, and, believe it or not, the road has considerably improved over the years.

Lowell Point Road begins west of the Alaska SeaLife Center and follows the rocky shoreline to Lowell Point Recreation Site, where motorists will find vehicle parking, picnic sites, and restrooms.

Camping facilities with waterfront RV parking is located at Miller's Landing. The landing operates a small country store, water-taxi service, and boat and kayak rentals. The Millers are knowledgeable folks and pass

Kayak launch and retrieval beach at the south end of Lowell Point Road.

along helpful information. Also scattered around the waterfront are bed and breakfast and cabin rentals. An unpaved road loops around Lowell Point, making it impossible to get lost.

The southern shore of Lowell Point is an important staging area for launching kayaks for a paddle to Tonsina Point and the Caines Head State Recreation Area. Adjacent to the public beach is a day-use parking area with toilet facilities. The Alaska State Parks maintains the beach area and does not permit camping or boat trailers in the Lowell Point State Recreation Site. Tent and RV camping is available at Miller's Landing and the Silver Derby Campground and RV Park. Hikers and kayakers also may camp at Tonsina Point. The Caines Head Shoreline Trailhead is located in the upper parking lot of the Lowell Point Recreation Site. (See Chapter 10 Resurrection Bay for more details on the Caines Head Shoreline Trail).

FOURTH OF JULY CREEK WATERFRONT

Across the bay, the Fourth of July Creek outwash plain lies along the eastern shore of Resurrection Bay. The area provides an escape from the dense tourist activity near town. To reach the Fourth of July area by vehicle, take the Seward Highway north. After crossing the Resurrection River bridges, take the first right turn onto Nash Road. Follow the road for five miles to the Fourth of July Marine Industrial Park. Along the route, several overlook areas invite outstanding views of Resurrection Bay and Seward.

Spring Creek Waterfront, Fourth of July area.

Spring Creek descends onto the Fourth of July alluvial plain and enters Resurrection Bay north of the harbor and cannery. The City of Seward operates the Spring Creek Campground. RV camping lies adjacent the beachfront or at the parking area behind the waterfront. Campers with tents can set up base camp along the bank of the waterfront lagoon. Portable toilets sit near the bulletin board. An unimproved boat launch area (four-wheel drive advised) is located on the beach. The Spring Creek beachfront is among the best kayak launching spots on Resurrection Bay's eastern shore.

In July and August, salmon anglers will find the fishing action here fast and furious. Pink and silver salmon are the staple. At times, observers will see dozens of boats circling like gulls as they troll along the waterfront. Groups of beach anglers often line up along the shore and flog the water with snagging hooks and lures.

On the south side of the Fourth of July's industrial park at the end of Nash Road, rests one of Alaska's largest shipyard facilities. The City of Seward also operates a travel boat lift and provides acres of dry dock storage for large commercial vessels. Spring Creek Maximum Security Prison lies hidden up the valley away from the waterfront. Prison guard towers loom above a thick forest of spruce, alder and cottonwood trees.

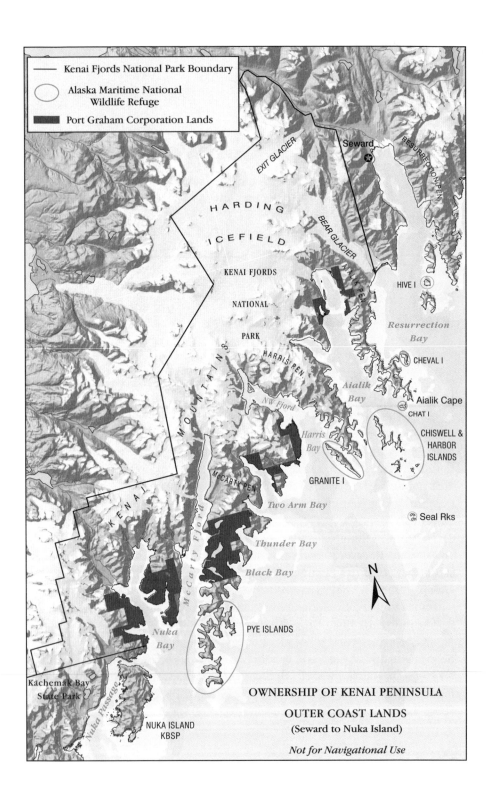

EXIT GLACIER

Seward

RESURRECTION PEN.

HARDING

ICEFIELD

BEAR GLACIER

AIALIK PEN.

KENAI FJORDS

HIVE I

NATIONAL

Resurrection
Bay

PARK

HARRIS PEN.

CHEVAL I

M O U N T A I N S

Aialik
Bay

NW Fjord

Aialik Cape

CHAT I

Harris
Bay

CHISWELL &
HARBOR
ISLANDS

McCARTY PEN.

GRANITE I

K E N A I

Two Arm Bay

Seal Rks

Thunder Bay

McCarty Fjord

Black Bay

N

Nuka
Bay

PYE ISLANDS

Kachemak Bay
State Park

OWNERSHIP OF KENAI PENINSULA

Nuka Passage

OUTER COAST LANDS

NUKA ISLAND
KBSP

(Seward to Nuka Island)

Not for Navigational Use

2

Kenai Fjords Land Ownership

A SUMMARY OF PUBLIC AND PRIVATE LANDS

The Kenai Fjords shoreline from Port Bainbridge to Port Chatham ranges from bold capes and glaciated valleys to deep fjords and cobble beaches. Hidden within this rugged seascape of mountains and glaciers are a wealth of remarkable places. Many of these wild scenic destinations lie on public lands within the Kenai Fjords National Park, Alaska Maritime National Wildlife Refuge, Chugach National Forest, Kachemak Bay State Park and State Wilderness Park, and five State of Alaska Marine Parks. Substantial lands are held privately, especially by Alaska Native Corporations. In the Kenai Fjords, and elsewhere, the Alaska Native Claims Settlement Act (ANCSA) provides for 17(b) easements (often unmarked) that reserve rights to the United States in the form of designated roads, trails and one-acre, short-term use, sites that enable the public to cross private property in order to reach public lands and major waterways.

KENAI FJORDS NATIONAL PARK

The Kenai Fjords National Park (KFNP) comprises a major portion of the Kenai Fjords seacoast southwest from Resurrection Bay. The KFNP encompasses more than half of the 50-mile-long by 20-mile-wide Harding Icefield, which blankets large segments of the eastern slope of the Kenai Mountains. The Harding Icefield contributes more than 38 glaciers that

Sea arch one-half mile south of McMullen Cove in Aialik Bay.

spill into the mainland fjords and valleys of the Kenai Peninsula. The park also includes a segment of the Grewingk-Yalik Glacier Complex located west of Nuka Bay.

The park's shoreline boundary begins at the southern end of the Bear Glacier moraine in lower Resurrection Bay and, after many twists and turns, ends south of Yalik Point in Nuka Bay. The 601,839 acre national park includes the main glacial fjords of Aialik Bay, Harris Bay and Northwestern Fjord, Two Arm Bay, McCarty Fjord, and the West and North arms of Nuka Bay. All these areas can be accessed only by aircraft, boat or kayak.

Presently, KFNP public use cabins available for summer use are located in upper Aialik Bay and Holgate Arm. Cabin stays are limited to three days. In winter, a public use cabin is also available at Exit Glacier. A fee is required for cabin use, and reservations should be made in advance.

Boaters and kayakers can contact rangers on VHF marine channel 16. Bear-proof metal food lockers (highly recommended) are at the more popular camping sites in Aialik Bay and Northwestern Fjord. Fires are allowed on the beach below the high tide line. Pack out what you pack in.

Visitors to the park should remember that it is against the law to disturb or remove Native Alaskan artifacts. If you discover an artifact, you should leave it in place, write down a description of the location or the GPS position and report the find to a park ranger.

ALASKA MARITIME NATIONAL WILDLIFE REFUGE LANDS

Nearly all of the islands, sea stacks, and rock spires located along the Kenai Peninsula outer coast are part of the Alaska Maritime National Wildlife Refuge (AMNWR). Included in the AMNWR are the Chiswell, Harbor, and Pye island groups and also, Granite, Hive, Cheval, and Chat islands. You do not need a permit to camp on AMNWR lands, but you must avoid disturbing any wildlife. Presently, the Alaska SeaLife Center has a video monitoring system used for studying Steller sea lion activity in lower Resurrection Bay, on Chiswell Island, and on other islands in the area.

PORT GRAHAM CORPORATION LANDS

The Port Graham Corporation (PGC) is an Alaska Native corporation that owns the surface rights to large tracts of land within the Kenai Fjords National Park boundary. The PGC also has land holdings outside the KFNP on the southern end of the Kenai Peninsula at Rocky and Windy bays and the Chugach Islands. Shareholders of the PGC have permission to access PGC lands. Non-shareholders and visitors can only access PGC land using ANCSA 17(b) public trail and campsite easements or by obtaining a special use permit issued by the corporation. The public easements have a 24-hour limit and have been established at Pedersen Lagoon, Paguna Arm, Delight and Desire lakes, Surprise and Yalik bays, and other areas. The PGC also owns a cabin in the Delight Creek area.

Public trail easements are 25 feet wide and follow along stream banks, traditional trails, and roads. They are unmarked in most areas. To check on current access policies, talk with the National Park Service in Seward. To directly contact the PGC, call (907) 284-2212. They can answer questions concerning use permits for camping on PGC lands.

ENGLISH BAY CORPORATION LANDS

The English Bay Corporation (EBC) owns large tracts of land on the lower Kenai Peninsula, especially around Port Chatham, Koyuktolik Bay, and Nanwalek. Contact the corporation, (907) 281-2328 regarding permits and access policies.

STATE OF ALASKA LANDS

The State of Alaska owns large tracts of land eastward from Resurrection Bay to Puget Bay. The state also owns lands southwest of the Kenai Fjords National Park. These lands include the Kachemak Bay State Park (KBSP) and Kachemak Bay State Wilderness Park (KBSWP). The KBSP encompasses Nuka Island and upper Nuka Passage, while the KBSWP includes the Tonsina Bay, Gore Point, and Port Dick areas.

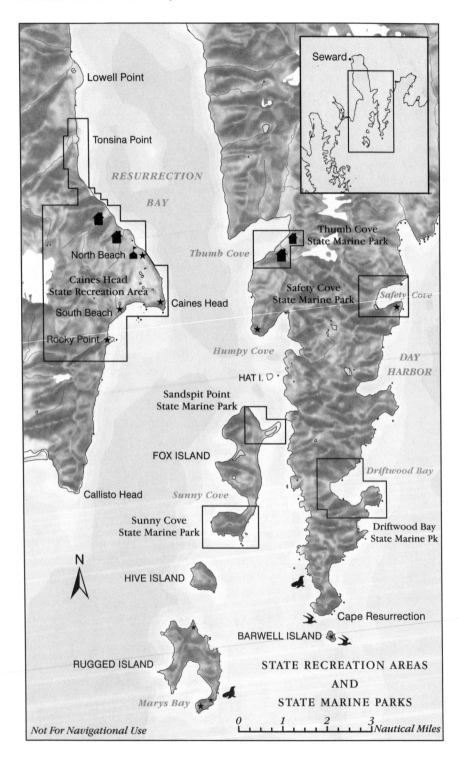

Seward

Lowell Point

Tonsina Point

RESURRECTION

BAY

North Beach

Caines Head
State Recreation Area

South Beach

Rocky Point

Thumb Cove

Thumb Cove
State Marine Park

Safety Cove
State Marine Park

Safety Cove

Caines Head

Humpy Cove

HAT I.

DAY

HARBOR

Sandspit Point
State Marine Park

FOX ISLAND

Driftwood Bay

Callisto Head

Sunny Cove

Sunny Cove
State Marine Park

Driftwood Bay
State Marine Pk

N

HIVE ISLAND

Cape Resurrection

BARWELL ISLAND

RUGGED ISLAND

STATE RECREATION AREAS

AND

STATE MARINE PARKS

Marys Bay

Not For Navigational Use

0   1   2   3
Nautical Miles

In addition to upland holdings, the State of Alaska owns coastal waters from three miles offshore to mean high water. State lands include tidal shores (below mean high water) of the Kenai Peninsula outer coast that abut uplands owned by the Kenai Fjords National Park, Alaska Native Corporations, Chugach National Forest, Alaska Maritime National Wildlife Refuge, and private landowners. No permit is required for short-term (less than two weeks), non-commercial activities including landing, beachcombing, or camping on State lands. There are exceptions. For specific information concerning allowed activities on State lands, contact the State of Alaska Department of Natural Resources.

The State of Alaska designated five State Marine Parks (SMP) in Resurrection Bay and Day Harbor. In Resurrection Bay they include Thumb Cove SMP, Sandspit Point SMP, and Sunny Cove SMP; in Day Harbor they include Driftwood Bay SMP and Safety Cove SMP. These parks are only accessible by boat, kayak, or aircraft. Each marine park has a beach area where camping is permitted. Pack out what you pack in. Toilet facilities do not exist and human waste must be buried away from streams and trails. Fires are permitted on the beach below the high-water mark. Respect private property. Many of the State Marine Parks lie adjacent to private property. There are no vessel moorings in any of the marine parks, except North Beach at Caines Head State Recreation Area and not all SMP locations are a suitable anchorage in foul weather.

The Caines Head State Recreation Area (CHSRA) sits atop the Caines Head bluff in lower Resurrection Bay. Here, the Army constructed Fort McGilvray to defend the Port of Seward during World War II. Caines Head SRA is only accessible by boat or foot (by hiking the shoreline trail beginning at the Lowell Point Recreation Site parking lot). Public use cabins are maintained at Callisto Canyon and Derby Cove. Two additional public use cabins are located on the eastern shore of lower Resurrection Bay in Thumb Cove SMP (Porcupine Glacier and Spruce Glacier cabins). For State public use cabin information call (907) 262-5581.

OTHER PRIVATE PROPERTY

Parcels of privately-owned waterfront property are primarily, but not exclusively, located in Seward and along the eastern shore of lower Resurrection Bay, Fox Island, the eastern shore of Day Harbor, Horsehead Bay, Whidbey Bay, Johnstone Bay, and the western side of Puget Bay. (The eastern shore of Puget Bay and Port Bainbridge is Chugach National Forest).

Immediately south of the Kenai Fjords National Park, on the mainland shore of Nuka Passage at Petrof Lake, is a large block of privately-owned parcels. On the Kenai Fjords seacoast, most privately-owned cabins are recreational.

Ogive Glacier with Striation Island (foreground) in Northwestern Fjord.

3

Key Vessel Destinations

SPECIAL BOATING DESTINATIONS IN THE KENAI FJORDS

RESURRECTION BAY

Thumb Cove State Marine Park is among the most scenic attractions in Resurrection Bay. The base of the cove's headwall is littered with piles of rubble and boulders from three melting glacial cirques. Scores of avalanche chutes furrow the cliffs, and dozens of waterfalls erupt during rainy weather. Thumb Cove is the best all-purpose anchorage of the five State Marine Parks located in Resurrection Bay and Day Harbor.

Eldorado Narrows is a 4.5 nm long water passage dividing the Resurrection Peninsula mainland from Fox and Hive islands. The spectacular passage is a regular stop for Resurrection Bay sightseeing tours and kayakers. The Eldorado Narrows begins at Sandspit Point, which protrudes from the northeast shore of Fox Island. The passage runs southward to the tip of Cape Resurrection.

Remarkable pillow basalt formations create the southern portion of the Resurrection Peninsula. These rounded bubbles of pillow lava also provide important habitat for scores of sea lions and nesting seabirds. At water level it is easy to be mesmerized by the vertical grandeur seen along Eldorado Narrows. The top sightseeing stops are Waterfall Bight, Sea Lion Rocks, Emerald Cove, and Cape Resurrection.

Bear Glacier, a part of the Kenai Fjords National Park, dominates the western shore of the Harding Gateway. The glacier reigns as the longest ice

15

Salmon trolling for kings in front of Bear Glacier.

tongue in the Kenai Fjords National Park. A glacial lake occupies the valley floor adjacent to the ice terminus. From the deck of an offshore vessel, visitors often can see the tops of icebergs floating in the lake.

Resurrection Bay Islands consist of the five islands seen at the mouth of Resurrection Bay. North to south, they include: Hat, Fox, Hive, Barwell, and Rugged islands. Fox Island is the most frequently visited island in the group. Camping and sightseeing are available at Sandspit Point SMP and Sunny Cove SMP. In 1918, the famous artist Rockwell Kent spent a winter living with his son on a fur farm in Halibut Cove. Today, a lodge and several private recreation cabins lie along the waterfront of both Sunny and Halibut coves. On Fox Island's southern tip stands a collection of giant sea caves, rock pinnacles, and sea cliffs comprised of layers of siltstone.

Most visitors will agree that Rugged Island is appropriately named. Along the island's steep, eastern shore is a collection of wave-washed sea cliffs, pinnacle rocks, and protruding rock ledges. Groups of sea lions use some of these rock ledges as haulout locations. In Mary's Bay, in the southeast corner, rests the remnants of a World War II dock. On the hillside, partially hidden in the dense undergrowth, lies evidence of a road and a steel-railed tramway that once hauled supplies to the soldiers who manned the bunkers, barracks, and observation stations atop the island's ridgeline. Another pair of cement observation bunkers and a powerhouse stand out on the rocky sea cliffs above Carol Cove on Rugged Island's north shore.

Harding Gateway occupies the lower western portion of Resurrection Bay and lies exposed to the Gulf of Alaska. The mainland shore from Callisto Head to Aialik Cape is among the most rugged sections of seacoast in the region. It also exhibits the finest collection of rock spires along the coast. Good examples may be seen at Bear Glacier Point, Pillar Point, Adz Rock, and Pony Point.

Cape Resurrection is a bold 1,430-foot-high headland at the southern tip of Resurrection Peninsula. The Gulf of Alaska swell and salty sea air generate an oceanic flavor near the cape. On any given summer day, 30,000 marine birds may gather on the steep sea cliffs of Cape Resurrection and Barwell Island. Black-legged kittiwakes nest along the steep cliffs. Smaller numbers of common murres, pigeon guillemots, cormorants, tufted and horned puffins occupy nests and burrows in rocky crevices and sea caves. At times, hundreds of kittiwakes, in unison, swoop down from their rocky perches, glide across the water's surface, and quickly reassemble on their nests. Not to be missed are the large floating seabird rafts comprised of hundreds of black and white murres that congest the passage between Cape Resurrection and Barwell Island. On a calm day, stop the boat engine and listen to the loud, relentless squawking from the thousands of kittiwakes perched on the vertical cliffs.

The passage between Cape Resurrection and Barwell Island is an excellent area for marine mammal observations. Frequent visits by pods of gray, humpback, and orca whales begin in spring and continue through fall. Groups of sea lions remain in lower Resurrection Bay during the winter and build in numbers in spring when schools of herring enter the bay.

HEADING EASTWARD

Driftwood Bay SMP in Day Harbor is similar in grandeur to Thumb Cove but with a pronounced ocean flair. Driftwood Bay is a physical place, strongly influenced by the Gulf of Alaska. Although Driftwood Bay is a State Marine Park, it is not always a secure anchorage, especially in easterly winds. Rugged mountains and sea cliffs comprised of basalt dikes ring the bay. In heavy rains, the towering cliffs awaken with dozens of waterfalls. At the southern entrance rests Davidson Point, a precipitous headland wiped clean by storm waves. A narrow band of colorful lichen clings to the wave-washed rocky shore a few feet above the algae-stained, high-water mark. Along Driftwood Bay's exposed northern shore rests a series of steeply sloped, jagged sea cliffs measuring more than 2,800 feet high. Beneath these ragged cliffs lie a handful of tall crumbling rock pinnacles and several sea caves, along with an impressive 100-foot-tall waterfall tucked in a vertical crevice. Its vapor plume radiates a rainbow in morning light.

Puget Bay lies 23 nm east of Cape Resurrection. The bay hosts a pair of anchorages in Goat Harbor and Kid Cove. At the bay's head rest Puget Glacier and a roaring glacial stream. Excellent halibut and silver salmon fishing surround Cape Puget and Cape Junken.

Port Bainbridge is situated at the western entrance to Prince William Sound, a 45 nm boat trip from Seward. Breathtaking Bainbridge Glacier dominates the western shore and sets the tone for this mountainous region. At Hogg Bay, mariners will find a secure anchorage with a handful of inviting beaches and hospitable camping areas. At Puffin Cove, a small boat basin at the head of Port Bainbridge, visitors will discover challenging hiking terrain in a wild, secluded setting.

HEADING WESTWARD

Chiswell and Harbor Islands (AMNWR) reside at the mouth of Aialik Bay, 30 nm south of Seward. The Chiswell Islands combine an assortment of tree-crowned islets and inaccessible sea stacks into a marine wildlife spectacle. The Chiswell Islands are remnants of mountain peaks, now slowly subsiding into the sea. These remarkable islands create an ideal habitat for thousands of marine birds that return each summer to nest. The Chiswell Islands maintain the largest concentration of marine birds found on the Kenai Peninsula. During an abundant year, approximately 75,000 marine birds and more than 200 sea lions gather on these offshore islands.

Holgate Arm is a long, narrow indentation located midway up the western shore of Aialik Bay. At the head of the arm towers Holgate Glacier, the single most visited tidewater glacier in the Kenai Fjords National Park. As for ice-calving, Holgate Glacier delivers the goods. Most sightseeing vessels entering Aialik Bay steer directly for either Holgate Arm or more northerly Aialik Glacier. A public use cabin sits along the arm's north shore.

Aialik Glacial Basin, approximately 40 nm by boat from Seward, includes all the water north of the moraine bar that crosses Aialik Bay between Pedersen Lagoon and Coleman Bay. Aialik Glacier dominates the raw landscape on the basin's western shore. The Harding Icefield stands out above the glacier. Slate and Squab islands rest near Aialik Glacier and hosts small marine bird colonies. Glacial ice drifting in the basin is home to one of the largest gathering of harbor seals in the Kenai Fjords. Abra Cove, a small indentation along the basin's east shore, is lined by a spectacular 1,000-foot-high granite headwall. A series of waterfalls (Abra Falls) have deposited colorful mineral stains on the wall's granite surface. Also growing on the wall are a variety of lichens and bright green algae. At the base of the headwall rests a rock-strewn, tidal spit protruding from the cove's northeast shore. The spit is easily explored by foot during lower stages of the tide.

Bear Glacier Point area, Harding Gateway.

Pedersen Glacier and Lagoon lie on the western shore of Aialik Bay adjacent to the submerged moraine bar abandoned by both Aialik and Pedersen glaciers as they retreated. Pedersen Lagoon and its spacious wetland area is rich with shorebirds and marine life. Sockeye salmon enter Pedersen Lagoon in June and July and spawn in Addison Lake at the north end of the lagoon. Large numbers of harbor seals migrate in and out of the lagoon and glacial lake, spring through autumn. The Pedersen Glacier Lake is often filled with drifting icebergs that serve as resting platforms for hundreds of harbor seals.

Granite Passage knives between the vertical shore of Granite Island and the cove-riddled shoreline of Harris Peninsula. This 4.5 nm long passage regularly attracts pods of humpback and killer whales, in addition to sea otters. The sheltered waters of Granite Passage are a major thoroughfare for vessel traffic heading into or departing the icy waters of Northwestern Fjord.

Taz Basin (AMNWR) occupies a tiny granite alcove on the western shore of Granite Island. Towering cliffs surround the basin, which during rainy weather cuts loose with countless cascading waterfalls. At the north entrance point stands an inviting rock peninsula with terrific hiking terrain, beautifully textured granite outcroppings, and water-carved spillways. Taz Basin is among the most idyllic small boat anchorages on Alaska's North Gulf Coast.

Taz Basin, Granite Island.

Cataract Cove is a steep-walled, circular basin near the eastern head of Harris Bay. A melting glacial cirque sits high atop the 1,000-foot-tall headwall and supplies a stream of meltwater down the wall's vertical face. Nearly hidden in the east corner of the headwall is a grotto recessed into the granite wall. A pair of cascading waterfalls tumbles into the basin. The grotto is a regular stop on the itinerary of many tour vessels. Small boats can nose their bow into the grotto to capture a closer look at the waterfalls.

Northwestern Fjord may be the single-most spectacular glacial enclave on the Kenai Peninsula. It is a prime destination for adventurous mariners, independent kayakers, and organized paddle tours. A handful of charter vessels and water taxis visit this fjord daily — as weather permits. Northwestern Fjord is a glacial paradise. The enclave is filled with valley glaciers, towering cirques, hanging valleys, and three tidewater glaciers. The recent retreat of many Northwestern Fjord glaciers has uncovered miles of polished and scoured granite walls that were covered by thick ice less than a century ago.

Two Arm Bay comprises two independent fjords: Paguna and Taroka Arms. This large, secluded bay tucked between Surok Point and Cloudy Cape rests approximately 48 nm by boat from Seward. Recreational boaters seldom visit the area. Both arms of the bay have unique and worthwhile characteristics including secluded lagoons and miles of reliable beaches on which to land a dinghy or to hike and camp.

Thunder Bay remains a wild and isolated location situated 50 nm southwest of Seward. The bay gushes with a half dozen powerful waterfalls. At the south entrance point rest the 2,000-foot-high Black Mountain and a series of towering sea cliffs. The steep shoreline leads into a dogleg-shaped indention that provides secure anchorage in most weather. One of the bay's most impressive physical features lies high above the water in the bay's northwest corner. Here, a massive waterfall, fed by an alpine lake, freefalls over a vertical rock cliff. Along the Thunder Bay shoreline, a sprinkling of rarely visited pocket beaches stands ready for the curious beachcomber.

Pye Islands (AMNWR) are a trio of heavily wooded cone-shaped islands at the mouth of Nuka Bay. A beautiful cream-colored granite shoreline with contrasting green hillsides decorates this spectacular island group. The Pye Islands — Ragged, Rabbit and Outer islands — are remnants of nearly submerged mountains. Their shorelines form a continuous series of intricate coves and bays. Separating the three islands are narrow but navigable water passages. The largest sea lion rookery in the Kenai Fjords occupies the southern shore of Outer Island. The National Marine Fisheries Service has designated the Pye Islands a critical habitat area due to the diminished sea lion population in the Gulf of Alaska. Both Outer and Rabbit islands remain temporarily closed to camping, fishing, and boating. The three-mile closure zone does not include Ragged Island or prevent vessel traffic in Wildcat or McArthur pass.

Sailing vessel, Northwestern Fjord.

McCarty Fjord is the longest glacial fjord (more than 20 nm long) on the Kenai Fjords coast. McCarty Glacier terminates at the head of the fjord. Areas to visit include Midnight Cove, Delight and Desire lakes, and the James Lagoon area. A shallow moraine bar, where McCarty Glacier terminated in the mid-1800s, crosses McCarty Fjord between McCarty and James lagoons.

Nuka Bay occupies a multi-armed fjord complex. The bay is one of the most hospitable fjords on the outer coast. Favorite destinations in Nuka Bay include Surprise, Quartz, and Yalik bays, in addition to Shelter Cove, Beauty Bay, and the Nuka River area. Nuka Bay radiates with gold mining history left over from the prospecting and glory years of the 1920s and 30s. Nuka Bay also exhibits miles of secluded beaches, beautiful tree-laced islands, and wilderness terrain to hike, camp, and explore. The Yalik Bay anchorage is 65 nm by boat from Seward.

Nuka Passage, approximately 12 nm long, stretches from the north end of Nuka Island southward to Front Point. Yalik and Petrof glaciers stand out on the mainland shore of the passage. A series of conspicuous sand and gravel beaches punctuate the passage's mainland shore, most notably Yalik Glacier moraine, Petrof Point, and the crescent-shaped barrier beach forming Petrof Bight. Also tucked along the mainland shore is Tonsina Bay, a jewel of a harbor and the last secure anchorage before rounding Gore Point. Tonsina Bay provides diverse terrain including wooded islands and islets, a hidden tidal lagoon, and scores of treasure-filled beaches standing ready for inspection.

Nuka Island is the largest island along the Kenai Fjords coast. It is part of the Kachemak Bay State Park. The island, 70 nm by boat from Seward, emanates its own wilderness mystique. Just the thought of Nuka Island conjures visions of soaring bald eagles, wary harbor seals, and blue foxes. Herring Pete and Josephine Sather operated a fur farm along the island's western shore from 1921 to 1961. The Sathers were local legends during the Nuka Bay mining era. The tattered remains of their cabin and fox feeding sheds still stand out along the island's shoreline. Dozens of wooded islets and hundreds of rocks litter the island's picturesque, cove-riddled shore.

Gore Peninsula protrudes into the Gulf of Alaska from the southeastern end of the Kenai Peninsula. The long, tall, and narrow peninsula forms a perfect hook-shaped catch basin. Isthmus Beach is the focal point and graveyard for tons of flotsam aimlessly drifting on the Alaska Coastal Current. All this, and more, gives Isthmus Beach the well-deserved reputation as the premier beachcombing destination on the Kenai Peninsula.

Anchorage, Thunder Bay.

Port Dick is a large multi-arm bay west of Gore Peninsula. This secluded bay includes a semi-protected access to beachcombing opportunities by hiking across the one-quarter-mile-wide Gore Peninsula isthmus to the exposed east side beach. Port Dick has many anchorages including Takoma Cove and the head of Taylor Bay. Large rafts of furry sea otters feed along the clam-infested tidal flats scattered throughout the coves and bays of Port Dick.

Rocky Bay lies tucked into the rock-riddled mainland of the southern Kenai Peninsula. At the bay's head rests Picnic Harbor, where mariners can find secure anchorage. Nearby the lower Rocky River delta is navigable by kayak or inflatable at higher stages of the tide, weather permitting.

Port Chatham is nestled into the mainland shore at the top of Chugach Passage. The rusted remains of cannery equipment lie scattered along the tidal lands surrounding the former townsite of Portlock, now abandoned. Port Chatham's strategic location makes it a popular vessel destination. Productive bottom fishing locations in lower Cook Inlet and the Barren Islands lie nearby.

Upper Northwestern Fjord.

4

Kayak Destinations

SPECIAL KAYAKING AND CAMPING DESTINATIONS

Large portions of the Kenai Fjords lie fully exposed to the wrath of the Gulf of Alaska. Crossing large bodies of open water presents considerable risks, even to an experienced sea kayaker, and should only be done with extreme caution and sound judgment (weather permitting). A calm sea may change into breaking waves when a tidal current collides with an opposing wind. Afternoon day breezes and katabatic winds (see Chapter 5, Wind in the Fjords) are common phenomena on the Kenai Fjords seacoast. For planning purposes, kayakers should consider following the shoreline as well as utilizing a water taxi to access sheltered waters where paddling is more enjoyable. Remember, a 10–15 knot sea breeze has the potential to turn a peaceful kayak adventure into an exhaustive ordeal, especially for an inexperienced, or out-of-condition paddler. Be sure to carry extra provisions and survival equipment, and leave a float plan with a responsible person.

RESURRECTION BAY

Lowell Point is the main kayak staging area on the western shore of Resurrection Bay. The launch and retrieval beach lies on the south side of Lowell Point at the end of the road. Nearby, a state maintained parking lot sits adjacent to the public access beach. Check the VHF weather forecast before launching. A predictable southerly bay breeze usually begins by late morning. Several reliable landing beaches lie along the 5.5 nm long paddle route to North Beach at the Caines Head Recreation Area.

Tonsina Point, situated just 1.5 miles south of Lowell Point is a quick escape for kayakers. Tonsina Point can also be accessed by water taxi or by simply hiking the Caines Head Shoreline Trail, which begins at the Lowell Point Recreation Area parking lot. Tonsina Point is a quiet camping and picnic location off the beaten path, far from the crowds and commotion in Seward. Pitch a tent along the beachfront or in the woods. A pit toilet sits near the trail close to the first wooden foot bridge.

Caines Head State Recreation Area has evolved into a popular kayak and camping destination. North Beach is the target landing spot. A trail from North Beach climbs to the top of Caines Head, where visitors can hike along the bluff among the remnants of army gun emplacements and cement fortifications at Fort McGilvray. The Caines Head Shoreline Trail has links to an alpine nature trail and forks into another trail that descends to South Beach. At North Beach is an Alaska State Park ranger station, picnic and camping shelters, an outhouse, and a bulletin board. Arrange tents and kayaks along the top of the beach berm.

Spring Creek at the Fourth of July industrial area, across the bay from Seward, is a staging area and kayak launch site for a paddle excursion along the eastern shore of Resurrection Bay. Thumb Cove SMP is a 5.5 nm long paddle trip from the Spring Creek beachfront. A few cobble landing beaches exist along the way. On the south end of the marine industrial area, south of the shipyard, is another beach area, closed to motor vehicles and near the mouth of Fourth of July Creek. This beach offers a secluded camping area.

Thumb Cove State Marine Park rests along the steep, wooded eastern shore of Resurrection Bay. Don't let the cove's proximity to civilization (7.5 nm from Seward's boat harbor) discourage you from visiting. Thumb Cove is an impressive place. The cove's 4,000-foot-high ridgeline displays scores of avalanche chutes and rock slides. Three glacial cirques dominate the cove's steep headwall. Kayakers and landlubbers will find excellent beachfront camping along the cove's southern shore, which falls within the State Marine Park. Rugged hikes are available throughout the area, especially up Likes Creek and the shoreline around the cove's head. Expect to see a flotilla of sailing craft, touring kayaks, and small inflatable boats on holidays and weekends.

Sandspit Point State Marine Park lies 10.5 nm south of Seward. The conspicuous sandspit stands out along the northeast shore of Fox Island. Its northern shore is an ideal water taxi drop-off location, camping spot, and reliable kayak haulout beach, except in strong northerly winds. The spit measures one-half-mile-long and is mainly visited by kayakers and drop-off campers. Check out the lagoon that occupies the middle of the spit where a ghost forest encircles the lagoon's perimeter.

Kayaker Cove is a funnel-shaped recess carved into Resurrection Peninsula. The cove sits across from the Fox Island Sandspit. Kayaker Cove enjoys a westerly exposure and is surrounded by a towering ridgeline. At the cove's head is a cobble beach cleaned up to permit easy kayak landings. Behind the beach berm are private land holding as well as several rustic wooden buildings belonging to an outfitter who provides valuable local information, cabin space, tent sites, and kayak rentals.

Eldorado Narrows begins at Sandspit Point

Sandspit Point (State Marine Park) on Fox Island.

and runs 4.5 nm alongside Resurrection Peninsula to Cape Resurrection. Along the narrows are traditional sea lion haulout areas and dozens of intricate nooks and crannies that paddlers can leisurely explore. No dependable kayak landing beaches exist in the Eldorado Narrows. Note the ocean swell and water movement increase the further one paddles southward toward Cape Resurrection.

DAY HARBOR

Driftwood Bay State Marine Park is the first bay encountered after rounding Cape Resurrection into Day Harbor. The barrier beach at the bay's head reveals piles of driftwood and an assortment of Pacific Rim flotsam. A log pond lies behind the berm. In summer, beach landings are possible when the swell off the gulf is light. Easterly weather significantly influences sea conditions in the bay. A series of vertical sea cliffs run for miles along the bay's north shore, all the way to Killer Bay and Safety Cove. A close examination of the sea cliffs reveals a scattering of sea caves, rock pinnacles, tree-crowned islets, and waterfalls, which make for exciting sea kayaking, weather permitting. Camping is best at the head of Driftwood Bay.

Aialik Glacial Basin at the head of Aialik Bay.

Safety Cove State Marine Park has a reliable landing area at the cove's head. A small alpine lake occupies the valley floor. Driftwood piles litter the 300-yard-long cobble beach. Safety Cove is camper friendly with several cleared camping areas located in the woods behind the beach berm. At the south end of the beach are the ruins of an Army supply building.

Bootleg Cove is a tiny, partially protected cove on the western shore of Day Harbor accessible during mid- to high-tide. Bootleg Cove sports a soft, sandy beach at the head, which is perfect for landing a kayak or small landing craft. Adjacent to the cove is Bootleg Lagoon, which is a very secluded area visited by waterfowl, black bears, river otters, and a late summer run of chum salmon.

The Head of Day Harbor occupies a lowland area filled with alder and spruce groves along with rye grass and wetlands. Ellsworth Valley sits behind the beach moraine abandoned by Ellsworth Glacier. The harbor's head lies relatively protected from the gulf swell, but the moraine beach is difficult to access when the swell is moderate or when a southerly day breeze is blowing.

The beachfront provides generous camping space. Ellsworth Glacier rests about four miles from tidewater. A glacial lake sits at the base of the glacier's ice terminus. Icebergs float and lie grounded along the shore. A stroll along the glacier stream on the valley's west side leads to the glacial lake.

KENAI FJORDS NATIONAL PARK

Bear Glacier dominates the western shore of the Harding Gateway at the mouth of Resurrection Bay. A powerful glacial stream on the northern end of the Bear Glacier moraine leads to a large glacial lake encumbered by huge floating and grounded icebergs. Bear Glacier Lake is one of the premier kayak attractions on the Kenai outer coast. The lake is accessible only by air or boat. A few local kayak outfitters work the Bear Glacier area, and they will arrange travel to the lake. Unfavorable weather and adverse tidal conditions can delay scheduled service. Independent mariners should note that the stream mouth is shallow and obstructed with sand bars and can be extremely dangerous. *Do not enter without local knowledge.*

Aialik Glacial Basin, Pedersen Lagoon, and Holgate Arm provide ideal kayaking among thundering tidewater glaciers, turquoise icebergs, and hundreds of harbor seals that ride atop calved ice floating in the icy waters. Abra Cove's north shore and the entire northeastern shore of Aialik Glacial Basin exhibit miles of accessible beaches and wetlands. Camp spots and reliable landing beaches litter the basin's shoreline.

The Pedersen Glacier and Lagoon area is wild and secluded and offers a glimpse of many species of waterfowl and shorebirds. Wary harbor seals colonize the ice floating in the glacier lake at the base of Pedersen Glacier. Kayakers typically reach the lake by paddling up the glacial stream located on the lagoon's western shore.

Non-campers who wish to enjoy the beautiful Pederson Lagoon area have the option to stay at a well-equipped lodge with a series of satellite cottages planted along the lagoon's waterfront. Contact the Kenai Fjords Glacier Lodge for reservations. The lodge provides vessel transportation to and from Seward as well as guided hiking and kayaking tours to Pedersen Glacier Lake and around Aialik Glacial Basin.

Northwestern Fjord stands out as the top kayak destination for tour groups and independent paddlers visiting the tidewater glaciers of the Kenai Fjords. Kayakers can choose from a host of camping sites and pocket beaches scattered around the glacial basin. The Harding Icefield stands atop Northwestern Fjord. Glaciers surround the basin on three sides. Eight major glaciers and three tidewater glaciers spill down from the icefield into the fjord. Several hundred harbor seals spend the summer in the fjord's upper arm. Sea otters gather in the clam-infested waters around the moraine bar and Otter Cove.

McCarty Fjord encompasses a 20 nm long steep-walled shoreline connecting a series of alder and willow covered outwash deltas, beaches, and tidal lagoons. The outwash beaches in front of James and McCarty lagoons are good base camp areas. A pair of outwash deltas around Delight and

Desire lakes provide expansive terrain to explore. Both lakes are spawning areas for a summer run of red salmon. A score of excellent landing beaches lies scattered throughout the area.

Nuka Bay comprises a remote region of partially sheltered water perfectly suited for kayak and small boat exploration. Within Nuka Bay, the indentations of Surprise and Beauty bays reveal signs of their gold mining history that began in the 1920s.

The Nuka River delta attracts large migrating flocks of waterfowl and shorebirds. In the North Arm gushes incredible Kvasnikoff Falls, a 900-foot-high cataract.

KACHEMAK BAY STATE PARK

Nuka Island and Nuka Passage are perhaps the most idyllic kayaking spots in the Kenai Fjords. The sheltered waters of Nuka Passage and the meandering western shore of Nuka Island display miles of secluded islets and alluring beaches. Groups of harbor seals haul out on the rocky tidal ledges surrounding the island. Islet Basin, Home Cove, Mike's Bay, and Berger Bay are only a few of the wonderful destinations worth getting to know.

GLACIAL BASINS AND TIDEWATER GLACIERS

Glacial basins are wonderful places to visit. Tidewater glaciers emit a barrage of sounds ranging from booming artillery to a sharp crack of a rifle. These sounds can be unexpected and jarring, especially in front of a steep tidal face where the amphitheater effect is focused. These earthy noises are harmless but emphasize the powerful physical forces taking place.

Dangers abound in glacial basins such as Aialik, Holgate, Northwestern and McCarty fjords. Beware of glacier waves generated by calved ice. Waves are produced when sections of calved ice displace water in front of the glacier's tidal face. For example, Aialik Glacier's ice face is capable of creating waves more than 20 feet high. Squab Island rests only one mile from Aialik's tidal face. At times, waves have been known to sweep over the island's north and south rocky shelfs and wash high on the island's shore. Glacier waves also influence portions of the basin's northern shore, especially the low-lying beaches and mud shoals that wrap around the basin's head. On an average day, Aialik Glacier dumps approximately 70,000 tons of ice into the basin. During periods of active calving, waves repeatedly wash the shoreline. Deep water is relatively safe. Shallow water and low-lying beaches are riskier areas to access as glacier waves break when they approach shoals and shallow water before surging onto the beaches. Kayaks and dinghies should be hauled to high ground to avoid being washed away.

West shore of Nuka Island.

Also, special care must be taken when landing or exiting beaches within the influence of glacier waves. Never anchor a boat in shallow water or close to the beach. All watercraft should avoid going any closer than one-quarter mile from any tidewater glacier.

When calving ice creates glacier waves, the floating ice in front of the glacier is set in motion by the water's movement. A kayak or small boat can easily capsize or be crushed in an iceberg sandwich. It may also be tempting to hike around on some of the barn-sized bergs, but beware! Floating pieces of ice can, without warning and very quickly, flip upside down or split into fragments.

In the Kenai Fjords most floating ice is classified as brash ice and growlers, although bergy bits and icebergs may be encountered. In cold weather hard crusted surface ice found in the glacial basins is dangerous and damaging to boat hulls.

- Brash Ice — An accumulation of floating ice fragments
  < six feet in diameter.
- Growler — Blue or Greenish in color and > six feet in
  diameter and < three feet above water.
- Bergy Bit — A cabin size piece of floating ice, showing three to
  five feet above water.
- Iceberg — A large piece of floating ice showing >15 ft above water.

Tour vessel, Holgate Glacier.

TIDAL LAGOONS AND GLACIAL LAKES

Tidal lagoons exist in nearly all the fjords along the Kenai Peninsula outer coast. They are wonderful places to watch wildlife and waterfowl. Harbor seals often congregate at the entrance channel to lagoons. Bald eagles, river otters, harlequin, goldeneye, and merganser ducks inhabit most tidal lagoon areas. In late summer the lagoons often fill with salmon, which also attract hungry bears.

In winter, the channel entrances leading into many tidal lagoons become obstructed by gravel and sand washed up during storms, especially on extreme tides. By late winter, tidal lagoons freeze over and become sealed off from the sea. In spring, the increasing water pressure from meltwater entering the lagoon eventually breaches the gravel obstructing the entrance channel and creates a new channel. Each year channel entrances may change.

Caution must be taken whenever entering or exiting a tidal lagoon with a kayak or skiff, especially when the entrance channel lies exposed to the wind and wave action, particularly during spring tides. Tidal velocity in the entrance channel can be accentuated by the stage of the tide, a narrow or obstructed channel, and a rapid drop in elevation, all of which can make it easy to lose control of a kayak or skiff. A strong tidal current in a channel also can sweep over rocks or slam into a grounded iceberg. Beware never enter or depart a lagoon channel entrance without first checking if the passage is safe. If necessary, wait for slack high water and calm sea conditions before proceeding.

During a flood tide, the water level in a tidal lagoon often sits lower than the actual water level at the channel entrance. Entering the channel on a fast moving flood current can be like riding a river down through rapids without knowing what is awaiting at the end. Slack high water is the best time, and often the only time to safely enter or leave a tidal lagoon. At times, a layover period of 6 to 12 hours may be prudent. Exiting a tidal lagoon channel by riding the ebb current, even only one hour after the tide change can be dangerous. Waves, perhaps breaking, can completely obstruct an entrance channel during the ebb tide. When paddling with a fast moving current, always travel cautiously. Closely watch the route in front for bottlenecks, submerged rocks, and rapid changes in elevation.

Glacier lakes with icebergs exist in front of Bear, Pedersen, Ellsworth, Excelsior, and Petrof glaciers. Pedersen Glacier is unique among the other fjords because Pedersen Lagoon lies between the glacier lake and tidewater. Both floating and grounded brash ice may partially obstruct the glacier stream, which is unnavigable by kayak at low water.

The tide table may only give an approximation as to the actual time of tidal change at a lagoon. For example, high tide in Pedersen Glacier Lake is 30 minutes to one hour after the Pedersen Lagoon entrance channel begins to ebb. Low water in Pedersen Lagoon also can lag more than one hour from the tide table estimate.

Harbor seal perched atop drifting ice.

5

Wildlife in the Fjords

MARINE BIRDS AND MAMMALS

The large seabird concentrations along the Kenai Peninsula outer coast play a major role in the overall marine experience. Between Resurrection Bay and Point Adam, an estimated 200,000 marine birds of 30 species nest annually on the islands and capes during the summer months. Also, an estimated two to five million birds, mostly waterfowl, and shorebirds, migrate along the Kenai Peninsula. Seabirds begin arriving on the outer coast in April. By late June and early July, hatching is in full swing and adult birds gather in large feeding aggregations, collecting fish for the young. Most fledglings appear in August and soon depart to winter farther south or in offshore waters.

The Kenai Peninsula's largest seabird nesting concentration lies 30 nm southwest of Seward in the Chiswell Islands, part of the Alaska Maritime National Wildlife Refuge. More than 75,000 marine birds of 16 species, including 40,000 tufted puffins mingle on these offshore sea stacks.

On calm summer evenings, commotion in the refuge grows to a fever-pitch, as tens of thousands of puffins swirl above Beehive Island and its sister island. Likewise, Matushka Bight on the west side of Matushka Island often overflows with flocks of rhinoceros auklets, parakeet auklets, and horned puffins. A pair of resident bald eagles and a handful of black oystercatchers sound the alarm to the local wildlife whenever intruders come near. A careful observer may also spy a peregrine falcon lurking along the craggy shoreline.

Kittiwake family at Cape Resurrection.

At Cape Resurrection, only 15 nm from Seward, is the second largest and undoubtedly among the noisiest concentration of breeding seabirds on the Kenai Fjords coast. Here, more than 10,000 screaming black-legged kittiwakes nest on steep, volcanic sea cliffs. Only one-half mile to the south, on 400-foot-tall Barwell Island, an estimated 10,000 common murres occupy the rocky sea cliffs. Barwell Island's murre rookery reigns as the largest murre colony in the Gulf of Alaska east of the Barren Islands.

Other large marine bird colonies occupy the Pye Island group, where 13 species of seabirds nest. The densest concentrations gather along the southern and eastern slopes of Outer and Ragged Islands.

Marine Mammals

Visitors venturing into the Kenai Fjords will quickly discover that marine mammals may appear at any time or place. More than 12 marine mammal species inhabit or pass through the area during the spring and summer months. Most commonly observed are the Steller sea lions, harbor seals, and sea otters that reside in the shoreline areas and offshore islands. Dall's and harbor porpoises frequently roam the outer coast, as well as pods of humpback and killer whales. Other less commonly seen marine mammals include gray, fin, and minke whales. Rarely, Pacific white-sided dolphins, elephant seals, California sea lions, and even walrus have made excursions along the Kenai Fjords.

Steller Sea Lions

Steller sea lions are the largest member of the family of Otariidae, or "eared seals" in Alaska. Sea lions differ from harbor seals in that sea lions have external ears and rear flippers which turn forward, allowing them to "walk" on their hind flippers. Underwater, Steller sea lions, gracefully 'fly' with their long, broad foreflippers.

At birth Steller sea lions weigh about 50 pounds. At eleven years, adult males grow to an average weight of 1,250 pounds while adult females, at six years of age, weigh 600 pounds.

Males establish their territories on rookeries in late May. Females arrive at the

Sea lions strike a pose in the Chiswell Islands.

rookery a few days before giving birth, anytime from mid-May through July, and breed with the territorial males a few days after giving birth. Young born the previous year may or may not accompany their pregnant mother. Once the pup is born, the mother cares for the pup and weans any previously born young. Occasionally, however, the mother may care for both or even abandon the new pup for the older offspring.

The Chiswell and Pye islands contain the largest Steller sea lion rookeries on the Kenai Peninsula. In the 1960s Outer Island, in the Pye Island group, maintained a summer colony between 2,000 and 4,000 animals. Today the island's numbers hover in the hundreds. Sea lions consistently haul out on Chiswell and Natoa islands, Seal Rocks, Rugged Island, around Cape Resurrection, Cape Puget, Point Elrington, Gore Point. and Nagahut Rocks.

The population of sea lions in the Gulf of Alaska has declined 80% since the late 1950s. In 1997, the National Marine Fisheries Service listed Steller sea lions from near Cape Suckling (northeast Gulf of Alaska) westward as endangered. To protect critical habitats, a three-mile vessel exclusion zone encircles major rookeries. No owner or operator of a vessel may enter the exclusion zone, except during an emergency. Chiswell Island is not considered a major rookery. However, Outer Island, of the Pye Island group is.

MARINE MAMMAL VIEWING GUIDELINES

The Marine Mammal Protection Act prohibits disturbances that result in marine mammal injury and alterations of their behaviors. The following guidelines outline recommendations and regulations that help minimize marine mammal disturbance. More details can be obtained at the National Marine Fisheries Service website (https://alaskafisheries.noaa.gov/pr/mm-viewing-guide).

- Remain at least 100 yards from marine mammals and 500 yards (without compromising safe navigation) from harbor seals on glacial ice. Regulations prohibit approaches of humpback whales within 100 yards.
- When in the vicinity of whales, avoid placing your vessel in the path of oncoming whales and operate your vessel at a slow, safe speed. Whales should not be encircled or trapped between boats, or between boats and shore. If approached by a whale, put the engine in neutral and allow the whale to pass. Remember, breaching, feeding and other whale behaviors may endanger people or vessels that are too close or are so quiet that the whales cannot detect them (an occasional tap on the hull may help).
- Travel in a predictable manner that avoids direct approaches and abrupt acceleration when entering and leaving marine mammal occupied areas. Avoid approaching animals already being observed by other vessels. Minimize loud noises and abrupt movements of people onboard vessels and limit observations to 30 minutes or less. When possible, keep downwind from harbor seals.
- In glacial ice, avoid traveling through waters with greater than 50% ice cover. When possible, target visits during early morning and evening hours when fewer seals are hauled out.
- Offering food, discarding fish or fish waste, or any other food item, and pursuit of marine mammals is prohibited by law.
- Note: harbor seal and sea otter pups may be left alone while their mothers feed. They are not abandoned and should not be disturbed. If concerned, contact the: Alaska SeaLife Center Stranding Hotline: (888) 774-7325 to report potentially abandoned pups or injured or dead marine mammals.

Harbor Seals

Harbor seals, a "true" or earless seal, inhabit nearshore coastal waters throughout the Gulf of Alaska. Harbor seals haul out on a variety of substrates, including mud and sand flats, rocky beaches and shorelines, and even glacial ice. They use haulouts as a place to rest, give birth, and nurse their pups. Harbor seals weigh about 24 pounds at birth and grow to about 180 pounds in adulthood; males are slightly larger than females. In summer, harbor seals congregate on glacial ice in Aialik Bay, Northwestern Fjord, and McCarty Fjord as well as on rocky shorelines in the Harding Gateway, Day Harbor, Cape Junken, Procession Rocks, Nuka Bay, and Nuka Island.

In the Kenai Fjords, seals give birth in mid-May through June. Within an hour of birth, seal pups leave their birth site and accompany their mother on their first swimming foray. The pup stays with its mother until weaned

Sea otter.

at about three weeks of age. Young pups with thin blubber layers are limited in the length of time they can remain in the cold waters of the fjords. Occasionally, pups remain on haulouts several hours while their mother forages. They have not been abandoned and should not be disturbed. NMFS recommends remaining 500 yds from harbor seals on glacial ice.

From July through September, seals return to haulouts to molt, where they shed their worn brown coats for shiny black, gray, and silvery white coats.

Harbor seals are well adapted to life at sea. Seals can dive to depths exceeding 600 feet and can remain submerged for more than 20 minutes. Typically, they dive for less than five minutes and remain within 100 feet of the surface. Harbor seals are graceful and efficient swimmers. They use their hind flippers for propulsion and foreflippers as rudders. Movement on land, however, is slow and laborious, typically involving incremental hopping on their belly, aided by their foreflippers.

Sea Otters

Sea otters are members of the weasel family. Adult males typically weigh 70 to 90 pounds and reach 4.5 feet in length. Females are smaller weighing less than 60 pounds.

Sea otters are clearly adapted for life at sea and seldom travel more than a few yards from the water. On land and ice, their gait is clumsy. Sea otter fur is among the finest in the world. It consists of a very dense underfur of inch-long fibers and sparse guard hairs. The underfur ranges from brown to almost black. Guard hairs may be black, pale brown, or silver, often giving a veiled effect of silvery hairs on a dark background. The fur is so warm that sea otters can easily overheat when onshore.

The slaughter of sea otters, which began two centuries ago with Russian fur hunters and continued with American profiteers, ended with the Fur Seal Treaty of 1911. Since then, the nearly exterminated sea otter has made a remarkable comeback. Today an estimated 1,300 otters dwell along the Kenai Peninsula seacoast. The largest concentrations of sea otters in the Kenai Fjords reside in Port Bainbridge, Northwestern Fjord, McCarty Fjord, Nuka Bay and Island, Port Dick, Chugach Islands, and the bays at the southern tip of the Kenai Peninsula.

Sea otters feed on sea urchins, crabs, clams, mussels, octopus, other marine invertebrates, and fishes. For an otter to obtain the 8 to 15 pounds of solid food needed daily (approximately 25% of their body weight), it may have to bring up 40 to 50 pounds of whole shellfish. They usually dive to the bottom in five to 250 feet of water and return with several pieces of food. Most feeding dives last less than one minute, although some otters are capable of staying underwater for five minutes or more.

In Alaska, most sea otter pups are born in late spring. Unlike river otters and most other members of the weasel family, only one pup is born a year. A pup weighs three to five pounds at birth and grows to about 30 pounds before weaning. When traveling, sleeping, or preening, a pup rides on its mother's chest as she floats on her back. The female seldom leaves her pup except when she dives for food. During this time, pups may be particularly vulnerable to predation or disturbance. It is important not to approach otter pups when their mothers are absent, so as not to inhibit the mothers' foraging or reunion with their pups.

Resurrection Bay, including the Seward boat harbor, is a convenient place to observe and photograph sea otters. Otter rafts containing a dozen or more individuals are frequently observed in the bay.

Gray Whales

Gray whales are among the most primitive of the living baleen whales. They are mottled gray in color with light baleen, covered with abrasions, blotches, scars, and clusters of parasitic barnacles. Mottling is especially abundant on their heads and backs, particularly on surfaces that are exposed to air when they breathe. Gray whales have no dorsal fin but have a low hump followed by a series of nine to 12 knobs on the dorsal ridge of the tailstock. Their flippers are large and paddle-shaped, and the tail flukes are very broad.

The eastern Pacific stock of gray whales winters in the warm coastal waters of Baja California and the southern Gulf of California and travels to the Bering and Chukchi seas to feed in summer. They pass by the Kenai Peninsula outer coast in March and April. Gray whales begin migrating back southward in mid-October and pass near the Kenai Peninsula in November through January.

Gray whales are the only baleen whales that are mainly bottom feeders. They feed by lying on their sides and sucking up sediment from the sea floor. Small amphipod invertebrates are captured by the baleen while sediment and other particles are expelled between the plates. Oblong bowl-shaped pits, measuring about three by six feet, are left behind as a record of their feeding, which provide habitats for recolonization by amphipods.

Humpback Whales

Humpback whales are the most commonly seen whales along the Kenai Fjords. Humpback whales are large black whales, reaching 50 feet in length, with moderately arched mouths and black baleen. When seen at a distance, humpback whales are easily recognized by their moderately tapered spout, which reaches 20 feet into the air. Their dorsal fin often has a broad knobby base with a more pronounced tip that ranges from being low and rounded to sharp and sickle-shaped. Their pectoral fins are long, with white coloration. Likewise, their scalloped flukes are marked with unique patterns of white on black.

Throughout the summer, humpbacks swim within the fjords feeding on krill, herring, and other small schooling fishes. They frequently can be seen breaching or tail slapping and occasionally will vocalize.

Each spring the central North Pacific migratory stock of humpback whales inhabiting the Kenai Fjords returns to summering areas in southeast and southcentral Alaska from wintering grounds in Hawaii, where the whales breed and give birth to their calves. Photo-identification studies indicate that humpback whales use discrete, geographically isolated feeding areas to which individual whales return year after year.

Rorqual Whales

Rorqual whales comprise a group of similar appearing, relatively slender baleen whales that include the giant blue whale. Two species of rorquals frequently seen along the Kenai Peninsula coastline include the minke and fin whales.

Minke whales, the smallest and most common of the group, are the easiest to identify. Minke whales are less than 30 feet in length, with a sharp, sickle-shaped dorsal fin located toward their flukes. They have white bands on their pectoral flippers, whitish baleen, and a grayish-white throat

A traveling Orca.

that is visible when viewed up close. They may travel singly or in small groups and have a weak, often invisible, blow when they surface. Minke whales visit nearshore areas within the fjords. They often surface in island passages and at the mouths of fjords, feeding on small schooling fishes.

Killer Whales

Killer whales, also called orcas, are the largest porpoise swimming in the ocean. They live up to their reputation as highly efficient predators. An adult male killer whale grows to approximately 27 feet in length and lives to 50 to 60 years of age. A female reaches an average length of about 23 feet and may live 30 years longer than the male. Killer whales are predominantly black in color with large white patches above and behind each eye, under the jaw, belly, genital area, and behind the dorsal fin. The dorsal fin of the male may reach six feet in height. Dorsal fins in females usually do not exceed three feet in height.

Killer whales roam the Kenai Fjords singly or in pods composed of a few to more than 40 individuals. Three distinct types of killer whales visit this region: resident, transient, and offshore whales. Resident killer whales often travel in large matriarchal family groups. More than a half-dozen family pods are known to visit the Kenai Fjords. Their numbers far exceed those of the transient whales in this area. Resident whales principally feed on schooling fish such as salmon, especially silver salmon, but are also known to eat king salmon, halibut, ling cod and herring.

Transient killer whales, also known as Bigg's killer whales, are less frequently observed. The "AT1" and Gulf of Alaska transient pods are known visitors to the Kenai Fjords. They do not appear to eat fish but prefer marine mammals including porpoises, whales, seals, and sea lions. Transient killer whales typically hunt prey singly or in small groups but do not vocalize much. They do not appear to interact with resident killer whales at all. Transient killer whales can appear anywhere along the Kenai Fjords. They are most often seen cruising the shorelines of islands and points of land where sea lions and harbor seals traditionally haul out and will enter tidewater glacial basins where seals haul out on ice floes. Offshore killer whales are less frequently observed in the region. Prey of offshore killer whales are not well known but include sharks.

Dall's and Harbor Porpoises

Two smaller species of porpoises reside along the Kenai Fjords: the flashy, black and white Dall's porpoise and the quieter, stealth-like inshore harbor porpoise. At first glance, Dall's porpoises can be mistaken for small killer whales. Any porpoise that rides the bow wake or frolics tirelessly near a speeding boat is undoubtedly a Dall's porpoise. This black and white cetacean is among the fastest swimmer in the ocean. Typically, Dall's porpoises are observed near the mouths of fjords and in the gulf. The slower, slate-gray harbor porpoise with its triangular dorsal fin usually travels alone or in small groups. Harbor porpoises rarely approach moving boats and seldom venture far from the shallow waters of bays and fjords.

LAND MAMMALS

A variety of small land mammals inhabits the Kenai Fjords including pygmy shrews, red-backed voles, red squirrels, hoary marmots, and beavers. Many species of mustelids (weasel family) including short-tailed weasels, mink, marten, river otters, and wolverines reside in the fjords. Canids (dog family) including foxes, coyotes and wolves inhabit the Kenai Peninsula, as do both black and brown bears. Ungulates, including moose, Dall sheep, mountain goats, and Sitka black-tail deer, roam the mountains and forest areas.

The wet outer coast favors different large mammals than interior regions of the Kenai Peninsula. Some species more typically seen in Alaska's interior may be observed in the upper reaches of Nuka and Resurrection bays. These areas have direct corridors into the interior not blocked by icefields.

Brown bears are most common in the western and interior Kenai Peninsula, although they can be observed near the heads of fjords such as Resurrection Bay and Day Harbor. Along the outer coast, however, black

Mountain goats.

bears are very common. Likewise, in interior areas of the Kenai Peninsula, Dall's sheep reside on steep mountainsides; conversely, on the coast, the white spots on the hills are mountain goats. Although moose reside at the heads of some fjords, they rarely roam along the outer coast. Sitka black-tailed deer periodically venture to the eastern Kenai Peninsula from Prince William Sound; however, they fare poorly during heavy snow years, and their numbers remain low.

A land mammal frequently seen swimming in the fjords is the river otter. River otters occupy many of the same waters as sea otters, although they tend to remain closer to shore. They inhabit burrows on shore and make forays into the water to feed on crabs, fish and other fresh and saltwater organisms. River otters can be distinguished from sea otters by their slimmer, snake-like appearance, and their tendency to swim facing forward, where sea otters prefer to swim on their back.

Not all mammals that swim in the water are considered marine mammals. Besides river otters, most other mammals will swim considerable distances. Bears, moose, and deer are not deterred by water and may opt to swim to good foraging areas rather than take a long walk.

Mountain Goats

Mountain goats are one of two species of all-white, hoofed mammals found in Alaska. They may be confused with Dall sheep but can be easily distinguished by their longer hair, black horns, and a "beard" of white hair hanging down from the chin and lower jaw.

Mountain goats normally spend summers in high alpine meadows where they graze on grasses, herbs, and low-growing shrubs. Goats winter at or below tree line and sometimes are observed along the shoreline in spring. Usually, a single kid (rarely twins), is born in late May or early June. Kids can keep up with adults when only hours old. Although females are reclusive before giving birth, they soon join other females with young kids to form nursery groups while males roam singly or in small bachelor groups. Kids typically remain with their mothers until the following November breeding season. Mountain goats may live 14 to 15 years, though most live fewer than 12. Many goats show healed wounds and missing teeth, probably related to falls and other accidents.

Black Bears

Black bears are the smallest, most abundant and widely distributed of the three species of Alaskan bears. Black bears are most often associated with forests, but depending on the season of the year, they may be found from sea level to alpine areas. Adult bears stand about 29 inches at the shoulders and measure about 60 inches from nose to tail. Males are larger than females. An average adult male in spring weighs about 200 pounds.

The fur color of black bears varies. Black is the most often encountered color, but brown or cinnamon bears may also be seen in southcentral Alaska. Some black bears have a patch of white hair on the front of their chests. Despite the color variation, black bears can be easily distinguished from brown bears by their straight facial profile and smaller claws. Black bears have adequate senses of sight and hearing but an excellent sense of smell.

Mating takes place anytime from June through July. Apart from that time, black bears are usually solitary except for sows with cubs. In mid-winter, one to four cubs (typically two) are born in dens, blind and nearly hairless, weighing less than a pound. Upon emerging from the den in May, they have gained about five pounds and are covered with fine woolly hair. Cubs remain with their mothers through their first winter. Typically, sows breed every other year.

Black bears are opportunistic feeders. Upon emergence in the spring they consume freshly sprouted green vegetation although they will eat nearly anything they encounter. Winter-killed animals are readily eaten, and some black bears are effective predators on newborn moose calves and goat kids. As summer progresses, feeding shifts to salmon, if they are available. In areas without salmon, bears rely primarily on vegetation supplemented by ants, grubs, and other insects. Berries, especially blueberries, are an important late summer-fall food item.

BLACK BEAR TIPS FOR CAMPERS AND HIKERS

In most of the Kenai Fjords, black bears far outnumber humans. They are regularly observed from June to October. They can show up any time or place, including beaches with or without salmon streams, offshore islands, and even on glacial ice. Bears are excellent swimmers.

Black bear, Slate Island, Aialik Bay.

In spring, bears feed on roots and bulbs in meadows and grasslands. Prime foraging occurs along beaches and meadows around lagoons, often near inviting camping locations. In summer, bears regularly loiter around streams mouths and river deltas, where they eat salmon, walk the bank and lounge in the grass. If you are in an area where you see or smell fresh scat, rotting fish carcasses on the stream bank, and patches of trampled down vegetation, you may want to move away from the area. A bear is likely in the vicinity and may aggressively defend its food cache. Avoid setting up a campsite on a bear trail or near a salmon-spawning stream. In bear areas, try setting up camp on islets and islands, where bear encounters are less likely.

When camping, remember that bears are always on the prowl for food. They take food seriously, and their highly-developed sense of smell may lead them to your camp. Always prepare food away from your camp area and do not leave discarded food scraps on the ground. Avoid eating or storing food in your tent! Be sure to clean up around the campsite, including washing all dishes, pans, and utensils. Hang the food cache away from the camp in a tree or over a cliff inside air-tight bags, or, if possible, in a bear-proof metal container. Bear-proof containers exist at many of the popular campsites in the Kenai Fjords National Park. Smelly garbage attracts bears, so do not bury or store it nearby. It is best to completely burn all garbage on the beach, well below the tide line. It is folly to feed a bear on purpose or by accident. Besides, the bear will return and demand more food.

People and bears commonly travel on the same game trails. When hiking in the woods, grassy wetlands, and clearings, make your presence known, particularly when bushwhacking in thick vegetation. Bears do not like to be surprised, so give them a chance to avoid you. Make noise! Break sticks, talk, sing, wear a bell.

If you see a bear before it sees or smells you, try to avoid it. Always give it plenty of space. Some black bears will immediately bolt when they encounter a person, while others appear mildly curious and unafraid. If encountering a black bear at close range, and it does not move away, do not panic. Start by talking to the bear in a normal voice while waving your arms. Give the bear a chance to recognize that you are not a threat. Then slowly retreat diagonally. If the bear follows or moves closer, you must stop and stand your ground. It is likely the bear will lose interest and leave, but if the bear continues to approach, keep waving your arms and talking to it. Do not turn and run. Bears are faster than humans and are known to chase down fleeing animals. If you have no means of escape, bear experts recommend that it is better to try and drive a black bear away than let it follow you. If attacked, you should fight a black bear. Curl up and play dead if attacked by a brown bear. Fortunately, bear attacks on humans are rare, in fact, more people in Alaska are killed and injured by dogs than by bears.

Prince William Sound Woman (Courtesy of the Alaska State Library).

Part II

History
of the
Kenai Fjords

Lower Northwestern Fjord.

Folded layers of tuff and siltstone from the earth's mantle have been thrust to the surface and form the eastern side of Fox Island in Resurrection Bay.

6

Birth of the Kenai Fjords

ORIGIN OF THE KENAI PENINSULA

The Kenai Peninsula is a land in constant motion. It began taking shape about 42 million years ago but remained submerged beneath the ocean. A period of uplift was initiated about 20 million years ago by the collision of two of tectonic plates. The Kenai Mountains, island peaks in Prince William Sound and Kodiak Island were uplifted by the compression of the two landmasses, but not all areas gained new heights. The colliding landmasses have manifested in a wave-like manner, down-warping certain areas while uplifting others. The headlands of the Aialik and Harris Peninsulas, west of the entrance to Resurrection Bay, are deeply indented by drowned cirques, which form steep-walled, semicircular bays and coves. The cirques, once breeding grounds for glaciers during the Pleistocene glaciations, have since been carried below sea level by tectonic subsidence during the last 10,000 years. The stands of dead trees lining the shorelines of the Kenai outer coast bear evidence of the downward thrust continued by the 1964 Alaska earthquake.

Resurrection Peninsula and Fox Island stand distinct from the rest of the Kenai Peninsula. In general, the Kenai Peninsula consists of poorly sorted sediments, slightly metamorphosed volcanic rocks and granite outcrops. The Resurrection Peninsula represents an Ophiolite formation. Ophiolite is a piece of the oceanic crust that has been uplifted and carried by tectonic movements to become part of a continent. Ophiolite formations are made up of magnesium and iron-rich volcanic basalts, which erupted from long cracks in the ocean floor. Basalt that erupts underwater can contract and develop a texture resembling rounded pillows as it cools. Such formations are known as "pillow basalt." Beneath the pillow basalt, slower cooling basalt forms coarse-grained gabbro. Gabbro forms from the same magma as the basalt, but instead of erupting onto the sea floor, it is forced

beneath the outer layers of basalt. Columns or dikes of basalt that supply magma to the ocean floor can produce in a distinct formation known as a sheeted dike complex, characterized by parallel sheets of basalt. The Resurrection Peninsula exhibits one of the most complete Ophiolite formations in Alaska — a cross-section of the earth's crust, tilted at a 45-degree angle.

The western side of Resurrection on Peninsula, from Thumb Cove south, is dominated by pillow basalt from the surface of earth's crust, whereas the peninsula's peaks and eastern side are dominated by basalt dikes and gabbro with occasional pockets of peridotite from the earth's mantle, just

Basalt sea cliffs at Elephant Head Point, Cape Resurrection.

beneath the crust. The rocks exposed on the east side Fox Island show the highest metamorphic grade of any in the area. Folded layers of tuff and siltstone lie conspicuously exposed on the eastern shore of the island. In contrast, Hive and Rugged islands, just south of Fox Island, are not part of the Ophiolite complex but are composed of the same rocks found in the Harding Icefield to the west.

SCULPTING THE KENAI FJORDS – RECURRING GLACIATION

During the Eocene (37–58 million years ago), the Alaskan climate was subtropical. Three major global cooling periods followed, separated by extensive warming periods. The third, most recent cooling period began about three million years ago. By about two million years ago, glacial ice extended onto the continental shelf. Around this time, average summer temperatures were colder than today, and vast glaciers began to fill the valleys of high and temperate latitudes, eventually covering most of North America and much of Northern Europe and Siberia. Four major glacial episodes (Nebraska, Kansas, Illinois, and Wisconsin) occurred during the Pleistocene. Between these episodes, three milder interglacial periods took place in which temperatures and the extent of glaciation were similar to the present.

It was not until the last glacial advance of the Wisconsin age (the last of the Pleistocene Ice Ages), climaxing about 20,000 years ago, that Prince William Sound began to assume its present form. Ice extended more than 50 nm offshore and covered Middleton Island in the Gulf of Alaska. The hard, compressed ice gouged submarine trenches nearly a mile deep into the sea floor. The deep fjords, glacially sculptured mountains, and the bathymetry (bottom depth and contour) all clearly indicate that glaciers covered and scoured this area for thousands of years.

Resurrection Bay rested beneath glacier ice at least 2,000 feet thick during the late Pleistocene. The reach of the Resurrection Bay glacier into the Gulf of Alaska is unknown, but bathymetry suggests the glacier carved a submarine trough extending 30 nm beyond the present mouth of the bay.

Roughly 12,000 years ago, the earth's climate began to warm dramatically, initiating the Holocene Retreat. Although the Holocene had been warmer than the Pleistocene, this warming fluctuated. Within the past 800 years, a cooling of the North Pacific initiated glacial advances throughout southcentral and southeastern Alaska. This period of glacial advance is known as the "Little Ice Age." It began around 1200 A.D. and extended into the early 1900s on the Kenai Peninsula. Snow lines were depressed about 300–450 feet below present levels. Glaciers in the Kenai Fjords reached their maximum extended positions at various dates between the 1600s (Aialik and Holgate Glaciers) and 1900 (Northwestern and Bear Glaciers). A general period of glacial retreat continues today.

Teben'kov (1852) published a coastal atlas with hydrographic notes for southcentral Alaska. Two of his charts depicting the Kenai Peninsula outer coast show the limits of Northwestern, Holgate, Pedersen, Bear, and seven other glaciers that terminated at tidewater or a short distance inland. The terminal glacier positions recorded by Teben'kov around the Kenai Peninsula are nearly the same as those mapped in 1909 by Grant and Higgins, indicating that little change occurred during the late 19th century. Between 1950–51 and 1984–85, however, the Harding Icefield lost about five percent of its total glacier cover, and many small glaciers around the periphery of the icefield at altitudes below 3,000 feet have disappeared

Northwestern Glacier at the head of Northwestern Fjord.

entirely. Northwestern Glacier has receded more than nine nautical miles during the last century. Presently in the Kenai Fjords, six tidewater glaciers (Aialik, Holgate, Northwestern, Anchor, Ogive, and McCarty Glaciers) actively calve ice into the sea.

THE FJORD ENVIRONMENT

"A long, deep, arm of the sea, occupying a portion of a channel having high steep walls, a bottom made uneven by bosses and sills, and with side streams entering from high-level valleys by cascades or steep rapids." (Hubbard, G. D. 1901).

Two major fjord regions exist in the world, located in a belt north of 43 degrees north and a belt south of 42 degrees south. The fjord coastline of Alaska, consisting of at least 200 major fjords, extends more than a thousand miles from the Kenai Peninsula and merges with the contiguous fjord province of British Columbia. However, only five degrees of latitude separate the northern and southern limits, and there is little difference in the mean ambient climate (northern temperate or subarctic maritime) or external oceanographic conditions affecting this coast.

Alaskan fjords are geologically youthful features. On the Kenai Peninsula outer coast, nearly all the fjords consist of one or more basins separated by sills that may be either bedrock or moraine deposits. In Resurrection

Beach rye grass.

Bay, a deep (60–158 fathom) sill links Caines Head with Humpy Cove, partially constricting water flow from the nearly 1,000-foot (158 fathom) deep basin to the north. Elsewhere on the outer coast, such as in McCarty and Northwestern fjords, sills reach close to the water's surface and can be hazardous to marine navigation. Sill constrictions limit deep water flow and mixing across the sill and reduces the transport of oxygen to the bottom of deep basins.

Fjords typically are estuarine environments. Nearly all fjords receive significant amounts of fresh water which flow as surface plumes from the fjord's head toward the mouth. Fresh water sources include tidewater glaciers, streams flowing from grounded glaciers, seasonal rainfall, and snowmelt. The fresh water often floats above the denser salt water until winds and waves mix the two layers.

A part of the scenic grandeur exhibited in the Kenai Fjords comes from its hanging valleys. These gouged-out areas often terminate in steep cliffs carved by glacial ice above sea level. Hanging valleys range along the shores of Resurrection, Aialik, and Harris bays, as well as Northwestern Fjord and portions of the outer coast. Rivers and streams flow through these high valleys and enter the main fjords as spectacular waterfalls and cascading streams. Similar features occur in subaquatic landforms, like Thumb Cove, where tributary fjords enter main fjords at shallower depths.

Recolonization of an emerging glacial environment.

Habitats and Plant Communities

The glaciers and icefields of the Kenai Fjords generate forces that continuously grind and fracture rock into talus, gravel and powdery silt. The erosion of exposed mountain surfaces is enhanced by freezing, thawing, and heavy coastal rains. These processes also create dynamic habitats and foster a variety of plant and animal communities.

Throughout the Kenai Fjords, in the alpine zone at the 1,500–2,000 foot level, cold temperatures, harsh snow, and windy conditions limit the vegetation to small alpine plants including a variety of lichens and dwarf willows interspersed among the rock and boulder landscapes. Frequent snow and rock avalanches on steep rock and talus slopes strip all but the most tenacious vegetation. Likewise, rushing torrents of water flowing down steep mountainsides and over gravel alluvial fans may wash the unstable substrates clean of soil, nutrients, and colonizing plants.

Below the alpine zone, a succession of vegetation takes root in the mountain areas. Lichens, mosses, and herbaceous plants such as fireweed and cow parsnip colonize exposed areas. They eventually yield to dense thickets of hardy woody species including alder, salmon berries, and blueberries. Over time, these colonizing species create soils and stabilized habitats for spruce and hemlock forests. Cottonwood forests and meadows exist in low wetland areas, especially near streams and rivers. Throughout the Kenai Fjords, however, Sitka spruce dominate the forest ecosystem.

Shoreline vegetation often lies exposed to the encroachment of salt water during high tides and storms. The composition of plants and their shoreline location provides valuable information. Along the exposed outer coast, the vegetation line often marks the reach of winter storm waves. In protected waters, the vegetation line indicates the extent of eroding effects from residual waves and tides. Initially, rye grass, sedges, beach greens, and beach peas establish themselves on rocky beaches above the intertidal zone. The presence of these plants indicates places susceptible to spring tides and storm surges and may not be safe areas for camping or leaving equipment. Beyond the rye grass, a variety of mosses thrive as do herbaceous plants such as saxifrages, angelica, cow parsnip and woody plants including Sitka alder, blueberries, huckleberries, salmonberries, red and black currents, and the ever-present devil's club. Moist meadows and bogs found near streams and in poorly drained areas contain a variety of grasses and delicate herbaceous plants and are well worth exploring.

WIND IN THE FJORDS

Winds strongly influence the Kenai Fjords. Katabatic winds — strong down-fjord movements of air from the icefields and high mountains — frequently occur in the winter. These winds often exceed 60 knots and occasionally exceed 100 knots. Forested areas may present different weather patterns. Rainfall can persist over forested regions because moisture evaporating from the warm vegetated land rises then cools and returns as precipitation. Glaciers, on the other hand, lose much less water to evaporation and reflect light (albedo effect). Consequently, clouds are fewer and appear lighter near a glacier. Because of the icefield and glaciers' colder temperatures, local high-pressure systems form over them, while the adjacent, warmer waters tend to be at lower atmospheric pressures. The difference in pressure causes air to move from the area of higher pressure to areas of the lower pressure creating local glacier breezes.

The opposite effect is seen with bay breezes (day breezes). These 10–20 knot shoreward breezes are caused when the warm air over land rises and cooler, replacement air flows in from the sea. Bay breezes frequently blow in the afternoons, especially on sunny summer days. They are common in the Kenai Fjords, especially in Resurrection Bay where the Harding Icefield and associated glaciers have relatively weak influences.

Prince William Sound Man (Courtesy of the Alaska State Library).

7

The Sugpiaq People

EARLY DWELLERS OF THE KENAI FJORDS

The earliest inhabitants of the Kenai Fjords were the Chugach Sugpiaq, also known as Alutiiq. The Sugpiaq is a Pacific Yupik culture whose territory encompassed the Alaska Peninsula to Prince William Sound, including Kodiak Island and the Kenai Peninsula outer coast.

The Sugpiaq migrated to the outer coast more than 1,800 years ago, and possibly as early as 7,500 B.C. Their territory ranged along the seacoast from lower Cook Inlet near Seldovia to Cape Puget. The Sugpiaq were well suited to survive in the extremely harsh living conditions of the Kenai Fjords. They lived a maritime subsistence lifestyle and excelled at fishing and as hunters of land and marine mammals. These were adaptable people residing in a hostile environment. They used a variety of stone tools shaped and designed for woodworking, hunting, fishing, and processing animal products for food, clothing, and shelter. They built shelters of wood planks, split from trees with stone wedges. The floor was partially dug into the earth and the roof framed with sticks and waterproofed with layers of bark as well as seal and sea lion hides. Masterpieces of their ingenuity were the one and two-hole kayaks or bidarkas. These small boats were fashioned with a bound hemlock frame, covered with tightly stretched sewn seal or sea lion hides, and waterproofed with oil and pitch. A seaworthy kayak in the hands of a skilled Sugpiaq seafarer could not only navigate year-round in temperamental gulf coast waters but could also travel great distances when necessary.

After the Russian fur traders had arrived in Alaska, Natives in large fleets of bidarkas began to hunt sea otters. In the late 1700s, the Sugpiaq began to build a larger three-hole bidarka. The middle cockpit was often used to carry a Russian trader or other important person.

Present archaeological evidence suggests that the Chugach Sugpiaq were widely distributed along the southern Kenai Peninsula and outer coast. They resided in summer and winter settlements in addition to smaller hunting and food gathering camps. Success of the tribes were linked to the geographic placement of settlements and camps. Settlements needed to be reasonably close to multiple marine food resources. Hunting and food gathering camps were established adjacent to salmon streams, lagoons, and spits, near tidewater glaciers, and close to seabird rookeries. High-ground vantage spots with commanding views were vital for sighting whales and other potential food sources as well as for detecting visitors, friends, or enemies, approaching from the sea.

Sugpiaq stone tools from the Kenai Fjords.

Permanent settlement sites often were placed in semi-protected bights near the mouths of fjords, particularly when an adjoining sand or gravel beach provided a reliable haulout area to launch and land kayaks. Regrettably, centuries of wilderness reclamation from storm wave erosion and a rising sea level have obliterated most evidence of the indigenous people who lived on the ragged edge of the outer coast.

The great earthquake of 1170 A.D. caused severe subsidence which likely washed away signs of many early settlements and camps. Subsequent coastal subsidence and cyclic glacial advances further eradicated evidence of Native habitations.

CULTURALLY MODIFIED TREES

The thick spruce and hemlock forests growing along the shoreline perimeter of the Kenai outer coast was a highly-prized resource of the Sugpiaq. Many products from the spruce and hemlock tree were used including the limbs, roots, needles, and cones. Each product could have multiple applications, which were woven into the Sugpiaq culture.

In the Kenai Fjords, physical evidence of Native habitation is seen in the form of a culturally modified tree (CMT). The harvest of bark, pitch, and wood was used for food, medicine, dye, and construction material. The Sugpiaq cut, peeled, and pulled sheets of bark from trees and used the material as siding and roofing for their steam bath houses, smoke-houses, and other buildings. They also used spruce bark to form the sides of bowls and food containers. In the spring or during periods of food shortages, the cambium on the inside of the bark was scraped off and eaten alone or with seal oil as food. Some CMTs are easily recognized from the conspicuous scars left behind from the inten-tional removal of bark from around the tree's base. Large strips of bark were removed with the help of a long, flat, wooden stick. CMT scars

A large culturally modified tree with two opposing scars forms a hollowed-out window.

can be large or small depending on the produce that was produced. Many CMT scars stand out as vertical, oval impressions, three-to-eight-feet tall and one-to-three-feet wide. The scared area is recessed where the bark was removed. The scar's perimeter may be partially covered by layers of pitch from the tree's healing process.

Another type of CMT scar seen is a relatively small, rounded, recessed area, where a hole was deeply gouged into the tree's heartwood for the purpose of collecting pitch when the sap ran in the spring. Spruce pitch was used not only for waterproofing skin kayaks, wooden boats, and wooden cooking bowls, but also as a medicine for sore throats and colds. It could be used as a fire starter, chewing gum, and warmed and softened for placement on a cut to stop bleeding.

Today, hundreds of CMTs can be observed at dozens of locations scattered along the entire outer coast. CMTs are usually discovered adjacent to landing beaches, around lagoons, salmon streams, the heads of bays, and near ancient Native settlements and campsites.

The bark removal process can weaken or even kill the tree, so the wilderness has already reclaimed the vast majority of ancient CMTs, but a few still survive. Even today, it is not unusual to find a standing grove of CMTs in a small, well-defined area. Good examples are found on the western shore of Nuka Island.

Some CMTs have multiple scars, symmetrically spaced around the base. After the tree dies, the heartwood is first to decay. As the heartwood decomposes, all that remains standing is the tree's outer shell with the scars appearing as eerie hollowed-out windows.

DISEASE AND SOCIAL CHANGE

After the initial contact with foreigners in the late 1700s, the Chugach Sugpiaq people of the North Gulf Coast experienced rapid economic, religious, and social change. Perhaps the darkest period of Kenai Peninsula history occurred during the mid-19th century. Between 1836 and 1843, and again in the 1860s, an estimated one-third to one-half of the inhabitants living on the shores of Cook Inlet, Prince William Sound, and the Kenai Peninsula outer coast died of smallpox. The cruel epidemic hit the Native populations hardest and disrupted the social harmony within tribes, contributed to panic and flight, caused mass starvation, and decimated villages. The aftermath led to the consolidation of families and villages. Many small settlements on the North Gulf Coast disappeared or relocated after the epidemic years.

Former settlements sites mentioned in archaeological documents, Sugpiaq legends, stories, and interviews, refer to numerous villages or campsites located in Day Harbor and Resurrection, Aialik, Harris, Two Arm and Nuka bays. Additional camps and refuge sites existed in McArthur and Nuka Passage, Nuka Island, Port Dick, Rocky Bay, Port Chatham, and Koyuktolik (Dogfish) Bay.

In the 19th century, outer coast settlements existed in Aialik Bay and Nuka Bay (Yalik Bay). The Yalik Bay settlement was the largest community, with outlying camps existing throughout the Nuka Bay region. Unfortunately, only a few documented visits to the Yalik Bay settlement are

A group of Natives pose alongside a barabara (wood plank hut) near Seldovia, Cook Inlet, in 1901 (Courtesy of the Anchorage Museum of History and Art).

known. In the late 1850s, a Russian priest Abbot Nicholas from English Bay (Nanwalek) visited the Yalik Bay settlement for a week. Upon his arrival, the priest sent messages to the neighboring camps calling the people together for prayer, confessions, and communion. Nicholas recorded performing one marriage and gave communion to 48 people. In 1880, Ivan Petrof, an agent for the United States Government, visited Yalik Bay to gather census information along the Kenai outer coast. Petrof reported 32 people were living in the settlement. Within a few decades, the remaining residents of Yalik Bay relocated to Port Graham and Nanwalek in Cook Inlet, thereby leaving the outer coast mostly uninhabited by year-round residents.

ВИДЪ СЕЛЕНІЯ ПРИ УГОЛЬНЫХЪ КОПЯХЪ ВЪ КЕНАИСКОМЪ ЗАЛИВѢ.
съ южной стороны.

Coal Harbor, near Port Graham, in 1860. Russian-American Company (Courtesy of the Bancroft Library).

8

Russian Fur Traders

A FOREIGN INVASION

Shortly after Captain Cook explored Prince William Sound and Cook Inlet in 1778, a steady stream of Spanish, English, and Russian sailing ships began visiting the diverse and resource-rich waters of the Kenai Peninsula. The earliest expeditions arrived with differing motives. A few expeditions were seeking scientific knowledge, collecting data and surveying the Alaska seacoast, while others came to trade for sea otter furs or to establish trading settlements. The Russian fur traders (promyshlenniki) were the first foreigners to arrive (1780s) on the Kenai Peninsula and stay. Their occupation began a period of social change and widespread exploitation of the indigenous people, which culminated in the 1790s.

The primary person responsible for changes coming to coastal Alaska was Grigorii Shelikhov, a Siberian fur merchant. The Shelikhov-Golikov Northeast Trading Company eventually became the influential Russian-American Company that controlled the economic resources of America's northwest coast from the Pribilof Islands in Alaska to Fort Ross in northern California. In 1784, Shelikhov appointed Evstratii "the Greek" Delarov as chief manager of the trading company based on Kodiak Island. During this time, Delarov began organizing large Native hunting fleets that could muster hundreds of bidarkas. In summer, a flotilla of Native hunters with Russian support roamed coastal waters hunting sea otter and collecting pelts. This lucrative strategy continued for decades.

Each spring, Native hunters from Kodiak Island gathered at Three Saints Bay, before setting out across the mouth of Cook Inlet, where they collected additional hunters from the settlements and camps scattered along the shores of the Kenai Peninsula. At Port Etches (Nuchek) in Prince William Sound, the entire hunting fleet, including dozens of Russian fur traders, several ships, 200 to 600 bidarkas and often a 1,000 Aleut, Koniag, and Chugach hunters rendezvoused. During the late 1780s, Delarov and his master navigator Grigorevich Izmailov expanded Shelikhov's fur trade business throughout the North Gulf Coast with hunting activities spreading eastward to Yakutat Bay.

Delarov and Izmailov explored the North Gulf Coast for many years and knew the region firsthand. Delarov was keenly aware of the ancient Native overland trade routes that linked the Kenai Peninsula outer coast to Cook Inlet and Passage Canal in Prince William Sound. Recognizing the logistic importance of the Native trail at the head of Resurrection Bay, the Russians named the place Delarov Harbor.

In 1786, Shelikhov ordered Delarov to establish Fort Alexander and a trading post at English Bay (Nanwalek) on the western shore of the Kenai Peninsula. That same summer, the English Captain Nathaniel Portlock sailed sufficiently close to the Kenai Peninsula's outer coast to chart and bestow place names to features including Day's Harbor, Point Barwell (Cape Resurrection), Port Andrews (lower Resurrection Bay), and the Chiswell and Pye Islands. Portlock failed to record any contact with local Natives until he dropped anchor at Coal Harbor on the northern shore of Port Graham. Two years later, in 1788, Captain Izmailov surveyed the Kenai Peninsula outer coast and western Prince William Sound. Izmailov also left no record of contact with Natives of the outer coast, although he had many encounters with the Chugachmiut in the western Sound.

The first recorded contact with Sugpiaq residents in the Kenai Fjords occurred at the mouth of Nuka Bay in July 1790. On an expedition to assess Russian possessions on America's northwest coast, Captain Joseph Billings and Lieutenant Gavrila Sarychev, in the vessel *Slava Rossiy* (*Glory of Russia*), entered the uncharted waters of Nuka Bay. As the ship appeared at the bay's mouth, a bidarka with two Natives paddled close to the *Slava Rossiy* and offered gifts of a river otter, sea otter, seal, and petrel. The Natives invited the ship to follow them to their settlement and informed Captain Billings that other small bays within the main bay provided sand bottoms that would serve as good stations for trading. Reluctantly, Captain Billings sailed into Nuka Bay, but upon observing a rock, well-offshore, he changed his mind, altered course, and sailed for open water. Although he came close, Captain Billings and the crew of the *Slava Rossiy* never sighted the Yalik Bay settlement.

Baranov's sea otter hunting fleet at the mouth of Port Dick, in the summer of 1794. (Courtesy of the Anchorage Museum of History and Art).

Another significant contact between English explorers and north gulf coast Natives occurred in May 1794. Captain Vancouver, at the helm of the flagship *Discovery*, rounded Gore Point *en route* to Cook Inlet and encountered two hundred bidarkas at the mouth of Port Dick. The bidarka fleet comprised a portion of Baranov's sea otter hunting flotilla. Vancouver and his crew traded with the hunters as they passed alongside the *Discovery*. This chance encounter recorded by the ship's artist Henry Humphreys endures among the most recognized images of the outer coast.

ALEXANDER BARANOV

In 1790 Alexander Baranov, at 43 years of age, sailed from Siberia with orders from Shelikhov to replace Delarov as manager of the Northeast Trading Company. Baranov's trip to Alaska was impaired by a shipwreck in the Aleutian Islands. Baranov and the Russian crew were forced to spend the winter camped on the beach. In the spring, they built two small boats from the ship's debris and sailed toward Kodiak. Nearly a year after casting off from Siberia, Baranov reached Three Saints Bay on Kodiak Island.

After replacing Delarov as manager of Northeast Trading Company, Baranov's first objective was to personally survey the seacoast and visit the Native settlements from Cook Inlet to Prince William Sound. In May

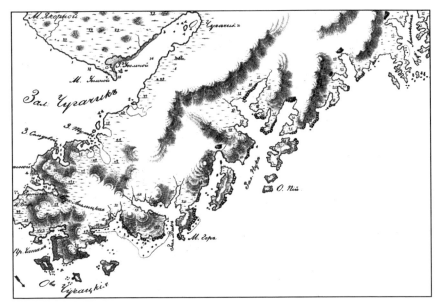

Teben'kov Chart #5 (Detail) Southern Kenai Peninsula coast in 1852 (Courtesy of the Alaska State Library).

1792 Baranov, with a fleet of 50 bidarkas, paddled from Kodiak Island across Cook Inlet to the mainland where they worked their way to Delarov Harbor. Here, Baranov was impressed with the harbor's protection and by the spruce forest that grew to the water's edge. His visit inspired him to change the harbor's name to Resurrection Bay (*Voskresenskaia Gavan*) as his arrival occurred close to Easter Sunday on the Julian calendar.

After departing Resurrection Bay, Baranov's fleet continued to Prince William Sound, following the lee shore of Montague Island, then across Hinchinbrook Entrance to Port Etches. Here, they camped at Nuchek and met with local Native hunters. While Baranov visited Nuchek, a fortuitous event took place. A strange ship with a broken mast and British flag limped into Port Etches and anchored. Baranov seizing the opportunity paddled out to the ship where he met Captain Hugh Moore, who commanded the 75-foot-long ship *Phoenix* used in the East India trade

Captain Moore was in Port Etches hoping to replace a mast damaged in a recent gale. A helpful Baranov volunteered his men to aid with the repairs, which Moore accepted, and the two men began to trade information and develop a relationship. Moore informed Baranov of the vast resource of sea otters that inhabited the coastal waters of southern Alaska. This chance meeting with Captain Moore in Port Etches made a lasting impression on Baranov and influenced his plans. Moore inspired him with the idea to build a ship, a beautiful ship like the *Phoenix*.

JAMES SHIELDS AND THE BUILDING OF THE PHOENIX

In 1789, while in Irkutsk, Shelikhov, known as a man to spot ambitious talent, acquired the services of second lieutenant James Shields from the Russian Ekaterinburg Field Battalion. At the time, it was not uncommon for Englishmen to serve in the Russian military. Shields, unlike many of his English countrymen, spoke fluent Russian. He also was respected as a shipwright and knowledgeable seafarer. Shelikhov quickly placed Shields under contract with the Northeast Trading Company and ordered him to construct a small schooner, *Northern Eagle* (*Severovostochnyi Orel*) at the company shipyard at Okhotsk.

In 1791, with the construction of the *Eagle* completed, Shields along with a Russian crew and four English seamen set sail from Okhotsk across the North Pacific Ocean to Alaska. Shelikhov's master plan was to have Shields and his English comrades build other ships so that Baranov could expand Shelikhov's fur empire. In the *Eagle's* hold were tons of food, trading supplies, and a handful of Russian workers.

In the summer of 1792, Baranov returned to Kodiak Island from his coastal survey to Port Etches and his visit with Captain Hugh Moore. The trip was plagued with bad weather and a fight with Tlingit Indians on Montague Island where Baranov almost died. Upon his arrival on Kodiak Island, he was surprised to find the *Eagle* moored in the harbor. In fact, it was like a dream come true, especially after he met with the red-headed, tattooed Englishman who built the ship and delivered it to his doorstep. Equally essential to fulfilling Baranov's dream of building a ship were the much-needed supplies in the *Eagle's* hold.

By autumn, Baranov and Shields stood together on the deck of the *Eagle* as they surveyed the shores of Resurrection Bay. The shoreline exhibited miles of suitable spruce and hemlock timber. The bay provided adequate protection from the gulf storms and sufficiently large tides for launching a ship from the beach. After returning to St. Paul Harbor, they spent the winter planning the construction of Baranov's *Phoenix*.

In the summer of 1793, Shields, along with 75 Russian workers and his English apprentices, landed at the head of Resurrection Bay. The names of three of the Englishmen that sailed with Shields were recorded as Scott, Borsley, and Short. A fourth Englishman may have died shortly after arriving in Alaska.

Russian work crews began with the construction of a fort with several outbuildings and a shipyard. The site existed near the present location of the Alaska SeaLife Center. Timber for the building of the fort and shipyard was cut from the local forest. Hand-picked, high-quality timbers needed for shipbuilding were harvested from the spruce forests on Green and

Montague islands. The felled logs were stripped of limbs and then towed by Shields with the *Eagle* and Izmailov with the *Simeon*, more than 70 nm through open water back to the Resurrection Bay shipyard.

Construction of the *Phoenix*, from the laying of its 66-foot-long keel to its launch, was plagued with logistic and supply problems. Competing Russian fur traders in Prince William Sound threatened and harassed the workers in Resurrection Bay. They also attacked Baranov's men while they harvested timber on Montague Island.

The builders lacked critical shipbuilding materials including sufficient nails for fastening the planks, iron for bolts, and ground tackle. Essential shipbuilding tools were also missing including a large saw, which made it necessary to hand-hew each plank from a single log. Caulking and pitch were in short supply, so tree moss was used to caulk the planks above the waterline. The lack of proper materials caused delays and resulted in ingenious, but sometimes crude, solutions. The Russian workers were continuously on the verge of starvation and mutiny.

Although not entirely complete, the 180-ton merchant vessel *Phoenix* was launched in September 1794. It was the first ship built on the Alaska mainland. The *Phoenix* measured 73 feet along the lower deck. The beam pushed 23 feet. When launched, the ship sported an array of exterior finishes and a colored patchwork of sails that hung from its three tall spruce masts.

The following year, the *Phoenix* with three-years harvest of sea otter pelts in its hold was assigned to Captain Izmailov for a trans-Pacific voyage to Okhotsk.

After building the *Phoenix*, two more vessels, *Pegas* and *Oleg*, named after winged-animals, were constructed at the Resurrection Bay shipyard. Baranov then transferred shipbuilding activities to the Woody Island shipyard near Kodiak Island.

In 1796, Shields, in the *Eagle*, was the first Russian navigator to sail into Sitka Sound. He informed Baranov that the area was rich with sea otter and suggested a settlement should be constructed at Sitka. At the same time, the fort at Resurrection Bay was downsized to a trading post (artel). A few Russians and Natives remained in Resurrection Bay well into the 19th century. The overland trade route from the head of Resurrection Bay to Kenai Lake and the river system into interior Alaska continued to be used.

The *Phoenix* sailed three successful voyages, transporting furs across the North Pacific Ocean to Okhotsk. However, in May 1799, while *en route* to Alaska from Siberia, the *Phoenix* encountered a spring storm and sank near its final destination of Kodiak Island. All 88 passengers and crew were lost at sea, including Captain James Shields along with several high-ranking members of the Russian Orthodox Church.

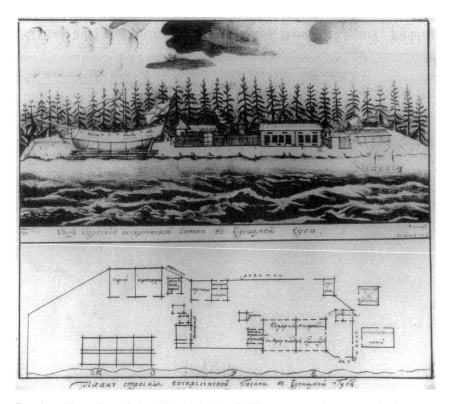

Russian shipyard and fort design at the head of Resurrection Bay drawn by James Shields in 1795 (Courtesy of the University of Alaska, Fairbanks).

The loss of the *Phoenix* was a severe blow to Baranov. Many of his closest friends were aboard the ship, in addition to vital supplies he desperately needed. The loss of the *Phoenix* and the dwindling sea otter population along the north gulf coast sowed seeds of discontent, which led to the rapid relocation of the Russian-American Company's headquarters to Sitka Sound. Another setback to the Russian colony, also in 1799, occurred when the first ship built by James Shields, the schooner *Eagle*, was wrecked on Montague Island.

In the brief time that James Shields lived in Resurrection Bay, he left behind several notable sketches of the Russian fort and shipyard. He also drew a fine collection of navigational charts of Resurrection Bay, the Kenai Fjords, and the Gulf of Alaska from his sea voyages (1791–1799) aboard the *Eagle* and *Phoenix*. Captain Shields along with his English comrades and Russian workers who built the Phoenix were the earliest known non-Native inhabitants to reside in the Kenai Fjords.

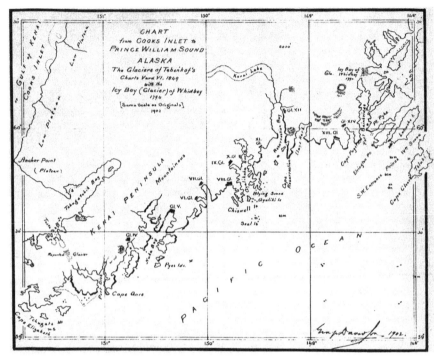

George Davidson's map of the Kenai Peninsula outer coast and glaciers in 1902 (Courtesy of the Bancroft Library).

9

Charting the Fjords

EARLY MARINE SURVEYS

The English and Spanish explorers who visited the Kenai Fjords generally passed through the area without investigating further. Upon sighting the mountainous capes and walls of ice, they prudently kept their ships offshore out of harm's way. Accordingly, the charts depicting the Kenai Peninsula coastline were inaccurate and lacked physical detail. The successful Russian fur traders, on the other hand, were often expert navigators who spent years living in and learning about an area. To protect themselves and guarantee their strategic position, they were reluctant to share their charts and sea knowledge with others. Additionally, many early records of their intimate knowledge of this region have been lost.

Early cartographic surveys of the Kenai Peninsula outer coast, Cook Inlet, and Prince William Sound were conducted by James Cook (1778), Nathaniel Portlock (1786–87), Gerasim Izmailov and Dmitrii Bocharov (1788–89), George Vancouver (1794), James Shields (1795), and Ivan Kashevarov (map of Resurrection Bay in 1790s). At the beginning of the 19th century, the most notable surveys of the outer coast were conducted by Danilo Vasil'evich Kalinin (date and survey lost), Bubnov (1804, survey lost), Gavrila Sarychev (published in 1826 from the 1785–1792 Billings Expedition), and Illarion Arkhimandritov (1849).

The steamer McArthur surveyed the Kenai Peninsula outer coast in 1906–07 (Courtesy of the NOAA Photo Library).

In 1794 Captain Vancouver completed a highly-detailed exploration of Prince William Sound and the eastern Kenai Peninsula. Vancouver's two lieutenants, James Johnstone and Joseph Whidbey, were given the task of surveying the sound by launch. Johnstone's job was to survey the northern and eastern sound. Whidbey surveyed the western sound, its islands, and fjords. The survey crews spent weeks camping on beaches at night while rowing or sailing by day. At the time, the survey of Prince William Sound was a grand achievement, and mariners used the resulting charts for more than one hundred years. Today, the survey work of Whidbey and Johnstone serve to document the position of tidewater glaciers that were near their maximum extent during the Little Ice Age.

In the late 1840s, the Russian Navigator I. Arkhimandritov gathered and completed the most comprehensive coastal survey of the Kenai Peninsula outer coast and lower Cook Inlet that was undertaken in the 19th century. The results of this survey were included in the Atlas of the Northwest Coast of North America, published by the Russian Governor M. D. Teben'kov in 1852.

George Davidson, the renowned English-born cartographer, took a particular interest in Alaska. In 1904 he published a map of the Kenai Peninsula outer coast that included many of the area's glaciers. Davidson's chart incorporated survey work from earlier sources including information gathered from Whidbey's survey of the eastern Kenai Peninsula in 1794 and Teben'kov's charts of 1852. Unfortunately, physical features added by Davidson to the Kenai Peninsula chart include many glaciers that were inaccurately drawn or misplaced. Davidson also published the first volumes of the United States Coast Pilot of Alaska.

From 1905–1913, a pair of talented geologists U. S. Grant and D. F. Higgins, working for the United States Geological Survey (USGS), surveyed and published an in-depth and accurate survey chart of the Kenai Peninsula. They also added many place names to the dominant physical features of the region. Their detailed information gathered over many years, focused on mapping, geology, glaciers, and early mining activity on the Kenai Peninsula. In 1913, Grant and Higgins spent the summer months in the field, rowing a small launch *Agnes* and sometimes beach camping along the coast. Grant and Higgins authored the USGS Bulletin #526, Coastal Glaciers of Prince William Sound and the Kenai Peninsula, Alaska, which contains dozens of drawings, charts, glacier photographs, and interviews. It remains one of the most important sources of geophysical baseline data gathered from the outer coast during the early 20th century.

In the late 1970s, Austin Post from the USGS spent several summers surveying the bathymetry and glaciers in Aialik Bay, Northwestern Fjord, and McCarty Fjord. The study involved radio-carbon dating of trees found in recently deglaciated areas. Post also graphed a glacial timeline for the Little Ice Age advance and retreat of the major tidewater glaciers in the

The survey launch Wildcat in Nuka Passage in 1929 (Courtesy of the family of Rear Admiral A. Smith, USC&GS, and the NOAA Photo Library).

Kenai Fjords. Post's bathymetry work produced unofficial charts of each glacial basin that indicate depth and position of glacial sills. He also identified prominent physical features, including hazardous rocks and shoals. Since his work, high resolution bathymetric and glacial surveys have been conducted by NOAA and the University of Alaska that provide a contemporary status of the fjords and its glaciers.

NOTABLE MARITIME DISASTERS ON THE NORTH GULF COAST

EAGLE

In 1799, the Russian schooner *Northern Eagle,* built by James Shields eight years earlier in Okhotsk, Siberia, ran aground and was wrecked on Montague Island. Six people were lost. The ship was commanded by Captain Talin who survived.

PHOENIX

In 1799, the Russian frigate *Phoenix*, built on the shore of Resurrection Bay, was near the end of its long voyage, across the North Pacific Ocean from Siberia, when it sank in a May storm near Kodiak Island. Some debris washed ashore on Shuyak Island. All 88 people on board were lost, including its builder Captain James Shields and the Archimandrite Joseph of the Kodiak Mission.

NATIVE BIDARKAS

In 1799, Baranov's hunting fleet was overcome by a spring gale near Hinchinbrook Entrance, Prince William Sound. Sixty bidarkas and 200 Native hunters were lost. It remains the worst human-loss sea disaster in Prince William Sound history. This tragic event discouraged Natives from participating in the annual sea otter hunts. In addition to the loss of the *Phoenix* and *Eagle,* the tragedy hastened the Russians to relocate to Sitka Sound.

TORRENT

In 1868, the US-flagged *Torrent* floundered and went aground in a winter storm at the mouth of English Bay, Cook Inlet. The crew abandoned the ship as the vessel broke up on the rocks.

YUKON

On February 4, 1946, at 4:16 a.m., the steamship *Yukon* (375 feet in length) encountered foul weather and poor visibility in Blying Sound and ran aground at Cape Fairfield. The ship was held fast between the cape and Pinnacle Rock. Most of the passengers initially huddled in the forward part of the ship as waves pounded the vessel. At daybreak, waves estimated

*The Torrent wrecked on the rocks at the mouth of English Bay in the winter of 1868
(Courtesy of the Anchorage Museum of History and Art).*

between 30 to 50 feet high washed over the ship's stern and broke the
vessel into two pieces. The ship's aft section was driven by powerful waves
toward the beach, while the forward section remained pinned to Pinnacle
Rock.

A massive rescue effort was mobilized from around the North Gulf
Coast and Seward. After three days on the scene, Coast Guard vessels,
minesweepers, power scows, tugs, and fishing boats rescued more than 485
people from the forward part of the ship and a narrow strip of beach near
the cape. Only 11 people were lost.

EXXON VALDEZ

On March 29, 1989, Captain Joseph Hazelwood ran the tanker vessel
Exxon Valdez aground on Bligh Reef at the mouth of Valdez Arm in Prince
William Sound. The disastrous event oiled the coastline from Bligh Island
to Chignik Bay, affected a thousand miles of pristine seacoast and to killed
fish, seabirds, and marine mammals. The oil tanker was salvaged after
spilling more than 11 million gallons of Alaska north slope crude oil.

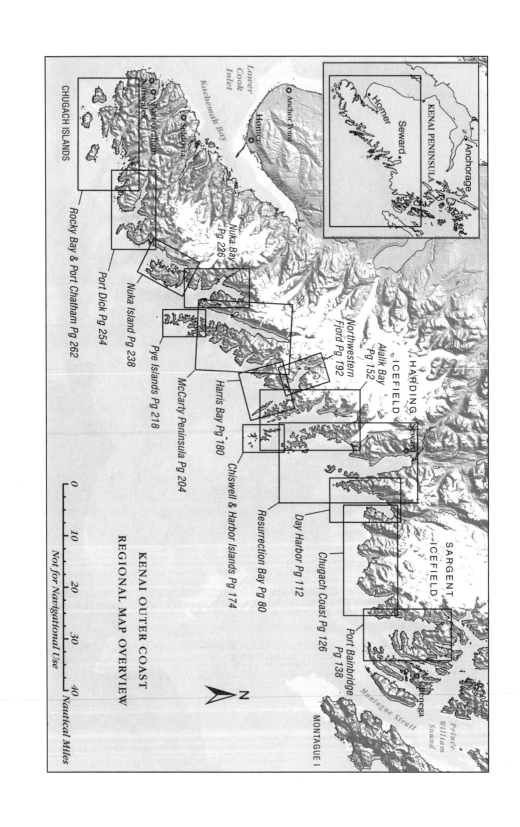

KENAI OUTER COAST
REGIONAL MAP OVERVIEW

CHUGACH ISLANDS

Rocky Bay & Port Chatham Pg 262

Port Dick Pg 254

Nuka Island Pg 238

Pye Islands Pg 218

McCarty Peninsula Pg 204

Harris Bay Pg 180

Chiswell & Harbor Islands Pg 174

Resurrection Bay Pg 80

Day Harbor Pg 112

Chugach Coast Pg 126

Port Bainbridge Pg 138

Nuka Bay Pg 226

Northwestern Fiord Pg 192

Aialik Bay Pg 152

HARDING ICEFIELD

SARGENT ICEFIELD

Lower Cook Inlet

Kachemak Bay

Nanwalek

Port Graham

Seldovia

Homer

Anchor Point

Seward

Prince William Sound

Montague Strait

MONTAGUE I

KENAI PENINSULA

Anchorage

Homer

Seward

0   10   20   30   40   Nautical Miles

Not for Navigational Use

N

Part III

Coastal Guide
to the
Kenai Fjords

Sailboats raft-up in Thumb Cove, Resurrection Bay.

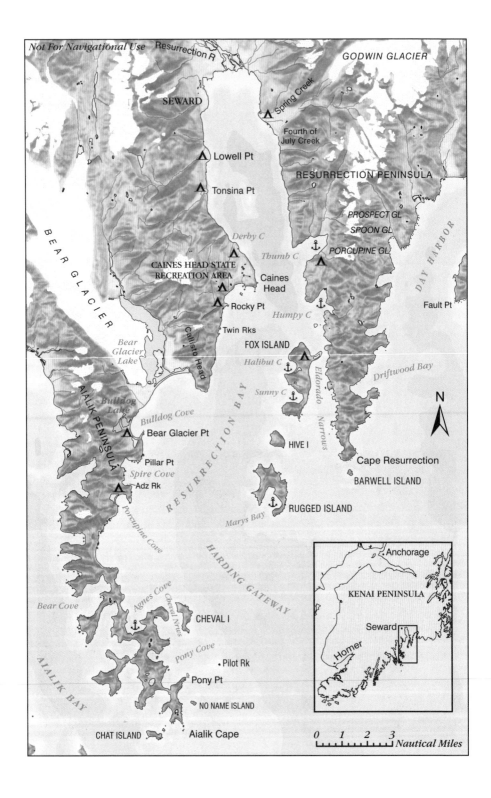

Not For Navigational Use
Resurrection R
GODWIN GLACIER

SEWARD
Spring Creek

Fourth of
July Creek

Lowell Pt
RESURRECTION PENINSULA

Tonsina Pt

PROSPECT GL
SPOON GL
PORCUPINE GL

Derby C
Thumb C

CAINES HEAD STATE
RECREATION AREA
Caines
Head

DAY HARBOR

BEAR GLACIER

Rocky Pt
Humpy C
Fault Pt

Twin Rks

Callisto Head
FOX ISLAND

Bear
Glacier
Lake
Halibut C
Eldorado

Driftwood Bay

Sunny C

AIALIK PENINSULA
Bulldog
Lake
Bulldog Cove
Narrows

N

Bear Glacier Pt

HIVE I

Pillar Pt
Spire Cove
Cape Resurrection

Adz Rk
RESURRECTION BAY
BARWELL ISLAND

Porcupine Cove

RUGGED ISLAND

Mary's Bay

HARDING GATEWAY

Anchorage

Bear Cove
Agnes Cove
Cheval Nrws
CHEVAL I
KENAI PENINSULA

Pony Cove
Seward

AIALIK BAY
Pilot Rk
Homer

Pony Pt

NO NAME ISLAND

CHAT ISLAND
Aialik Cape

0   1   2   3
Nautical Miles

10

Resurrection Bay

INCLUDING THE RESURRECTION BAY ISLANDS

Wildlife Viewing:
> Waters encompassing Resurrection Bay, the Harding Gateway, and the Resurrection Bay islands provide outstanding wildlife viewing opportunities. May through August, thousands of kittiwakes, murres, and puffins nest on the cliffs of Cape Resurrection and Barwell Island. Dall's and harbor porpoises as well as humpback, gray, and killer whales routinely roam and feed in the Harding Gateway. Sea otters range along the bay's outwash deltas as well as in the small boat harbor at Seward. Dozens of posturing Steller sea lions lounge along the pillow lava ledges in the Eldorado Narrows and Cape Resurrection.

Kayaking:
> The novice kayaker should stay in sheltered waters, close to shore, and pay attention to wind and weather. An alternative is to use a water taxi to reach a sheltered kayak destination. The bay's accessible western shore from Lowell Point to the Caines Head Recreation Area provides numerous landing beaches, popular with summer kayakers. Thumb Cove, Sandspit Point, Kayaker Cove, and the Eldorado Narrows on Resurrection Bay's eastern shore are ideal destinations for paddlers and tour groups. Fair summer weather and ocean kayaking expertise are necessary for kayakers paddling south of Fox Island or into the Harding Gateway to view the remarkable sea stacks and rock pinnacles that punctuate the mainland shore. Bear Glacier Lake is a particularly rewarding kayaking destination in Lower Resurrection Bay. Reaching the lake, however, requires setting up travel arrangements with one of the local outfitters. Access to the glacier lake is dependent on weather and tidal conditions so travel delays may occur.

Hiking:
> The 7-mile-long Caines Head shoreline trail between Lowell Point and South Beach at the Caines Head Recreation Area is the only maintained hiking trail on the outer coast. Wilderness bushwhacking and exploring are available at Thumb Cove, Sandspit Point, Eldorado Trail, and in Mary's Bay.

Camping:
> Waterfront camp areas exist along the Spring Creek and Fourth of July beaches, Tonsina Point, Caines Head Recreation Area, Thumb Cove SMP, Sandspit Point SMP and Sunny Cove SMP. Beach landings at Bulldog Cove and Porcupine Cove are weather dependent.

Fishing:
   Excellent silver salmon fishing takes place late June through August in
   Resurrection Bay. Hotspots include Fourth of July Creek, Lowell Point, Caines
   Head, Eldorado Narrows, the south end of Fox Island, and legendary Pony
   Cove. The bottom fishing is best in the Eldorado Narrows and around the
   Resurrection Bay islands, on the shelfs or off a cape, headland or point of land.

Anchorages:
   Anchorages in Resurrection Bay tend to be deep and situated at the heads of
   bays and coves, where the bottom is likely more than 10 fathoms deep. In
   places like Agnes Cove, mariners must be prepared to anchor more than 20
   fathoms deep. Primary anchorages in Resurrection Bay include Thumb Cove,
   Humpy Cove, Kayaker Cove, Sunny Cove, Mary's Bay, and Agnes Cove.

Flanked by icy peaks with year-round snow, Resurrection Bay lies atop the northern Gulf of Alaska, sandwiched between the massive mile-high Harding and Sargent icefields. Unlike the adjacent glacial fjords indenting the outer coast, Resurrection Bay lacks a significant glacier at its head. Instead, a deglaciated valley and highway stretches northward into the Kenai Peninsula's interior. Resurrection Bay is Alaska's largest, year-round, ice-free seaport with road, railway, and air routes linking south-central to interior Alaska. The bay is also a gateway to the Kenai Fjords: a series of long, glaciated indentations that form the wildest stretch of seacoast on the North Gulf Coast.

Seward boat harbor.

The Resurrection Bay islands at the bay's mouth tame the ocean swell and partially protect the upper bay from the wrath of gulf coast storms. They also afford stunning scenery, with an assortment of anchorages, fishing, and camping opportunities.

By mid-summer expect to see salmon anglers lined up along Seward's waterfront, attempting to catch silver salmon. Nearby, rows of RVs and camp trailers stand beam to beam within a rock's throw of high water. Beyond the water's edge isolated stands of tilted pilings reveal, where once stood, a network of wooden docks and piers destroyed and washed away by the 1964 tidal wave.

THE WESTERN SHORE OF RESURRECTION BAY

LOWELL POINT TO AIALIK CAPE

Lowell Point

Lowell Point is a conspicuous outwash plain, two nautical miles (nm) south of Seward. The point is named for the Lowell family. Resurrection Bay was uninhabited in 1884 when Frank and Mary Lowell sailed into the bay, dropped anchor, and homesteaded at the present town site of Seward. In the early days, a shoreline trail linked Seward's waterfront to Lowell Point.

Later, in the 1920s, a local entrepreneur developed a rough tourist trail that followed Spruce Creek up the mountainside to gain access to the Harding Icefield. Promotional material advertised that the icefield trek only took one hour and 50 minutes and enticed tourists and locals to hike it with dog sled rides available on the icefield. Within a short time, however, enthusiasm died and the rough trail fell into disrepair. Nevertheless, the trail gained immortality as one of the earliest tourist ventures in the area.

Today, Lowell Point lies barely above sea level, built from deposits of sand and gravel washed down the mountainside by Spruce Creek. Elevated beach cabins and visitor facilities occupy the area. Most notably are Miller's Landing and the day-use and long-term parking areas at the Lowell Point Recreation Site.

Kayaking:
> Lowell Point is the main staging area for kayak groups and individuals intending to paddle Resurrection Bay's western shore toward Caines Head. The launch and retrieval beach for kayaks rests on the south side of Lowell Point, adjacent to the State Park day-use parking lot. The one-way paddle distance from Lowell Point to Tonsina Point is 1 nm and to Caines Head (North Beach) is 3.8 nm. If possible, catch the early morning ebb tide to beat the afternoon southerly day breeze.

Waterfront, Lowell Point.

Camping:

No overnight camping is allowed on Lowell Point Beach. The nearest camp areas are located at Tonsina Point (free) and Miller's Landing campground (Fee). Camping is also available at the Silver Derby Campground and RV park near the Spruce Creek Bridge on the Lowell Point Road.

Fishing:

In August, the Lowell Point waterfront is a focal point for salmon and anglers. At the height of the silver salmon season, schools of coho salmon mill about the shoreline where, at times, the water's surface explodes like popcorn as silvers leap and splash.

Often, when the salmon are plentiful, a flotilla of sports boats battle along the waterfront in a traffic snarl. The landlubber with an idle fishing pole, will find the action along the Lowell Point waterfront can be equally impressive, if the timing is right.

Hiking:

See Caines Head Shoreline Trail.

Anchorage:

In summer, vessel traffic around Lowell Point generates substantial wakes. Frequent day breezes and choppy seas make Lowell Point a temporary anchorage at best. Stay well away from the north shore where mudflats and shallow water reach out more than 200 yards.

Private moorings sprinkle the inshore contour of Lowell Point. These moorings are usually constructed with heavy ground tackle and should be given an extra-wide berth to avoid entanglement, if anchoring along the Lowell Point waterfront.

Tonsina Point

Tonsina Point is an undeveloped gravel outwash plain at the mouth of Tonsina Creek, approximately 3.2 nm south of Seward. Tonsina Point is accessible by kayak, skiff, or by foot. The easiest way to reach Tonsina Point by foot is to hike the Caines Head Shoreline Trail, but it is equally accessible to kayakers or water taxi drop-offs. Note that steep cliffs obstruct the beach route from Lowell Point to Tonsina Point.

Tonsina Creek empties into Resurrection Bay on the northern end of Tonsina Point. A steel footbridge, part of the Caines Head beach trail, carries hikers across the creek. Another footbridge allows access across a stream on the southern end of Tonsina Point.

Mariners, beware of the gravel shoal extending more than 0.25 nm offshore from Tonsina Point. Teetering corpses of spruce and hemlock trees stand out on the beach berm as a sobering reminder of the great earthquake and tidal wave that took place nearly six decades ago.

Tonsina Creek has a long history of attracting prospectors. Several gold claims briefly flourished in the early 1900s. Among the local miners was Alfred Lowell who worked several claims in the area as early as 1904. Today, recreational placer panning along the creek can still be rewarding, but collecting enough colored flakes to take to the bank may require overtime.

Kayaking:
Tonsina Point is an ideal sand and gravel landing beach as well as a convenient camping spot. A short hike from the beach along the stream's bank, on the N shore, leads to the footbridge and shoreline trail system.

Fishing:
In August, when silver salmon fishing peaks, experienced trollers work the tree-fringed shoreline off Lowell Point, Tonsina Point, and Derby Cove. Anglers also troll alongside the high cliffs of Caines Head, a traditional salmon derby hotspot.

Camping and Hiking:
Tonsina Point is a convenient stop for hikers along the Caines Head Shoreline Trail. It also attracts an assortment of tents and tarps on the beachfront, especially on weekends. In late summer, black bears forage for salmon carcasses along the banks of the creek. Kayak and backpack groups should set up shelter along the beach berm and away from the woods, stream bank, and bear trails.

Caines Head

Caines Head lies 10 nm southwest of Seward. The headland stands out as a steep bluff, 650 feet high, on Resurrection Bay's western shore. The head was named in 1905 for Captain E.E. Caines, the president of the Alaska Pacific Navigation Company that operated the memorable steamship *Dora*. Day visitors or overnight campers have several ways to reach Caines Head.

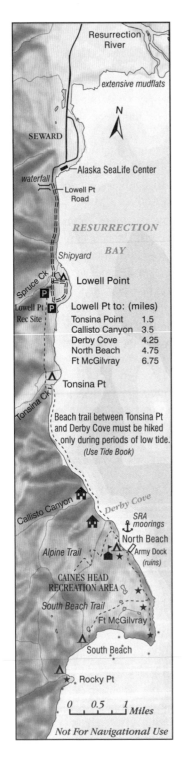

RESURRECTION RIVER

extensive mudflats

N

SEWARD

waterfall — Alaska SeaLife Center

— Lowell Pt Road

RESURRECTION

BAY

Shipyard

Spruce Ck

Lowell Point

Lowell Pt
Rec Site

Lowell Pt to:	(miles)
Tonsina Point	1.5
Callisto Canyon	3.5
Derby Cove	4.25
North Beach	4.75
Ft McGilvray	6.75

Tonsina Pt

Tonsina Ck

Beach trail between Tonsina Pt
and Derby Cove must be hiked
only during periods of low tide.
(Use Tide Book)

Callisto Canyon

Derby Cove

SRA
moorings

North Beach

Alpine Trail

Army Dock
(ruins)

CAINES HEAD
RECREATION AREA

South Beach Trail

Ft McGilvray

South Beach

Rocky Pt

0   0.5   1 Miles

Not For Navigational Use

Many visitors save time by catching a water taxi from Miller's Landing to North Beach, while others hike the Caines Head Shoreline Trail.

Caines Head Shoreline Trail:

The trail begins at the upper parking lot of the Lowell Point Recreation Site. The shoreline portion of the trail is only passable on a plus 5-foot tide or lower. Hikers are advised to leave two hours before low water. Consult a tide table for time and tide information. The trail extends 1.5 miles from the trailhead to Tonsina Point, following a hillside road with switchbacks that descends to Tonsina Point. The trail then follows the shoreline from milepost 2 to 4.25. A state park public use cabin (PUC) is located adjacent to the trail at Callisto Canyon, milepost 3.5, and another PUC is located in the woods at Derby Cove, milepost 4.25. Reservations are required for both cabins. At North Beach Army Dock, milepost 4.75, the trail climbs upward to the Caines Head bluff where visitors can investigate the ruins of Fort McGilvray. Along the way, approximately one-mile south of North Beach, an intersecting trail leads southwest for 1.5 miles, descending to a former garrison, now ruins, built in the woods at South Beach. Secluded South Beach has an exceptional scenic view of lower Resurrection Bay and is a terrific camp location. Nearby, at Rocky Point, a concrete bunker stands out on the low-lying tongue of land.

CAINES HEAD RECREATION AREA

Caines Head State Recreation Area (CHSRA) is a somewhat overgrown showcase for the Seward Harbor Defense network constructed by the Army during the early stages of World War II. Fort McGilvray, built atop Caines Head, was a 6-inch gun battery designed to sink enemy ships entering Resurrection

Bay. Other gun batteries existed on Rugged Island. Today, the fort with its deserted hallways and rusted gun platforms is part of the 5,961-acre CHSRA. The fort is open to the public. The Quonset huts and wooden garrison buildings lie flattened by heavy snow and appear to be melting into the wilderness landscape. The concrete ammunition and observation bunkers and the massive gun fortifications aligned along the Caines Head bluff will be visible for centuries.

Camping is encouraged in the Caines Head State Recreation Area; however, fires are restricted to the beach. There are toilets and a bulletin board near the trailheads at both North and South beaches. Otherwise, pack out what you pack in.

North Beach (CHSRA)

North Beach (Army Dock) is a pocket beach along the northern shore of Caines Head. It is easy to identify from the creosote ruins of the Army supply dock erected in 1941. The old pilings are unstable and to be avoided. A state park ranger cabin located on the hillside above the beach has maps and information. There also is a covered picnic shelter in the woods where stands of old growth Sitka spruce and mountain hemlock form a canopy.

Camping, Hiking, and Kayaking:
North Beach is a picturesque base camp for exploring the Caines Head area. The partially protected shale shoreline at North Beach affords reliable beach landings. Colorful tents and kayak hulls sometimes stretch the length of the

The Army Dock ruins at North Beach with Thumb Cove in background.

beach. A bulletin board sits on the south end of the beach, where the trail climbs the overgrown roadbed to Caines Head. Backpackers and campers, with or without a boat or kayak, can book a ride on one of the water taxis that regularly run to North Beach from Lowell Point. Check with Miller's Landing or the Seward water taxi service. For the convenience of vessel owners visiting the Caines Head Recreation Area, two public use moorings, maintained by the State Park lie near the Army Dock ruins in 4 fathoms of water. The partially protected beach is a mix of shale and gravel and makes an excellent landing site for a dinghy.

Fort McGilvray (CHSRA)

A Coastal Defense Plan for Alaska was rapidly put in place soon after the Japanese invaded the Aleutian Islands. The Fort McGilvray complex was the hub of Seward's coastal defense network during World War II. The design plan approved the construction of two 6-inch gun batteries, one at Caines Head and the other at the southern end of Rugged Island, as well as numerous observation outposts and searchlight stations, in and around the mouth of Resurrection Bay and in Day Harbor. Radio and a submerged telephone cable linked the network of remote outposts to each other and the gun batteries. High on the Caines Head bluff visitors will find two dismantled gun emplacements.

South Beach (CHSRA)

To visit South Beach, descend the trail 1.5 miles from Caines Head to the beach. The trail passes near the twisted metal skeletons of former barracks and utility buildings. In 1942–43, a garrison of 250 soldiers lived on South Beach, formerly called Minneapolis Beach. Heavy snow loads collapsed the Quonset huts long ago, but the cement bunkers and ammo magazines remain. On the beach, a splintered collection of wood pilings is all that remains of the army's supply dock.

South Beach Bight is a protected shore for small boats in northerly weather, especially when the choppy seas create lumpy trolling along Caines Head. Mariners should give a wide berth to the rock pile in the middle of South Beach Bight, 0.3 nm from the beach and marked on the marine chart. At higher stages of the tide, a noticeable swell or breakers often mark the rock pile. A sea cave along with perpendicular cliffs occupy the shore between South Beach and the outstretched tip of Caines Head.

The seacoast south from Rocky Point to Callisto Head consists of a steep, crumbling shoreline with adjacent peaks ranging from 1,500 to 3,500 feet high. A squad of men from South Beach once manned a 155 mm gun battery, power station, and searchlight on Rocky Point, one mile south of South Beach. Along the shoreline, south of Rocky Point lies a collection of rocky islets, most notably Twin Rocks. There are no reliable landing beaches between Rocky Point and Bulldog Cove.

Callisto Head shore with Bear Glacier.

Hiking, Camping, and Kayaking:
> South Beach is the last stop on the Caines Head Shoreline Trail. The gravel beach tends to be a poor landing spot because of the ever-present southerly swell, although in light sea conditions, beach landings are possible.
> The area is an ideal camp location with an expansive beach and valley to explore and miles of trails weaving around Caines Head. Behind the beach berm at South Beach are layered rock outcroppings and tall eroded cliffs. Nearby, a water plume from a gushing waterfall descends the hillside. A bulletin board and a small outhouse lie near the trail's base leading north to Caines Head.
> An alternative camp and landing beach with a generous freshwater stream rest on the north side of Rocky Point.

Anchorage:
> South Beach Bight is, at best, a temporary anchorage because of its exposure to the southeast. A swell rolls into the bight, so it offers only a restless night. During strong northerly winds, the bight can be a safe-haven.
> An anchorage for those wishing to go ashore lies between the rock pile (in the center of the bight) and the gravel beach, situated northwest of the rock pile, in 8-10 fathoms.

HARDING GATEWAY

In 1923 President Warren G. Harding traveled on a cross-country trip from Washington DC to the west coast. The presidential trip included a steamship tour of the Pacific Northwest and Alaska. On July 3rd, as the transport vessel *Henderson* entered the mouth of Resurrection Bay, the

Alaska Territorial Governor Scott Bone informed President Harding that Alaskans wanted to name a glacier (Bear Glacier) or mountain for him. The President told Governor Bone that of all the beautiful scenery and interesting features they had sailed past, he would rather have, more than anything else, the entrance to Resurrection Bay perpetuate his name. Governor Bone and the officers of the *Henderson* then ceremoniously christened the bay's entrance as the Harding Gateway. In 1950, the United States Geological Survey (USGS) also bestowed the massive icefield blanketing the mountains west of Seward with Harding's name.

Harding Gateway is a deep, 4.5 nm wide passage that extends from the mouth of Resurrection Bay into Blying Sound. Cruise ships and large ocean-going vessels visiting Seward use the main shipping lane that passes west of the Resurrection Bay Islands. The entrance, marked by navigational beacons placed on both Rugged Island and Pilot Rock, stands out from the offshore waters of Blying Sound.

In contrast to the deep waters of the upper Resurrection Bay, the upraised, irregular bottom of Harding Gateway forms a shoal that accentuates the swell from the Gulf of Alaska. The twisted shoreline and adjacent waters are natural catchalls, especially for drifting logs floated by storms and spring tides. At other times, the Harding Gateway bathes in a cool glacial breeze or remains veiled by summer fog. Highlights of the Harding Gateway are Bear Glacier and a rugged seascape of eroded rock spires that grace the inshore waters.

The steep crumbling headland standing vigil on the east flank of Bear Glacier is Callisto Head. The headland was named in 1930 for the nymph in Greek mythology who was changed into a bear and set in the heavens as Ursa Major. Westward from Callisto Head and the Bear Glacier moraine beach is the beginning of the Kenai Fjords National Park shoreline.

Bear Glacier

Bear Glacier was a local name reported in 1909 by U.S. Grant and D.F. Higgins, United States Geological Survey, when they first visited the area.

Bear Glacier descends from the 5,000-foot elevation of the Harding Icefield. The glacier's ice tongue is cracked and fissured. Icefalls appear along its surface where ice spilled over steep walls and broke into cabin-sized ice blocks. Two medial moraines, dark ribbons of rock and debris, stretch the length of Bear Glacier and reveal the merging of tributary glaciers.

One of the largest glaciers of the Harding Icefield, Bear Glacier extends 13 miles from the icefield to its terminus in a glacial lake filled with icebergs. Bear Glacier terminates only a short distance from terminal positions recorded in 1852 by Teben'kov and observed in 1909 by Grant and Higgins. Dendrochronological studies of the forest trim line above

Jagged rocks adjacent to Bear Glacier Point.

Bear Glacier indicate that recession probably began between 1835 and 1845 and that the glacier's 19th-century advance was its greatest since the early 1600s. Today, Bear Glacier continues to slowly retreat up the valley with its ice face resting 3 miles from tidewater.

In spring, Bear Glacier's 2.5-mile long moraine provides excellent beachcombing but only during calm sea conditions. Beach treasures can include bright red halibut buoys, snarled yellow crab line and other multi-colored plastic bottles and containers discarded from Japanese and Russian fishing vessels. With luck, beachcombers might find a glass ball mixed with nature's bounty of cedar, redwood, and fir logs from the West Coast or teak and mahogany carried from Asia by the Japanese Current.

Mariners unfamiliar with the Bear Glacier area should stay in deep water and away from the beach. The bottom rapidly shallows and accentuates the swell and surf, which can and has driven boats ashore. *Do not anchor in shallow water or try to drop people off on the Bear Glacier moraine beach.*

Kayaking, Hiking, and Camping:

Bear Glacier is among the premier kayaking destinations on the Kenai Peninsula. If paddling amid majestic icebergs sounds enchanting, then this is the adventure for you. Boat access to the Bear Glacier area is via the stream channel at the north end of the moraine beach. The lower stream channel runs parallel behind the beach and is only navigable to jet boats, shallow-draft vessels, and inflatables, and only during higher stages of the tide. Mariners without local knowledge of the channel entrance and stream should steer clear of the area. Guided and unguided kayak tour options to Bear Glacier can be handled by a kayak outfitter, water taxi or helicopter service. A visit to Bear Glacier requires patience and flexible scheduling due to changing weather and tidal conditions. The Bear Glacier outwash area and its wave-ravaged moraine offer miles of wilderness hiking.

Bulldog Cove

Tucked on the south side of Bear Glacier Bight is Bulldog Cove. At the entrance lies Bear Glacier Point and a picturesque collection of rock pinnacles that provide haulout ledges for dozens of harbor seals. Two beaches stand out in the cove with a rocky headland separating the north and south beach. Shallow water in the cove helps to magnify the swell off the Gulf. A lagoon lies behind both beaches, but in the northern lagoon, a crescent-shaped spit or former barrier beach nearly divides the lagoon. Bulldog Cove is black bear country, so stay alert if going ashore.

Kayaking:
Even in light weather, surf washes both exposed beaches of Bulldog Cove and creates unreliable landing conditions. Access the beach in the south corner. It requires calm seas to land on the north beach. Do not risk beach landings in marginal sea conditions unless prepared for an extended stay.

Camping:
The Kenai Fjords National Park allows camping in Bulldog Cove. Camp and store gear anywhere above the reach of high tide. Although lacking a bear-proof locker, the cove's southeast corner has good camping options, with access to the lagoon.

Anchorage:
Bulldog Cove is a fair-weather anchorage, most suitable in southwesterly weather. To anchor, mariners should favor the partially protected area inside Bear Glacier Point. Drop anchor in 7–10 fathoms. Be aware that early morning katabatic winds occasionally sweep down from the Harding Icefield via Bear Glacier and create choppy seas in the cove.

Spire Cove

This rocky alcove has a steep, storm-washed pebble beach at its head. Its southeast exposure makes beach landings tough even in calm sea conditions. Both majestic and prehistoric in appearance, the rugged shale and granite shoreline at Pillar Point reveals some of the finest monolithic rock features on the Kenai Fjords coast. Stationed at Spire Cove's south entrance point is Adz Rock, a 75-foot-tall rock monolith resembling a stone adz standing on end. One can easily imagine a fleet of skin-covered bidarkas plying this wild section of seacoast.

Porcupine Cove

Constantly crashing surf washes the sand and cobble barrier beach at the head of Porcupine Cove. Along the western shore, a notable rock formation lies 200 yards offshore. A scenic 20-acre lagoon rests behind the low-lying

Pillar Point at the northern entrance to Spire Cove, Harding Gateway.

beach and ghost-white trees. The beach at Porcupine Cove has developed a reputation for stranding boaters and campers and for dumping kayaks and dinghies when landing or launching from the wave-washed beach. Be cautious. The cove's north shore is a sensitive pupping haulout for harbor seals. When seals are present, avoid disturbing them.

Immediately south of Porcupine Cove are miles of exposed, inaccessible sea cliffs and wave-lashed shoreline. No protection or anchorages are available until Agnes Cove.

Kayaking and Camping:
The northeast end of the beach is usually the calmest place for beach landings. Waterfowl, both resident and migrating, inhabit the secluded lagoon along with families of river otters and flocks of ravens. Near the lagoon's entrance channel, a hillside stream offers a water source.

Anchorage:
A constant groundswell makes into Porcupine Cove, so only anchor overnight in weather that is light and variable. Drop anchor midway into the cove in 5–8 fathoms, gravel bottom. Nearby, Agnes Cove provides a more secure anchorage.

Agnes Cove

In 1910 Grant and Higgins named Agnes Cove after their launch *Agnes*, which was the small day boat used for their coastal survey work. The shoreline and hillsides of the cove are extremely rugged, densely wooded, and mostly inhospitable.

Anchorage:
> Agnes Cove affords adequate protection in most southerly weather. At times, katabatic winds from the direction of Bear Glacier influences the cove. Traditionally, mariners drop anchor in the eastern corner, where the bottom lies more than 20 fathoms deep. The bottom is mostly soft mud that can sometimes give way. During southeasterly gales, williwaws sweep down the eastern headwall and careen across the cove.

Cheval Island

Many vessels traveling between Resurrection and Aialik bays cruise the scenic shoreline route through the protected waters of the Cheval Narrows. The mile-long narrows is deep, clear and refreshing. Salmon anglers are commonly spotted trolling along Cheval Island's lee shore. The wildlife cruise vessels from Seward routinely watch pods of orcas and humpbacks that traverse the area. Dall's and harbor porpoises are summer regulars, as well as roving gangs of juvenile sea lions and skittish harbor seals.

Pilot Rock

Approximately an acre in size, Pilot Rock (100 feet high) is the conspicuous, round top sea stack protruding from the water's surface 1.3 nm east of Pony Point. An acetylene navigational light was installed atop the rock in 1914. Today, the Coast Guard maintains a navigation beacon in addition to a weather station. Although greatly influenced by Bear Glacier weather, Pilot Rock is an excellent source of weather information for mariners traveling outside the Harding Gateway. Listen to the latest Pilot Rock weather, updated every hour, on WX-1.

During easterly weather and spring tides, the irregular rocky bottom and counter-clockwise current in Blying Sound can create turbulent seas between Pilot Rock and the Chiswell Islands, especially with an ebbing tide from Aialik Bay. Even in light weather, the water in the vicinity of the Aialik Cape can be sloppy.

Pony Cove

Pony Cove is a towering oval-shaped basin resembling an amphitheater. A remarkable rock headwall rises to a trio of granite spires. Mariners entering the cove should steer south of mid-channel to avoid a collection of rocks and islets that extend from the northern shore. Inside the cove, the crashing sound of the surf, amplified by the surrounding sea cliffs, drown out the cry of gulls. Trapped logs and floating debris often aimlessly drift in the cove. A poor anchorage, the cove is deep and exposed to the east and the constant water movements from Blying Sound.

Fishing:
> Pony Cove annually reestablishes its legendary fishing status as the premier silver salmon destination on the outer coast. The trolling grounds around Pony Point to the Cheval Narrows are usually the first reliable area to produce consistently high catches of ocean-bright silvers. In mid-June, the local char-

Salmon fishing at Pony Cove, No Name Island (background).

ter salmon fleet begins silver mining around the cove, many weeks before schools of coho migrate into upper Resurrection Bay. During peak fishing, six-pack charters reel in bag limits within an hour or two.

No Name Island

Auspiciously named "No Name Island" lies between Pony Point and Aialik Cape. The rocky shore is a sea lion haulout area and coho trolling location. Small boats pass between the island and the mainland shore. In easterly weather, rough seas can rebound in the passage between No Name Island and the sea cliffs. In heavy easterly weather, mariners should give a wide berth to No Name Island and Aialik Cape by passing a mile or more eastward.

Aialik Cape

At Aialik Cape, a series of granite islets and rocks protrude from the southern tip of Aialik Peninsula. Aialik Cape forms the western extent of Blying Sound — an open bight (24 nm wide) stretching eastward to Cape Fairfield. On old Spanish charts, this strongly indented seacoast feature, with its outstretched capes and windswept islands was called Canal Blyings. Relative to offshore waters, the hollowed-out seacoast of Blying Sound is buffered from the strongest easterly and westerly winds and waves. The capes eastward from Cape Resurrection to Montague Island at the mouth of Prince William Sound provide additional protection to Blying Sound by directing the coastal current southwestward and offshore.

THE EASTERN SHORE OF RESURRECTION BAY

Fourth of July Creek to Cape Resurrection

Fourth of July Creek Area

Directly east of Seward, across the head of Resurrection Bay, is a wooded valley with an extensive gravel outwash plain. A large stream known as Fourth of July Creek descends the valley from Godwin Glacier, then drains into Resurrection Bay on the southern end of the outwash plain. Godwin Glacier straddles the ridgeline of Resurrection Peninsula, which separates Resurrection Bay from Day Harbor.

The outwash plain has the heavy metal look of an industrial park. The spacious waterfront is home to a harbor, fish processing plant, an extensive commercial dry dock facility, and the largest shipyard on mainland Alaska. Nearby, in the upper valley, surrounded by alder and razor wire lies the Spring Creek Maximum Security Prison.

Kayaking:
> The Spring Creek beach is an excellent kayak staging area from which to launch and paddle the eastern shore of Resurrection Bay. The distance from Spring Creek to Thumb Cove is 5.5 nm. Several optional landing beaches lie along the paddle route to Thumb Cove.

Camping:
> The Spring Creek campground lies at the N end of the Fourth of July waterfront. RV parking and tent camping arrangements are on a first-come basis. Portable toilets stand near the fee station. A small, picturesque lagoon adjoins the camping area.
> An out-of-the-way camp location sits at the southern end of the Fourth of July waterfront, south of the shipyard. Follow the access road on the back side of the shipyard to a waterfront parking area, where a mile-long secluded beach awaits.

Fishing:
> In June, red salmon fishing is popular at the head of Resurrection Bay. In July and August, salmon anglers can expect the action to become fast and furious. Pink salmon usually arrive in the upper bay before the silvers. Watch for jumpers off the Spring Creek beach.
> Salmon lures like Pixies, Krocodile, and Cripple-herring work well for pink and silver salmon. The area has produced many Silver Salmon Derby winners and is the most popular fishing location on the upper east shore of the bay.

Thumb Cove

Thumb Cove, 7 nm south of Seward, is the largest indention along Resurrection Bay's eastern shore. Thumb Cove, named in 1906, has worn other labels including Dickinson and Porcupine coves. The navigational light on the tree-crowned islet at the cove's north entrance point became

Thumb Cove State Marine Park Beach.

operational in 1938. In winter and spring, the rocky shore of the wooded islet also serves as a sea lion haulout. In the 1790s, the Russians called this feature Woody Cape.

In the early 1900s, prospector and local Seward resident S.E. Likes cut a trail from the mouth of Likes Creek up the rugged valley. It then traversed along the headwall below Prospect and Spoon Glaciers. For years, Likes worked a copper claim at the 1,500-foot elevation above the cove.

In 1911, Grant and Higgins described the head of Thumb Cove as follows: *"The Spoon Glacier, being so named on account of its smooth, glassy, round front, which reminds one, approaching from below, of the inverted end of a huge spoon. Between the Prospect and Spoon Glaciers is an abandoned medial moraine. Boulders of prodigious size are common, the largest nearly a 20-foot cube. Located, just north of the Prospect Glacier is a small ice cap covering the top and upper part of the western slope of Resurrection Peninsula."*

Today, Thumb Cove is recognized as a spectacular anchorage and terrific base camp for hikers, campers, and kayakers. The vertical grandeur encompassing Thumb Cove is hard to beat. At the cove's head, on the northern shore, a ghost forest of dead spruce trees reveals evidence of major land subsidence. Precipitous cliffs and glacial cirques dominate the headwall that rises more than 4,000 feet in elevation. From north to south, Prospect, Spoon, and Porcupine glaciers flow from the three cirques clinging to the headwall. At times, barges, fish processors, and ships that are too large to tie-up in the small boat harbor drop anchor in Thumb Cove.

Kayaking, Camping, and Hiking:

Thumb Cove's prominent and alluring south shore beachfront (State Marine Park) is a popular camping and hiking area, as well as the destination of touring kayak groups, backpackers, water-taxi dropoffs, and open-boat sailors needing a place to rest. Visitors can choose from a dozen well-worn sites or find a camping spot in a secluded grove of alder and Sitka spruce. Hillside streams created by meltwater from the glacial cirques cut a path through the cobble beach and drain into the cove.

If the cove's southern beachfront is too crowded, move across Thumb Cove to secluded Likes Creek and camp behind the beach berm in the woods. Nearby, at the cove's head, the shoreline leads through a wetland area of beach rye and eelgrass. The mudflats go dry at low water.

Public Use Cabins:

Two public use cabins sit along the cove's southern beachfront. The "Porcupine Glacier" public use cabin is located near the barge ruins and marked by a wooden walkway and state park signs. The "Spruce Glacier" public use cabin is on the southwest end of the beach.

Anchorage:

The alpine grandeur of Thumb Cove, with its glacial cirques towering overhead, makes this scenic location the most popular anchorage in Resurrection Bay. The bottom is deep throughout, except near the outwash streams and mudflats clogging the cove's head. A steeply sloped, 10-fathom contour extends around the cove's head from Likes Creek to the beach on the southeast shore. Try anchoring in 10 to 15 fathoms offshore from the barge ruins visible toward the bay's head.

Small vessels can drop anchor, off Likes Creek, on the north shore, in 10–13 fathoms. Avoid anchoring too close to the creek's outwash, where an anchor can be buried or dislodged. At the cove's head, is an inlet with shallow mudflats that go dry at low water. Shallow draft vessels can anchor at the mouth of the inlet in 5–10 fathoms. Be mindful of the limited swing room and the mudflats extending from the cove's head.

Vessels can drop anchor off the small stream and outwash area located 0.35 nm, west of Likes Creek, and marked 3.5 fathoms on the NOAA marine chart. Drop anchor in 6–8 fathoms on the shelf, away from the stream outwash. The alcove is an optional anchorage, especially in brisk northerly weather or when the cove's head is too crowded with vessels.

Thumb Cove is a better anchorage in northerly weather than in southerly weather when active water movement from Resurrection Bay and williwaws can directly influence it. In brisk southwest winds, the Seward Harbor is a better place to overnight. Thumb Cove also is susceptible to a residual swell from the afternoon day breeze, along with wakes from passing tour vessels.

Humpy Cove

Humpy Cove is a steeply walled basin with north and southeast arms. When the Russians occupied Resurrection Bay in the 1790s, the cove was known as Humpback Bay. Today, private summer cabins punctuate Humpy Cove's shoreline. Fleets of touring kayaks regularly paddle through the area.

Orca Island Cabins, North Arm, Humpy Cove.

The "Iron-Door" bunker at Topeka Point, on the north entrance point of Humpy Cove, is another memento of World War II. Along the hillside in the north arm, a road and trail system once traversed the mountainside to an observation site where army personnel with searchlights used to scan for enemy ships entering Resurrection Bay. At the time, Humpy Cove was called Butts Bay, and a communication cable stretched from Topeka Point across Resurrection Peninsula to an army outpost bunker perched atop Chamberlain Point, a rocky headland at the entrance to Safety Cove in Day Harbor.

Fishing:

A flotilla of serious anglers fishing in open skiffs and runabouts use the waters south of Humpy Cove as a base to troll or bottom fish around tiny Hat Island and the weathered shore along Sandspit Point. Even more popular for salmon trollers and those that love a majestic seascape are the intricate nooks and crannies from the Eldorado Narrows to Emerald Cove.

Anchorage:

Humpy Cove's northern arm is too deep for convenient anchoring except at the arm's head where the bottom is 10–15 fathoms deep. Powerboats and sailing vessels can find secure anchorage in the cove's southeast arm, although it does get crowded with boats on weekends. Drop anchor in 8–15 fathoms at the mouth or inside the southeast arm. The bottom is soft mud and sand. The anchorage provides partial protection from tour vessel wakes. A stream flowing at the shallow head of this inlet attracts schools of pink salmon as well as hungry harbor seals in summer.

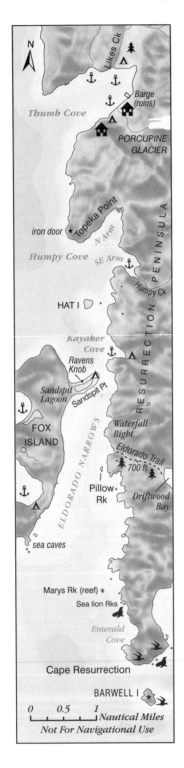

Not For Navigational Use

Kayaker Cove

Kayaker Cove is a steeply walled, funnel-shaped alcove located across from Sandspit Point. The cove's westerly exposure and towering ridgeline give protection in easterly weather. Private property occupies most of the accessible waterfront. At the head, a kayaking outfitter provides economical lodging options and valuable information. Highly recommended.

Kayaking and Camping:
Kayaker Cove is a popular destination. At the cove's head is a cobble beach, cleared of boulders, which offers a reliable landing spot for kayakers.

Anchorage:
Kayaker Cove is a suitable anchorage in mild summer weather. Avoid the anchorage in northwest winds. Anchor in the center of the cove, midway toward the head, in 8–10 fathoms.

ELDORADO NARROWS

The Eldorado Narrows is a water passage that extends 4.5 nm from Sandspit Point to Cape Resurrection and separates Resurrection Peninsula from Fox and Hive Islands. Its intricate eastern shore exposes miles of pillow lava formations, sea caves, and towering cliffs. On a calm sunny afternoon, the Eldorado Narrows is a spectacular place to paddle a kayak or to cruise in a boat.

Geology enthusiasts probably will recognize the volcanic bubble outcroppings along the mainland side of the narrows. These pillow basalt formations, created when molten rock rapidly cooled beneath the ocean, stretch from below sea level to the high ridges of the peninsula. The coarsely textured volcanic rock creates handy footholds for mountain goats and niches for nesting seabirds. In wet weather, dozens of waterfalls leap into space as they tumble down the overhanging lava outcroppings.

Waterfall Bight is located 0.8 nm southeast of Sandspit Point, where a roaring stream tumbles more than a thousand feet down a steep crevice etched into the Resurrection Peninsula. Vessels often stop here to obtain a close-up view.

Pillow Rock is the prominent 25-foot-tall islet near Resurrection Peninsula, 1.5 nm south of Sandspit Point. This bare islet is also simply known as "Good" because of the United States Geological Survey benchmark attached to the rock. Pillow Rock is a prime example of volcanic pillow basalt born and cooled beneath the sea. Deep water lies mid-channel between Pillow Rock and the mainland.

Eldorado Trail lies immediately northeast of Pillow Rock. At the bight's head is an unmarked, unimproved trail that ascends a 700-foot high saddle atop Resurrection Peninsula and descends into Driftwood Bay in Day Harbor.

The trail was first developed by John Davidson and Dan Bair in the early 1970s as an alternative land route to the Driftwood Bay homestead. The Davidson Family often used the trail when poor sea conditions at Cape Resurrection prevented them from entering Day Harbor. On August 2, 1976, John, Ginger, and Jesse, age 3, disappeared without a trace while traveling from Seward to Driftwood Bay in their 20-foot-long skiff.

Mary's Rock is a dangerous reef that reveals itself on a 3-foot tide or lower. The reef lies in the vessel traffic lane 1 nm northwest of Cape Resurrection, approximately 0.3 nm off the Resurrection Peninsula. Usually, a noticeable groundswell breaks over this reef, but in calm seas and high water, the reef hides beneath the surface. The reef's namesake Mary is just one of many unfortunate mariners to confront this navigational hazard.

Sea Lion Rocks are a trio of pillow lava rocks along the Resurrection Peninsula shore, 0.8 nm northwest of Cape Resurrection. The rocks are a destination where sightseeing tours view the posturing sea lions.

Emerald Cove is a rocky alcove tucked into Resurrection Peninsula's precipitous western shore, adjacent to Cape Resurrection. It is a majestic place, popular with anglers and sightseers. Visitors can scan the sea cliffs for mountain goats, bald eagles, and the occasional peregrine falcon.

Emerald Cove is not a secure anchorage, although occasionally, fish boats temporarily anchor in the cove while they mooch for silvers or attempt to bottom fish for halibut. Energetic water movement reverberates around the cove. In brisk easterly weather issuing from Blying Sound, it is normal for williwaws to blast over the peninsula into Emerald Cove.

Lower Resurrection Peninsula shoreline.

Cape Resurrection

Cape Resurrection marks the impressive eastern entrance to Resurrection Bay, is 16 nm from the Seward boat harbor. This bold headland, easily recognized from offshore, crowns the southern tip of Resurrection Peninsula. Cape Resurrection was originally named Point Barwell in 1787 by Captain Nathaniel Portlock. In 1869, the U.S. Coastal & Geodetic Survey christened Cape Resurrection with its current name and assigned Barwell to the adjacent offshore island.

When rounding Cape Resurrection in summer, thousands of seabirds are visible, nesting on the sea cliffs. It is a noisy spectacle that visitors young and old cannot ignore, so grab a camera and prepare for the onslaught. Dense rafts of murres float in the strait between the cape and Barwell Island. Tufted and horned puffins, cormorants, marbled murrelets, pigeon guillemots, black-legged kittiwakes, and glaucous-winged gulls also congest the passage. Overhead, squadrons of kittiwakes soar on the swift air currents.

Marine bird populations change seasonally and between years, but in an abundant year, more than 30,000 marine birds inhabit the Cape and Resurrection Bay islands. While inspecting the cape, watch for mountain goats that graze on the towering, thinly vegetated rock ledges.

Mariner Notice:

Summer sea conditions at Cape Resurrection can vary day-to-day, sometimes hour-to-hour. Typically, on a warm, sunny day, a southerly bay breeze of 5–15 knots will develop at the bay's mouth and spread northward by late morning. Breezy conditions usually calm by evening. Also, common sights in Blying Sound are large, dark squalls (low-pressure cells). The squalls bring increased wind, rain, and white caps.

Mariners heading into Blying Sound from May to September should scan the VHF radio for the weather action at Cape Resurrection. It begins around 7 am when the charter fishing fleet broadcasts live sea conditions from the cape. Also, check the VHF marine weather, which includes updated weather observations from Pilot Rock in Harding Gateway.

At Cape Resurrection, east and southeast winds can create rough seas, which can be treacherous in a small vessel or kayak. In some cases, tide rips may extend miles offshore to the east and south of Cape Resurrection and Barwell Island. Tide rips at the cape are enhanced when a strong ebbing current from Day Harbor and Resurrection Bay collides with a brisk east or southeasterly wind in Blying Sound.

RESURRECTION BAY ISLANDS

Hat Island

Hat Island is a thickly wooded, oval-shaped island located between Humpy Cove and Sandspit Point. In the 1790s, the Russians called it Round Island.

The shore is steep and laced with seaweed-covered boulders. During low tide, deep-keeled vessels should avoid the shallow underwater ledge and rocks that lie offshore, about 80 yards east of the island. To be on the safe side, mariners should favor the mainland shore when cruising east of the island.

Fox Island

Fox Island has undergone many name changes. In the 1790s, the Russians partially adapted the Sugpiaq name and called it Chiklyykhtak Island. Then, in the early 1900s, it became known as Lowell Island after Alfred and Billy Lowell established the first of many fox farms that took over the island's western shore. In 1905 it became Fox Island, but that quickly changed again in 1906 to Renard, meaning fox in French. Renard Island was designated on charts and maps for most of the 20th century, but local folks in Seward, who always referred to the island as Fox Island, finally got their way when the U.S. Geological Survey officially changed the name from Renard back to Fox Island.

Fox Island is the largest and most hospitable of the five Resurrection Bay islands. Along the crumbling eastern shore are talus piles from active slides. Rockhounds and kayakers should check out the island's southeastern point, where sea caves and rock arches exist amongst folded layers of rock. At the southeast end of the Fox Island, a reef lies less than 200 yards offshore, often revealed by cresting waves but hidden in calm seas.

Ghost forest at Sandspit Lagoon, Fox Island.

Sandspit Point

Sandspit Point rests at the tip of a half-mile long, narrow peninsula protruding into Eldorado Narrows from Fox Island's northeastern shore. The Sandspit Point State Marine Park is primarily used by kayakers and open boat mariners. The sandy north shore welcomes beach landings. Water taxis from Seward service the area.

Hiking:

Unencumbered hiking lies along the spit's north beach. The area presents a unique vantage point from which to view the lava outcroppings of the Eldorado Narrows. On the spit's ragged southern shoreline, beachcombers can hike among gnarled logs tossed ashore by winter storm waves.

A secluded lagoon occupies the inner portion of the sandspit. A skeleton spruce forest, killed by salt water moving in after land subsidence from the 1964 earthquake, surrounds the waterfront.

Sandspit lagoon offers a quiet place to observe wildlife and flora. During late summer, sheets of bright green algae float on the lagoon's surface. Furry rafts of sea otters sometimes invade the lagoon while clamming in the area. Usually, several eagles are observed hanging around the lagoon, perched atop dead spruce trees. River otters often patrol the spit and can also be found diving for fish in the lagoon. A thriving spruce forest is replacing the ghost forest.

Kayaking:

The Sandspit is positioned perfectly for paddle trips into the Eldorado Narrows, or for side trips to Kayaker Cove, Thumb Cove, and Caines Head. Paddlers may explore the Sandspit lagoon by portaging or by catching the upper end of the flood tide at the lagoon's channel entrance, near the hillside.

Camping:

The quarter-mile-long north shore of the spit is the natural place to set up shelter. Those campers seeking access to an ocean view and a camp area should check out Raven's Knob. The knob is an elevated rock outcropping that stands midway along the spit's north shore. Weekend mariners using inflatable boats and powerboats regularly camp on the beach. They either anchor the vessel off the beach or fasten it to shore.

Anchorage:

Sandspit bight lies exposed to the north and only provides marginal overnight anchorage. The area also is close to vessel traffic lanes, susceptible to boat wakes and the noise of diesel-powered tour vessels.

In summer, an occasional early morning north wind sends an annoying chop into the bight. The bottom is steeply sloped, and deep water runs close to the beach, except around Sandspit Point where shallow water extends well off-shore.

Sunny Cove

Sunny Cove is a State of Alaska Marine Park. The southern end of the beach is available for camping. Private property lies behind the beach at the cove's head.

Anchorage:

Drop anchor in the middle, 250 yards from the head in 12–15 fathoms, muddy bottom. Small boats can anchor at the northeast corner, near the head in 8–10 fathoms. Sunny Cove lies exposed to westerly winds from Bear Glacier and wakes from vessel traffic. Not surprisingly, williwaws careen across the cove in easterly gales.

The Eldorado Narrows shoreline.

Halibut Cove

In 1918 the famed artist and adventurer, Rockwell Kent, lived with his son and a fox farmer on the shore of Halibut Cove. Kent's book *Wilderness: A Quiet Adventure in Alaska* published in 1920, depicts the artist's winter experience. A copy of the book is on display in Seward at the public library and the museum.

In summer, Kenai Fjords Tours operate a dock at the head of the cove, along with an onshore lodge.

Hive Island

Hive Island's steep, conical profile well-depicts its current name. In 1905 the island was known as Sugar Loaf Island and then later as Guard Island. Hive Island's north shore rises perpendicularly from the sea. Except for a

Looking S from Mary's Bay, Rugged Island.

pocket beach located on the island's western tip, most of the island's shore is unnervingly rocky and unsuitable for landings. Waters around the island are increasingly fished when foul weather keeps the charter fleet captive in Resurrection Bay. The area is seasonally productive for bottom feeders as well as schools of silvers.

Rugged Island

Rugged Island, 15 nm south of Seward, is the southernmost island in the Resurrection Bay island group. The island's eastern shore is vertical and prone to erosion. It exhibits spectacular rock outcroppings and crumbling sea arches. Communication towers, used by the National Park Service and U.S. Coast Guard, dominate the skyline at the 1,500-foot-high north peak. Rows of solar panels power the equipment. Atop the island's SE end, 400 feet high, the Coast Guard maintains a navigational beacon that lights the entrance to Resurrection Bay.

During World War II, the U.S. Army constructed harbor defense fortifications in a handful of places around Rugged Island. At that time, the
island was known as Fort Buckley. A few reminders of World War II are
found in Carol Cove on the island's northeast point. Here, a searchlight
control bunker and concrete powerhouse sit on a cliff 150 feet above the
water. Access to the bunker area is from the shoreline where a gently sloped
rock ledge in the tidal zone was used to land men and supplies. Steel tie
rings, corroded from decades of exposure to salt water, stand out on the
rock ledge.

Additional army fortifications were constructed at Alma Point, on the
northwest tip of the island, and at Patsy Point, on the southeast entrance of
Mary's Bay. At times, Steller sea lions cling to the steep rocky ledges along
the island's spectacular eastern coast.

Hiking:

In Mary's Bay, the ruins of an army dock sit in the east corner. Here, a dilap-
idated steel-railed tramway ascends the mountainside to dismantled gun
emplacements and a multi-level observation bunker. A switchback trail at the
base of the tramway (hidden by vegetation) winds upward to the 672-foot
summit and follows along the ridge line. The uphill hike takes about 45 minutes with tough bushwhacking at the trail's end.

Anchorage:

Mary's Bay is a suitable anchorage in fair weather but is susceptible to sloppy
water movement and williwaws in moderate southerly weather. In the bay's
north corner, drop anchor near the head in 6–8 fathoms. Another anchorage
for small boats lies in 8 fathoms in the bay's southeast corner, about 100 yards
off the army dock ruins.

Barwell Island

Barwell Island, a precipitous 30-acre island immediately south of Cape
Resurrection, is part of the Alaska Maritime National Wildlife Refuge.
The ravaged sea cliffs provide Barwell Island with an austere appearance
and ideal marine bird habitat. In spring, thousands of kittiwakes, murres,
and puffins return to take up residence along the cliffs and in the cement
bunkers atop the island.

In the early 1940s, the U.S. Army built and operated an observation post
and a handful of bunkers atop Barwell Island's 414-foot high summit. From
an offshore vessel, a careful observer can still see the outline of bunkers
perched on the cliffs and summit. The soldiers stationed on the island must
have thought they were at the end of the world. Detailed graffiti preserved
on the concrete walls and steel doors describes the desolate, windswept
outpost as a "Hellhole." No surprise there. The bunkers were abandoned
shortly after construction.

Seabirds among Army observation bunkers, Barwell Island.

A former foot trail carved into the sea cliffs began from a rock ledge on the northwestern shore. The trail switchbacked steeply up the eroding cliff and then runs eastward to a sloping razorback ridge that lead to the bunkers on the summit.

Unfortunately, the old wooden steps, water pipe, and cable hand railings corroded away and dropped into the sea long ago. Steep sections of the trail have completely eroded away. Intense summer foliage, head high wild celery, and cow parsnip, well fertilized by marine birds, covers the island. The thick vegetation limits visibility to only a few feet and makes the climb dangerous. Climbing on Barwell Island is not recommended.

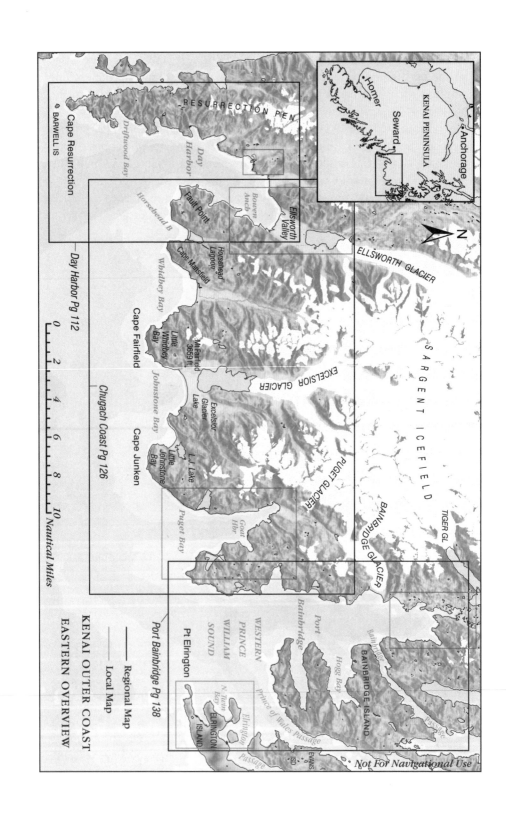

KENAI OUTER COAST
EASTERN OVERVIEW

Day Harbor Pg 112

Chugach Coast Pg 126

Port Bainbridge Pg 138

⎯⎯ Regional Map
⎯⎯ Local Map

0   2   4   6   8   10
Nautical Miles

Cape Resurrection
BARWELL IS

Day Harbor

Driftwood Bay

RESURRECTION PEN.

Bowen Anch.

Ellsworth Valley

Horsehead B.

Fault Point

Whidbey Bay

Cape Mansfield

Horsehead Lagoon

Cape Fairfield

Little Whidbey Bay

Mt Fairfield 3659 ft

Johnstone Bay

Cape Junken

Excelsior Glacier

Excelsior Lake

L.J. Lake

Little Johnstone Bay

EXCELSIOR GLACIER

PUGET GLACIER

Goat Hbr

Puget Bay

Pt Elrington

WESTERN PRINCE WILLIAM SOUND

Port Bainbridge

Hogg Bay

BAINBRIDGE ISLAND

Bainbridge Passage

Prince of Wales Passage

Elrington Passage

N.Twin Bay

ELRINGTON ISLAND

EVANS ISD.

ELLSWORTH GLACIER

SARGENT ICEFIELD

BAINBRIDGE GLACIER

TIGER GL.

N

Not For Navigational Use

Anchorage

KENAI PENINSULA

Homer

Seward

Section 1

Heading Eastward
from
Resurrection Bay

Vessels anchored near Bainbridge Glacier in Port Bainbridge.

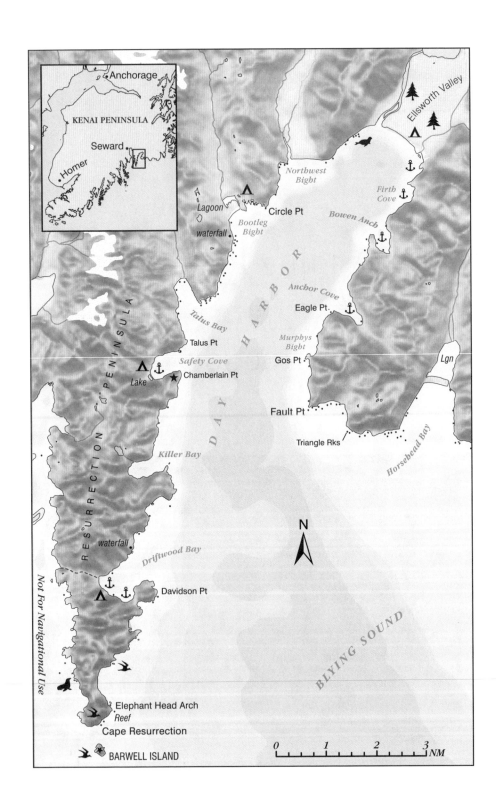

Anchorage

KENAI PENINSULA

Seward

Homer

Lagoon

waterfall

Bootleg Bight

Circle Pt

Northwest Bight

Bowen Anch

Ellsworth Valley

Firth Cove

Talus Bay

Talus Pt

H A R B O R

Anchor Cove

Eagle Pt

Murphys Bight

P E N I N S U L A

Lake

Safety Cove

Gos Pt

★ Chamberlain Pt

Lgn

D A Y

Fault Pt

R E S U R R E C T I O N

Killer Bay

Triangle Rks

Horsehead Bay

N

waterfall

Driftwood Bay

Davidson Pt

Not For Navigational Use

B L Y I N G   S O U N D

Elephant Head Arch
Reef
Cape Resurrection

BARWELL ISLAND

0   1   2   3
NM

11

Day Harbor

CAPE RESURRECTION TO FAULT POINT

Wildlife Viewing:
Cape Resurrection is a prime viewing area for marine birds, whales, and sea lions. Bootleg Lagoon attracts scores of common merganser and Barrow's goldeneye ducks. Count on seeing wildlife including river otters, black bears, bald eagles, and hundreds of glaucous-winged gulls. Upper Day Harbor is a summer playground to humpback whales, sea otters, and marbled murrelets.

Kayaking:
Lower Day Harbor lies exposed to the gulf coast weather and offers few landing beaches. The upper harbor and eastern shore provide partially sheltered waters with reliable landing beaches. A kayak journey from Safety Cove to Bootleg Cove onward to the harbor's head, and then along the eastern shore to Gos Point reveals Day Harbor's finest features.

Camping:
Driftwood Bay State Marine Park, Safety Cove State Marine Park, and Bootleg Cove are excellent camping areas. The harbor's head and Ellsworth Valley host the best camping and hiking destinations in Day Harbor.

Hiking:
Bootleg Cove and Lagoon provide wooded terrain to explore along the harbor's western shore. The Ellsworth Valley area is loaded with miles of wild glacial landscape to discover. The Eldorado Trail follows the path of least resistance from Eldorado Narrows over Resurrection Peninsula to Driftwood Bay.

Anchorages:
Day Harbor's eastern shore has two excellent vessel anchorages: Bowen Anchorage and Anchor Cove. On the western shore, Safety Cove provides the good shelter. As an anchorage, Driftwood Bay owns spectacular scenery, but lies exposed to easterly winds and should only be used in light weather.

In 1787 Captain Nathaniel Portlock noted a 2.5-nm wide indentation on his tract chart and named it Day's Harbor. It is unlikely Portlock recognized Day Harbor's main attribute — as one of the most hospitable fjords in the region. Today, only 20 nm from Seward, the harbor has become a backyard recreation area for mariners escaping Resurrection Bay, whether by air, sailboat, powerboat, paddle, or water taxi.

Davidson Point at the south entrance to Driftwood Bay.

When cruising from the east, a mariner's first visual contact with Day Harbor is the exposed, precipitous Resurrection Peninsula shoreline between Cape Resurrection and Driftwood Bay. Here, the 4 nm long shoreline echoes with the sound of surf and seabirds through a dramatic series of eroded sea caves, rock pinnacles, and sea cliffs. Mariners unfamiliar with the Day Harbor side of Cape Resurrection should be alert for a barnacle-encrusted reef located 60 yards offshore from Elephant Head Arch. This sea arch forms the easternmost point of Cape Resurrection. The nearby reef begins to show at a 6-foot tide or lower and is usually marked by cresting waves and breaking surf. Immediately northwest of Elephant Head Arch is an exposed rocky bight remarkable for its tall talus piles and steep shoreline. Starting in late June, the area is a convenient spot to wet a line for silver salmon that often school and mill between the cape and Driftwood Bay.

Driftwood Bay

Driftwood Bay is a breathtaking, semi-protected embayment surrounded by towering basalt dikes. The sheer cliff at Davidson Point on the bay's south entrance resembles a walled fortress and partially protects the bay from southeasterly storm waves. Inside the bay, spruce trees grow along the lichen-covered ledges of the sea cliffs. In wet weather, the encircling cliffs come alive with sounds of cascading water. The bay's hook shape, with a long lead exposed to the east, forms a natural catch basin for flotsam that drifts westward on the coastal current. Beachcombing at the bay's head can be rewarding, especially in spring after winter storms have raked over the Blying Sound region.

The rocky seacoast stretching north from the bay's head is nearly perpendicular. Approach it only during calm sea conditions. A semi-hidden, 70-foot-tall waterfall occupies a narrow rock crevasse 1 nm from the bay's head. At times a colorful rainbow radiates from the plume exiting the rock-walled grotto.

Kayaking and Camping:

Dependable landing beaches are scarce along the rugged western shore of lower Day Harbor. However, the barrier beach at the head of Driftwood Bay serves as a semi-reliable landing site in summer. Driftwood Bay State Marine Park permits beach camping but obtaining fresh water at the bay's head can be a problem in dry periods. A log pond lies behind the beach berm and overflows with marooned driftwood. Please be respectful of private property located on the hillside at the north end of the beach.

Hiking:

The Eldorado Trail links Resurrection Bay with Driftwood Bay. This wilderness trail is a collection of human and wildlife trails. It begins at the northwestern head of Driftwood Bay, then ascends the wooded valley. The trail crosses

over a 700-foot-high saddle atop Resurrection Peninsula and descends to a rocky alcove, 0.25 nm northeast of Pillow Rock, on the shore of Eldorado Narrows. The hike, approximately two miles long, is steep and becomes obscured by summer vegetation. Only attempt the hike under dry conditions during daylight hours.

Anchorage:

Driftwood Bay is a fair-weather anchorage frequently used by fishing boats and sailboats. Tucked on the inside of Davidson Point is a rocky recess that affords anchorage for small vessels. Drop anchor in 8–12 fathoms; the bottom is rocky with limited holding ability in heavy easterly weather. Many skippers prefer to anchor in 6–10 fathoms at the bay's head,

Beach at the head of Driftwood Bay.

Killer Point, southern entrance to Killer Bay.

favoring the south end of the beach. Seafarers planning to spend an extended period at the anchorage may consider setting a stern anchor to position the bow into the swell.

Note:

Periodically, easterly and southeasterly gales assault Driftwood Bay and raise havoc with anchored vessels, especially in late summer. Avoid the bay when such conditions threaten. In northwesterly weather, however, vessels can move in close to the beach at the bay's head. Typically, the northwesterly wind careens over the saddle of Resurrection Peninsula and then blasts out of the bay's entrance. At the head, the gusting winds may be strong, but the fetch is minor. Also, the offshore wind conveniently knocks down the swell entering the bay from Blying Sound.

Killer Bay

At the southeast entrance to Killer Bay stands a 12-foot-high rock, 100 yards offshore. A water depth of 25 fathoms or more runs throughout the bay, except close to shore.

In 1912, a U.S. Geological Survey team named Killer Bay when mapping the outer coast. While in the bay, the survey crew observed an orca whale locked in a bloody battle with another leviathan, hence the name.

A gravel beach, 100 feet long, is located at the bay's head. Deep water extends right up to the beach. Small boats can temporarily drop anchor close to the beach in about 15 fathoms of water, with limited swing room from the shore. A better choice is to anchor in nearby Safety Cove.

Safety Cove

Safety Cove is less spectacular than Driftwood Bay, but it is the best anchorage on Day Harbor's western shore. At the cove's south entrance stands the precipitous rock face of Chamberlain Point. Here, World War II ruins of a searchlight station, observation bunker, and powerhouse cling to the cliff, 150–300 feet above the water's surface. At the cove's head, the wooden remains of a military storage building rest on the S end of the beach. In an amazing feat of sheer will and determination, Army engineers, construction crews, and soldiers hauled and dragged a communication cable from Topeka Point at Humpy Cove in Resurrection Bay over the 1,500-foot high pass atop Resurrection Peninsula to link Chamberlain Point with the coastal defense fortifications in Resurrection Bay.

Behind the piles of driftwood scattered along the beachfront, a small lake decorates the valley floor. The lake's mirror-like surface reflects 3,800-foot high snowy peaks and glacial cirques. On minus tides, a rusted boat engine buried in beach gravel makes an appearance at the water's edge.

While brown bears are not common in Day Harbor, a record-sized brown bear was shot and killed in Safety Cove a few years back. Black bears are common.

Kayaking and Camping:
The cobble beachfront at the cove's head provides a landing beach with an easy portage to the lake. Typically in summer, a late morning, southerly day breeze develops in Day Harbor, and the wind chop at the cove's mouth can exceed 2 feet. Take advantage of summer daylight and calm sea conditions by traveling early morning and evening hours.
Safety Cove, a State Marine Park, is an excellent location to establish a base camp. A few well-worn campsites hide in the sheltered alder and spruce grove between the beach berm and the lake.

Anchorage:
Drop anchor near the head of Safety Cove in 10–12 fathoms, muddy gravel bottom. By favoring the S shore, anchored vessels can avoid some of the swells issuing from Blying Sound.

Fishing:
Halibut anglers may anchor or drift along the rocky 30-fathom shelf, 0.25 nm off Talus Point. During the summer, halibut come up from the harbor's depth and migrate over this rocky shelf area.

Talus Bay

Talus Bay lies exposed to the southeast and the swell. Inside the bay, vessels should stay on the deeper side of the 10-fathom curve. A roaring stream cascades down from a lake located on the hillside at the bay's head. Wave action exposing irregular patches of sand and boulders gives the beach a ravaged look. Offshore from the head is foul with rocks. Watch out for a rock 100 yards south of the east entrance point, which is exposed at low tide. Avoid overnight anchoring because of the uncomfortable swell from the gulf.

Approximately 2 nm north of Talus Bay is Bootleg Bight, where a prominent waterfall drops over a cliff on the south end of a half-mile-long, wave-beaten, barrier beach. The gravel beach stretches northward and terminates at the channel into Bootleg Lagoon.

Bootleg Cove and Bootleg Lagoon

Bootleg Cove and Lagoon together encompass one of the hidden treasures of Day Harbor. The area should only be visited during calm seas. Bootleg Cove is a tiny alcove with an ideal landing beach for an inflatable, kayak, or skiff, preferably less than 20 feet in length. The alcove is shallow with little room to maneuver. The entrance is only 10 yards wide, so keep to mid-channel. Immediately inside, on the north side of the entrance rests a conspicuous flat-top rock. Other boulders and submerged rocks are scattered around the perimeter, so keep to the center of the basin.

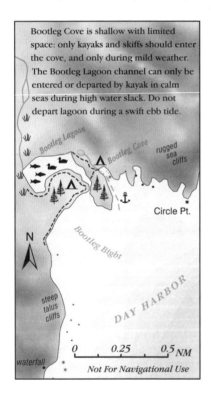

Bootleg Cove is shallow with limited space: only kayaks and skiffs should enter the cove, and only during mild weather. The Bootleg Lagoon channel can only be entered or departed by kayak in calm seas during high water slack. Do not depart lagoon during a swift ebb tide.

Bootleg Lagoon • Bootleg Cove • rugged sea cliffs • Circle Pt. • N • Bootleg Bight • steep talus cliffs • DAY HARBOR • waterfall

0   0.25   0.5 NM
Not For Navigational Use

Be aware that during low water with a moderate southerly swell, waves sometimes crest and break in the narrow entrance of the cove. In light weather and neap tides, skiffs and inflatables can anchor in the center of the cove or land on the sandy beach at the cove's head. Avoid anchoring in the cove during periods of extremely low water.

A local legend claims that during prohibition, a Seward tavern owner operated a secret whiskey still in the cove. A moss-covered wooden foundation of unknown origin, possibly the alleged still, lies buried beneath deadfalls and blueberry bushes on the hillside.

On the cove's west flank is Bootleg Lagoon. The lagoon's shoreline is abundant with alder, spruce, and fields of lupine and rye grass. Thick mats of eelgrass clog the 40-acre lagoon. A network of shallow streams and spawning channels fan out from the swampy head. A diverse array of wildlife

Sand and cobble landing beach, Bootleg Cove.

inhabits the lagoon. Groups of merganser, and harlequin ducks swim and dive along the shore. Visitors can often view half-dozen eagles perched atop spruce branches or loitering along the stream feeding on salmon carcasses. Watch for river otters that slink among the salmonberry bushes along the shoreline, harbor seals that navigate in and out of the lagoon channel at high water, and black bears feeding in the marshes.

In winter, mounds of gravel piled high by storm waves block the lagoon channel. The channel remains obstructed until meltwater, and spring tides blow it open in late May or early June.

Kayaking, Camping, and Hiking:
   Set up a camp atop the sandy beach berm in Bootleg Cove. An unreliable water source trickles on the west side of the cove.
   There are two ways to reach the lagoon. (1) Hike or portage over the 150-yard wide wooded peninsula on the southwest flank of Bootleg Cove. An over-grown trail obstructed by fallen trees meanders to the lagoon. (2) During calm sea conditions at the upper end of the high water, kayakers can enter or depart the lagoon via the stream.

Note:
   Exiting the lagoon during a swift flowing ebb current is dangerous. Be sure to check sea conditions at the mouth of the channel before departing the lagoon. An ebbing current along with a swell from Blying Sound creates breaking seas at the entrance (I once helped rescue three people and a dog, after a wave flipped their skiff onto the beach at the channel's mouth).

Looking north along the eastern shore of Day Harbor toward Ellsworth Glacier.

Anchorage:
> The Bootleg Bight area is a poor overnight anchorage. However, for day use, vessels can temporarily anchor on the gravel shelf, midway along the beach, in 6–8 fathoms. Small boats can also temporarily anchor, southeastward from the outer mouth of Bootleg Cove, off the wooded peninsula, in 7–8 fathoms, rocky bottom.

Northwest Bight

Northwest Bight is a wide indentation 1 nm north of Bootleg Cove. At the head lies a three-quarter-mile-long gravel beach. A wooded valley ascends four miles to an unnamed glacier, which is an extension of Godwin Glacier in Resurrection Bay. A wide, fast-moving stream flows on the west end of this beach. Chum salmon move into the stream in late summer. In the woods behind the beach are remains of an old logging camp that operated more than a half century ago.

Private land and a few recreation cabins sit behind the beach berm. Bush planes occasionally land on the beach, which is usually washed by waves generated in the gulf. Accessing the beach from the water is possible during calm seas.

Sports fishers can temporarily anchor in Northwest Bight, east of the stream mouth in 6–10 fathoms on a sandy bottom. Vessels should avoid the rocky alcove southwest of the barrier beach, as rocks and kelp patches lie near shore. At low water, harbor seals haul out along the bight's southern shoreline and are sensitive to vessels approaching too close.

HEAD OF DAY HARBOR

The long sloping waterfront at the head of Day Harbor is the former terminal moraine of Ellsworth Glacier, which withdrew from tidewater more than two centuries ago. Today, behind the moraine beach, thick stands of alder and spruce grow on the valley floor. Ellsworth Glacier dominates the valley skyline. The State of Alaska owns most of Day Harbor, although private property exists along the harbor's east shore.

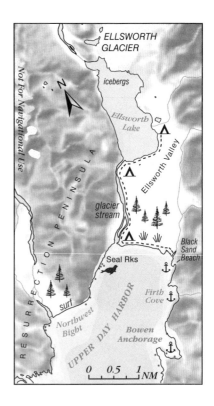

The bottom rapidly shallows within one-quarter mile of the beach. In 1909, geologists Grant and Higgins visited the Ellsworth moraine. At the time, they reported Ellsworth Glacier was about 1.7 miles from high water. In the past century, not only has the glacier continued to slowly retreat up the valley but also the surface elevation and thickness of the glacier have significantly diminished. Nevertheless, Ellsworth Glacier is easily visible from vessels passing the mouth of Day Harbor. This imposing glacier, with its two dark medial moraines, flows down from the Sargent Icefield and presently terminates about four miles from salt water. A glacial lake with icebergs and bergy bits lies in front of the ice terminus.

A silt-laden stream departs from the lake and meanders along the valley's western edge before entering Day Harbor. Harbor seals regularly surface in the stream mouth and feed throughout the area. Seals also haulout on the rocks that litter the western shoreline near the head. The population of harbor seals in Day Harbor is seasonal and varies between 100 and 200 seals. Avoid disturbing hauled-out seals, especially in June when females give birth and in August and September when seals molt and need to rest ashore.

Kayaking:

> During calm sea conditions, at high water, paddlers can enter the glacial stream at the western end of the moraine beach. A protected basin, created by the eroding stream current, lies immediately inside the entrance. This basin is a good place to beach a kayak or dinghy. Dependable landing beaches are located at the head's E corner and in numerous locations along the E shore.

Ellsworth Glacier at the head of Day Harbor.

Camping:

> The head provides numerous camping opportunities along the moraine. In summer, campers will find thick vegetation, alder and spruce groves, in addition to swampy, lowland areas north of the cobble beach.
>
> Mountain streams are at either end of the moraine beach. A water source lies at the eastern end of the beach approximately 100 yards from high tide at the base of the hillside. The Ellsworth glacial stream, on the western end of the beach, is silty.

Hiking:

> The low-lying glacial moraine at the head of Day Harbor contrasts with the fjord's nearly vertical shoreline. Hikers can bushwhack their way up the valley's east side (not recommended) or hike up the valley's west side along the glacial stream to the southern shore of Ellsworth Glacier Lake. The route is marked in places with survey tape. Thick brush, irregular push moraines, and occasional clearings line both routes. At the glacial lake, icebergs float and lay grounded along the shore. The glacial till terrain is raw and wild looking from recent deglaciation.

Anchorage:

> In calm weather, small craft can anchor at the head, in the east corner. Drop anchor approximately 0.3 nm southwest of the stream mouth and shallow tidal mudflats to gain easy access to the beach. The bottom shallows rapidly.
>
> Nearby, an optional spot to anchor lies near the wooded peninsula that forms the tiny, south-facing pocket beach known locally as Woelker's Bight. The place hosts a little, black sand beach. Drop anchor at the bight's mouth in 7–10 fathoms. Private land surrounds the black sand beach.

Firth Cove

Firth Cove (Resolute Cove) is located 1 nm from the head of Day Harbor. A handful of private cabins and recreation moorings occupy the cove. A powerful stream cascades down a boulder-filled streambed. A gravel outwash shoal at the stream mouth extends into the cove and goes partially dry at low water. In fair weather, small craft can anchor in 6–8 fathoms. All the upland property from mean high water is privately owned.

Bowen Anchorage

Bowen Anchorage is a secure place to moor a vessel and explore the head of Day Harbor by inflatable boat or kayak. Although exposed to northwest winds, the water's surface is usually flat calm. During southeasterly gales, williwaws can sweep down the mountainside into the anchorage. Thick stands of spruce and hemlock grow from the water's edge to a height of 1,200 feet where alpine terrain begins. Most of the waterfront property is privately owned, and several cabins lie scattered along the shore.

In 1927, Bowen Anchorage was named after William H. Bowen, a crew member of the USC&GS vessel *Surveyor*. Bowen drowned in an attempt to rescue two of his mates who were cast into Resurrection Bay when their skiff swamped in rough seas.

Modest logging activity has taken place at least twice in Bowen Anchorage during the past century, including the hillside above the southern entrance point and in the valley at the cove's head. Close examination of the beach at the head reveals rusted cables and overgrown skid trails. A small warehouse once sat at tidewater near the stream. Also, buried by thick vegetation are the remains of several cabins used by the logging families who lived there. In the 1920s, loggers used teams of horses to drag the trees to the beach. A boat would then tow rafts of logs to Seward.

Anchorage:
> Bowen Anchorage is the most sheltered anchorage in Day Harbor. Vessels anchor in the center of the outer cove in 14 fathoms on a sticky mud bottom. Small craft can anchor closer to the head in 6 fathoms. A significant rock along the south shore, near the head, periodically shows itself. Also, a few rocks and a shallow shelf extend off the stream's mouth.

Anchor Cove

Anchor Cove lies 2 nm north of Fault Point. In 1909, Grant and Higgins visited here and lost their anchor in the process. They also noted that the cove was the first safe anchorage in Day Harbor. Anchor Cove is a half-mile wide and shaped like a funnel with an outer and inner basin. When easterly gale winds slam the outer coast, vessels *en route* to or from Prince William Sound commonly find refuge in Anchor Cove. On occasions, fishing vessels have used the gravel beach at the head for emergency repairs. A homestead with several cabins sits in the inner cove at the head.

Looking west across Day Harbor from Anchor Cove.

Anchorage:

> Anchor Cove has a gently sloped bottom and offers shelter in all weather, except northwesterly gales. The cove's main navigational danger lies in the inner cove, off the northeast shore, where a boulder rests 75 yards offshore. A 6-foot or higher tide covers the boulder, which has been rammed by vessels more than once.
>
> Large vessels prefer to anchor in the middle of the outer anchorage in 10–15 fathoms, on a hard mud bottom. Small craft can drop anchor in 3–5 fathoms in the inner anchorage toward the head, slightly favoring the south shore. In summer, thick patches of kelp grow on the bottom of the inner cove and may foul an anchor.

Gos Point

Gos Point is a prominent rock headland protruding from the shore 1 nm south of Anchor Cove. The headland borders a small indentation to the north known locally as Murphy's Bight. Beautiful cobble beaches extend northward along the bight's shore. Most of the waterfront property behind the barrier beach north of Gos Point is privately owned.

Kayaking:

> In summer, the mile-long stretch north of Gos Point provides fairly reliable access to the beach. If traveling by kayak to Prince William Sound, Murphy's Bight provides the last reliable landing beach until Goat Harbor 24 nm away.

Fishing:

> July through August, Gos Point attracts milling schools of silver salmon in addition to a fleet of fishing boats. At times, the fishing is sensational with anglers quickly landing bag limits. On other occasions, when sloppy sea conditions

invade the Blying Sound, Gos Point and the partially sheltered waters along the eastern shore of Day Harbor stand ready to welcome boat loads of anglers.

Anchorage:

Small craft can find temporarily anchorage in Murphy's Bight in 6–8 fathoms on a gravel bottom. The shoreline from Gos Point to Fault Point lies broken with rock slides and talus mounds. Mariners wishing to avoid fouling or losing their favorite anchor should not drop it in rocky areas near the base of talus chutes.

Fault Point

Fault Point is the fissured rock headland at the eastern entrance of Day Harbor. The point is named for two obvious faults that give the headland a sawtooth appearance.

A pair of boulders located 40 yards south of Fault Point, appear during extreme low water and are sometimes marked by cresting waves. The fragmented graywacke cliffs along Fault Point are unstable. During local earthquakes, the fractured sea cliffs and headlands from Fault Point to Cape Puget are known to erupt in massive rock slides and billowing clouds of dust that reach hundreds of feet into the air.

The 40-fathom curve running southeastward from Fault Point along the Day Harbor trench marks good halibut fishing grounds.

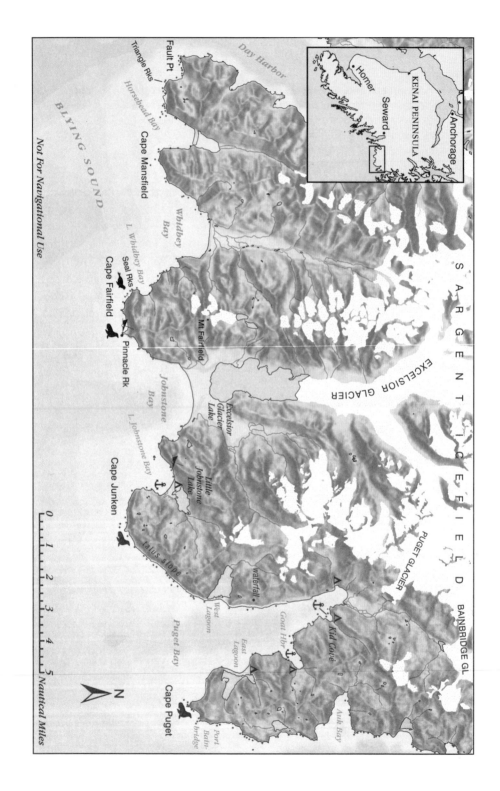

Day Harbor

Fault Pt

Triangle Rks

Horsehead Bay

Cape Mansfield

Whidbey Bay

Mt Fairfield

L. *Whidbey Bay*

Seal Rks

Cape Fairfield

Pinnacle Rk

Johnstone Bay

L. *Johnstone Bay*

Cape Junken

talus slope

Excelsior Glacier Lake

Little Johnstone Lake

waterfall

West Lagoon

Puget Bay

East Lagoon

Goat Hbr

Kid Cove

Ank Bay

Port Bain-bridge

Cape Puget

BLYING SOUND

Not For Navigational Use

S A R G E N T   I C E F I E L D

EXCELSIOR GLACIER

PUGET GLACIER

BAINBRIDGE GL

KENAI PENINSULA

Anchorage

Seward

Homer

0 1 2 3 4 5 *Nautical Miles*

N

12

Chugach Coast

FAULT POINT TO CAPE PUGET

Wildlife Viewing:
> The headlands of Cape Fairfield, Cape Junken, and Cape Puget provide dynamic viewing opportunities for Steller sea lions and marine birds. Migrating gray, humpback, and killer whales frequent the region. Rocks along the eastern shore of Whidbey Bay are important harbor seal haulouts.

Kayaking:
> Only a well-conditioned kayaker with ocean savvy should paddle this exposed seacoast. The landing beaches in this region are undependable. An ocean paddle of 22 nm against the coastal current separates Fault Point from a reliable refuge beach at Goat Harbor. Alternative landing beaches in Little Johnstone Bay and Little Whidbey Bay are precarious and require fair weather.

Camping and Hiking:
> Access to the exposed Chugach coast by sea is limited to a few partially sheltered spots and is totally weather dependent. Only the sheltered confines of Puget Bay provide regular access to shore. The beach at Little Johnstone Bay is a good camping and hiking destination. Bush or float plane is often the only means of access to this area.

Fishing:
> An extensive bottom fishing shelf stretches from Fault Point to Cape Puget. The Seward sport fishing fleet works the productive shelf for a diverse collection of bottom dwellers including halibut, gray cod, rockfish, and lingcod. From June through early August, silver salmon fishing is productive along the capes.

Anchorages:
> Only Puget Bay has reliable anchorages for small vessels. During mild summer weather, Little Johnstone and Little Whidbey Bays provide partial shelter from the gulf but should be considered only fair-weather anchorages.

Bold capes, crumbling rock headlands, and wide bays backed by valley glaciers are the dominant features between Fault Point and Cape Puget. Behind the rugged seascape, the Chugach Mountains lie buried in the thick ice blanket of the Sargent Icefield. The icefield spills into a complex system of glacial fjords stretching from Day Harbor to Port Bainbridge and northward along the western edge of Prince William Sound.

Triangle Rocks, east of Fault Point.

Visiting mariners need to keep a keen eye on the wind and weather and stay tuned for weather updates on the VHF radio.

Directly eastward from Fault Point is a rocky bight, where foul ground extends more than 150 yards offshore. Even in light weather, the steeply cut gravel beach at the head is rarely accessible for beach landings. A thickly wooded valley with a rambling stream lies hidden behind the beach berm. The only evidence of past human activity is the remains of a wooden staircase. At the eastern end of this bight stands a prominent group of inshore rock islets, locally known as Triangle Rocks. The islets are a convenient area to wet a line for rockfish and lingcod or to troll for silver salmon.

Horsehead Bay

Horsehead Bay is the first large indentation east of Day Harbor. At Horsehead Point, submerged rocks extend southeast of the west entrance point and end with a 3-foot-high boulder, approximately 0.3 nm offshore. Midway into the bay (0.5 nm from the head), the sandy bottom shallows to less than 10 fathoms.

Horsehead Lagoon sits behind the barrier beach in the low-lying, wooded valley. Some logging has taken place in the valley behind the beach. Float planes occasionally land on the lagoon while bush planes land on the beach. A private, plywood cabin sits at the base of a crumbling cliff at the lagoon's edge. The bay's ragged shoreline is active with avalanche chutes that reach below the water's surface.

Fishing boats temporarily drop anchor at the bay's head and along the east shore. Accessing the shore requires nearly ideal sea conditions. A landing spot (weather dependent) lies east of the stream mouth and the prominent rock boulder. A trail leads behind the massive boulder to the stream and lagoon.

Cape Mansfield

Cape Mansfield is named for Lt. Commander (later Rear Admiral) Henry Buckingham Mansfield, who skippered the USC&GS survey vessel *Patterson* (1889–91) while surveying and naming many features in southeast Alaska.

A rock awash at high water lies surrounded by deep water approximately 0.3 nm southeast of Cape Mansfield. Breaking seas or a cresting swell usually mark the rock's location but in calm seas, during periods of high water, the danger hides beneath the surface and presents a hazard to those mariners unfamiliar with the area.

A productive bottom-fishing shelf, 30- to 40-fathoms deep, lies south of Cape Mansfield. The shelf is a popular area for charter and weekend halibut anglers. Every summer, halibut weighing more than 200 pounds are hooked and landed in the waters around Cape Mansfield, Cape Fairfield, and Cape Junken.

Groups of mountain goats can often be seen browsing on the narrow rock ledges along the steep east side of Cape Mansfield.

Cabin at Whidbey Bay.

WHIDBEY BAY

When Captain Vancouver sailed past Whidbey Bay two-hundred years ago, glacial ice choked the valley. Today the glacier has withdrawn to a modest-sized glacial cirque at the bay's head.

In 1908, Grant and Higgins named the bay for Lt. Joseph Whidbey, an officer under Captain Vancouver. In spring, 1794, Whidbey undertook the job of surveying western Prince William Sound. After enduring multiple hardships, Whidbey's crew charted the nearby waters of Port Bainbridge, Bainbridge Passage, and all of Bainbridge Island.

Whidbey Bay is a south-facing seacoast 4 nm wide. At the bay's mouth, the bottom is mostly sand. The water shallows to less than 10 fathoms deep, 0.5 nm from the bay's head. As surf crashes along the entire beachfront, little opportunity exists for mariners to cleanly access the beach. A massive boulder (glacial erratic) obstructs the stream mouth at the west end of the beach. At high water, the lower stream entrance can be navigated by skiff or kayak, weather permitting.

A privately-owned cabin sits perched on the western hillside adjacent the stream. Bush planes occasionally land on the beach, which is the most reliable way to access the area. For mariners, the bay's southerly exposure makes it a poor anchorage.

Whidbey Bay's eastern shore has two exposed bights; Little Whidbey Bight is the first cove west of Cape Fairfield.

Little Whidbey Bight

This semi-protected cove is a handy spot to ease a queasy stomach after traveling through lumpy offshore seas. A beautiful, black sand beach spans the cove's head. A stream flows into the cove from the south corner. Thick stands of alder, spruce, and hemlock grow immediately behind the beach berm. The upland areas are mostly privately owned.

Harbor seals inhabit the rocky shoreline rocks and ledges between Little Whidbey and Cape Fairfield. This seal haulout area is the largest in the region. Although the numbers of seals vary seasonally, dozens of seals may be sighted, especially during low water. Keep a respectful distance to minimize disturbance of the seals.

Kayaking and Camping:
The black sand beach in Little Whidbey Bight is anything but a reliable place to land. However, when sea conditions allow, the beach provides a camp and landing area with a reliable water source.

Anchorage:
Little Whidbey is a fair-weather anchorage, primarily used by fishing vessels. Small boats can tuck inside the lee shore, favoring the east corner. Drop anchor in 6–8 fathoms, sandy bottom.

Offshore rocks along the east shore of Cape Fairfield.

Cape Fairfield

Cape Fairfield is the boldest land feature among a series of impressive headlands occupying this stretch of seacoast. At the base of the cape sits Pinnacle Rock, a 126-foot-high outcropping easily recognized from offshore waters. A series of rocks, some submerged, lurk inshore around the cape, especially to the northeast. Dozens of sea lions rest on the rock ledges etched into Pinnacle Rock. In summer, hundreds of kittiwakes nest on the steep cliffs near the cape.

Immediately west of Pinnacle Rock, rusted wreckage from the steamship *Yukon* rests on the beach. The wreck remains a curiosity for divers and treasure hunters. See Chapter 9 for *Notable Maritime Disasters on the North Gulf Coast.*

JOHNSTONE BAY

Johnstone Bay is the largest of the exposed bays in the area. Thick alder and spruce stands thrive in the deglaciated valley behind the 2-mile-long sand and gravel beach. Excelsior Glacier dominates the head. Beach landing are challenging and unreliable because of surf.

In the late 1700s, Excelsior Glacier was at or near tidewater. In 1909 Grant and Higgins reported the glacier was within 0.5 nm of the sea. Today, the ice terminus lies more than 5 miles from salt water and has ground out a significant glacial lake, strewn with icebergs.

Looking west across Little Johnstone Bay.

Grant and Higgins named the bay for Lt. James Johnstone, an officer aboard Vancouver's ship *Discovery*. Similar to Lt. Joseph Whidbey, who surveyed western Prince William Sound, Lt. Johnstone had the task of surveying the northern and eastern portions of the sound.

Little Johnstone Bay

Lying 1 nm west of Cape Junken, Little Johnstone Bay is a modest-sized indentation within Johnstone Bay, and is a popular destination among charter and sports fishers. In summer, the semi-protected bay is a great spot to mooch for silver salmon or just take a break from the washing-machine wave action commonly found offshore.

A tree-crowned islet with rocks awash rests 0.25 nm off Little Johnstone Bay's western entrance point. The eastern entrance and shoreline lie littered with rocks, bull kelp beds, and a pair of rocky islets that stand approximately 150 yards offshore.

A large lake sits behind the crashing surf and beach frontage of Little Johnstone Bay. A stream issuing from the lake runs parallel to the beach for more than a quarter-mile. In mid- to late-summer, the stream is abundant with pink and chum salmon. Private land holdings are scattered along the lake and the eastern head of Little Johnstone Bay. Float planes land on the lake, while wheeled planes land atop the beach berm west of the stream. The head of Little Johnstone Bay includes exceptionally wild and expansive terrain.

Salmon seiner working near Cape Junken.

Kayaking, Camping, and Hiking:
> In mild sea conditions, a dingy, raft, or kayak can access the gently slop-
> ing sand beach at the northeast corner of Little Johnstone Bay. The nearby
> kelp beds help to buffer the surf. Set up camp along the wave-ravaged barrier
> beach at the bay's head. Camp areas and hiking opportunities lie along the
> main beach. A network of game trails crisscrosses the thickly vegetated ter-
> rain to the lake.

Anchorage:
> Little Johnstone Bay is a fair-weather anchorage due to its southwesterly
> exposure. To anchor, favor the east shore. Here, approximately 0.25 nm north
> of the rock islets, at the outer edge of the kelp beds, is a suitable anchorage in
> 7 fathoms, sandy bottom.
> Little Johnstone Bay is a unique place with spectacular ocean scenery. Do not
> be fooled, however, the bay is not a good location for a vessel to stay in dete-
> riorating sea conditions. In heavy southerly weather, breakers are known to
> sweep across the offshore rocks and shallow-water areas near the east and
> west entrances. Vessels must move to deeper water in the exposed outer
> mouth to hope to hold anchor against the storm surge.

Cape Junken

Cape Junken is a bold headland stepped at its lower base. A large flat-top
rock is easily recognizable at the tip of the cape when cruising offshore. An
extensive 30- to 40-fathom-deep shelf adjacent to Cape Junken is good
halibut ground. Try anchoring a mile offshore from Cape Junken. For fishers
new to cape fishing, take a tip from the charter boat skippers, and watch

North shore, Kid Cove.

where they anchor or drift fish. Sometimes it pays to experiment and fish downstream from the other boats to take advantage of chum bags and bait scent that drift with the westward current.

Note: A pair of rocks, surrounded by 20 fathoms of water, but awash at low water, lie 0.25 nm south of Cape Junken. On spring tides during foul weather, occasional tide rips form in areas around the cape as currents and winds clash.

Puget Bay

A spectacular 3-mile-long stretch of crumbling sea cliffs lie along Puget Bay's western entrance. Cruising northward into Puget Bay is a welcome change of pace from the miles of open ocean that range eastward from Day Harbor. The 6 nm wide entrance to Puget Bay gradually tapers to less than a half-mile at the head, where Puget Glacier is clearly visible on the hillside. The glacier's reclining tongue clings to a rock ledge with recent signs of deglaciation. A century ago, Grant and Higgins reported that Puget Glacier terminated 1.25 miles from tidewater. Since then, the glacier has ever so slowly retreated up the valley.

Midway up Puget Bay, a noticeable 2-mile-long gravel beach stands out on the western shore. Here, most of the beachfront property stretching to the bay's head is privately owned. Thick stands of alder and spruce blanket the low-lying terrain, helping to camouflage a handful of private cabins built behind the beach berm. A scattering of private moorings collect algae on their buoys and tie-lines. At the bay's head, in the west corner, a muddy shoal clogs the stream mouth area. Here, the water rapidly shallows.

The Chugach National Forest lays claim to the upland areas of Puget Bay's eastern shore.

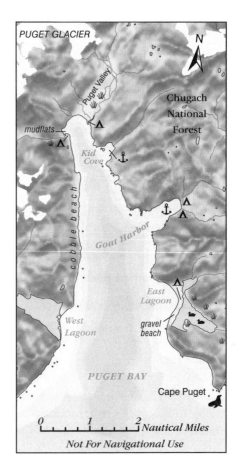

Kayaking and Camping:
A camp area with an inviting landing beach lies on the spit, in the W corner, adjacent the bay's head. Here, a treeless, gravel spit terminates at the mouth of a mud-clogged inlet. A lush valley spreads out behind the spit where stream winds through the valley floor. Nearby, on the spit, thick mats of beach greens and rye grass grow around piles of old driftwood marooned by storm waves. The N end of the spit is owned by the State of Alaska and OK for camping.

Kid Cove

Kid Cove rests along the bay's eastern shore approximately 0.7 nm from the head. It is a good destination with a spectacular view of snowbound peaks laced with glacial cirques. This anchorage is a handy base camp for further exploration, by dinghy or kayak, of the upper portion of Puget Bay. Unfortunately, the towering mountain ridges restrict VHF weather reception.

Anchorage:
Enter Kid Cove mid-channel or by favoring a pair of prominent tree-covered islets that protrude from the north shore. An offshore rock (covered by an 11-foot tide) is located 100 yards west of the southern entrance point. The cove is about 0.25 nm wide. Drop anchor east of the wooded islets in the center of the bight in 5 fathoms. Groundswells off the gulf can reach the cove.

Camping:
Mudflats fill the head and portions of the north shore of Kid Cove. A stream enters at the head by way of a narrow finger inlet. The cove has slim offerings for camping. Neap tides allow some protection from high water, but better camping options are located at the bay's head or in Goat Harbor.

Head of Goat Harbor at low water.

Goat Harbor

Signs of past human activity can be found in the old growth woods at the harbor's head where a few culturally modified trees, dead and alive, still stand. In the woods near the main stream are scattered signs of early 20th century endeavors, now mostly buried beneath moss.

Goat Harbor is a convenient and popular anchorage for sport and commercial fishing vessels that operate offshore and along the capes. It is one of the few secure places to get out of the weather. The cobble beach at the harbor's head also is a reliable place to land a kayak and provides a choice of hospitable places to camp.

Kayaking, Camping, and Hiking:

Goat Harbor offers a little of everything. Two streams drain into the harbor at the head. Former campsites exist near each of the streams.

Hikers can spend hours bushwhacking at the head. A variety of 20th century treasures (mostly moss covered) from fishing and hunting endeavors lie scattered in the woods. Pink salmon are plentiful in late summer.

Anchorage:

Goat Harbor is the main vessel anchorage in Puget Bay. Drop anchor near the harbor's head in 6 fathoms or more, hard mud bottom. Be aware that extensive gravel outwash areas extend into the cove from both streams at the harbor's head, so allow for extra swing room.

In summer, thick mats of kelp can be a bit of a problem when anchoring in Goat Harbor, especially in water less than 30-feet deep.

East Lagoon

On the eastern shore of Puget Bay, a prominent crescent-shaped barrier beach, 2 nm northwest of Cape Puget, is a worthwhile destination for beachcombers. A spacious, tree-lined lagoon lies hidden on the other side of the barrier beach.

Kayaking and Camping:
> In calm sea conditions, raft and kayak landings are possible inside the kelp beds midway along the beach. Hike the expansive beach or portage a kayak across the beach berm and explore the secluded waters of the lagoon. This is a beautiful location.

Cape Puget

Cape Puget rests at the western entrance to Port Bainbridge. In 1794, Lt. Whidbey named Cape Puget for Lt. Peter Puget, an officer, and aide to Captain Vancouver. Whidbey noted the cape while surveying the shoreline of Port Bainbridge.

Numerous rocks lie inshore near Cape Puget. One jagged rock lurks 350 yards offshore, south of the cape. This rock is a traditional haulout for dozens of Steller sea lions. During periods of stormy southerly weather, vessels should give the cape a wide berth.

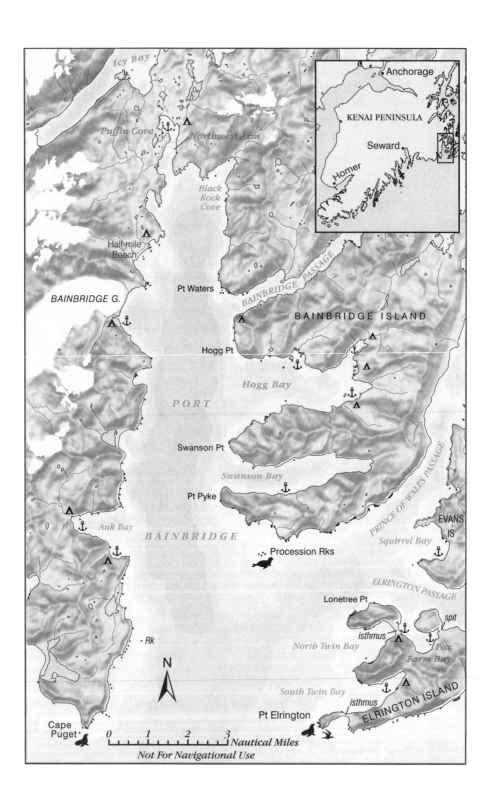

Icy Bay

Puffin Cove

Northwest Arm

Black
Rock
Cove

Half-mile
Beach

BAINBRIDGE G.

Pt Waters

BAINBRIDGE PASSAGE

BAINBRIDGE ISLAND

Hogg Pt

Hogg Bay

PORT

Swanson Pt

Swanson Bay

Pt Pyke

PRINCE OF WALES PASSAGE

EVANS
IS

Auk Bay

BAINBRIDGE

Squirrel Bay

Procession Rks

ELRINGTON PASSAGE

Lonetree Pt

spit

isthmus

Rk

North Twin Bay

Fox
Farm Bay

N

South Twin Bay

isthmus

ELRINGTON ISLAND

Cape
Puget

Pt Elrington

0   1   2   3
Nautical Miles

Not For Navigational Use

Anchorage

KENAI PENINSULA

Seward

Homer

13

Port Bainbridge

CAPE PUGET TO POINT ELRINGTON

Wildlife:
> Lower Port Bainbridge, between Point Pyke and Elrington Island, is an
> abundant marine wildlife area. Both Procession Rocks and Point Elrington are
> traditional haulout areas for harbor seals and sea lions. Transient and resident
> killer whales regularly cruise the island passages leading into Prince William
> Sound. Sea otters are likely to be seen feeding in the sheltered waters around
> Fox Farm Bay, Hogg Bay, and from Northwest Arm's glacial sill to Puffin Cove.

Kayaking:
> The gulf coast weather greatly influences lower Port Bainbridge. Upper Port
> Bainbridge resembles the sheltered waters of Prince William Sound. Fog and
> rain are common in summer. Strong northerly winds and heavy chop are
> frequently channeled down Port Bainbridge, especially in the spring, fall, and
> winter months. Access to landing beaches in the exposed locations of lower
> Port Bainbridge is weather dependent. The pocket beaches in upper Port
> Bainbridge, especially along the eastern shore, are reliable landing areas.

Camping and Hiking:
> A popular refuge known locally as Fox Farm Bay is located at the western
> entrance to Elrington Passage. A wooded isthmus links Fox Farm Bay with the
> head of North Twin Bay. The isthmus offers an excellent location to set up a
> base camp. Within Port Bainbridge, intriguing camping and hiking areas lie
> along the north shore of Hogg Bay and along Bainbridge Glacier's moraine.
> Touring kayakers also can take advantage of a convenient landing beach and
> camp location at the southwestern tip of Bainbridge Passage. The sheltered
> waters and hospitable terrain surrounding Puffin Cove at the extreme head of
> Port Bainbridge provide the best hiking opportunities in the region.

Anchorages:
> Many fine anchorages are scattered throughout the Port Bainbridge area. The
> most popular and secure anchorages are found in Auk Bay, Fox Farm Bay,
> Hogg Bay, and Puffin Cove.

Port Bainbridge, 15 nm long, sits at the western entrance to Prince
William Sound. Its semi-sheltered location seems caught in a tran-
sition between the oceanic ambiance of the outer coast, and the
back-bay, solitude of the sound. The port's western shoreline includes a

mixture of pocket beaches and steeply wooded sea cliffs punctuated by an occasional offshore rock pinnacle. Midway into the bay, the striking white hulk of Bainbridge Glacier descends from the Sargent Icefield to near tidewater. As mariners approach the head of Port Bainbridge, the bay narrows and a shallow glacial moraine, 1.5 fathoms deep, must be crossed to reach the inner sanctum of the Northwest Arm and Puffin Cove.

The port's eastern shoreline is a combination of bold headlands, island passages, and secluded indentations, including Hogg Bay, the most scenic and hospitable bay within Port Bainbridge. Port Bainbridge is no stranger to vessel traffic. Vessels traveling to and from western Prince William Sound typically use Bainbridge, Prince of Wales, or Elrington passages.

When approaching Port Bainbridge from the west, two notable navigational obstructions lurk at the surface northeast of Cape Puget. First, a foul rocky ledge, 0.5 nm north of Cape Puget, extends offshore more than 0.25 nm. Second, a barnacle and seaweed encrusted 9-foot high boulder, located 2.5 nm north of Cape Puget, lies 0.3 nm offshore. Both hazards are especially dangerous during periods of low visibility.

Auk Bay

Auk Bay is the southernmost bay on the western shore of Port Bainbridge. The bay, open to easterly winds, displays a scattering of pocket beaches and terrific mountain scenery.

The mouth of Auk Bay is deep and clear, although a prominent rock pinnacle sits off the southern entrance point. Even in light weather, a noticeable groundswell creates water movement within the bay. Retreat to the bay's head to buffer the swell.

Note, when approaching the head of Auk Bay, mariners should avoid a rock pile (covered during high water) located 150 yards off the north shore and 0.35 nm from the head. Additional rocks and shallow water hazards exist between the rock pile and the north shore.

Kayaking and Camping:
In light weather, the first pocket beach inside the south entrance point offers a suitable landing spot and camp area. Better yet, the bay's recessed head has a choice of landing beaches, water sources, and camp options.

Anchorage:
In calm weather, the crescent-shaped bight, immediately inside the south entrance point, offers a convenient anchorage for vessels. Drop anchor in 7 fathoms, sandy bottom.

Small craft mariners seeking more protection can move into the upper bay. Anchor in 6–11 fathoms, no closer than a 0.25 nm from the high-water mark at the head. Tidal mudflats clog the head, especially along the north and west shores.

An icy stream drains from Bainbridge Glacier Lake.

Bainbridge Glacier

Located directly across from the entrance to Bainbridge Passage stands Bainbridge Glacier; an imposing white ice tongue that reaches within a quarter mile of tidewater. Bainbridge Glacier springs from the 5,000-foot-high elevation of the Sargent Icefield in the Chugach Mountains. The glacier's moraine includes an expansive silt and gravel tidal zone that lies behind the beach berm. Brown bears are known to roam the glacial moraine.

In late summer, on the north and south end of the moraine, noisy gulls loiter along the banks of the glacial streams feeding on pink salmon carcasses. A beautiful collection of tree-covered rock islets lies adjacent to the headland point at the moraine's north end.

In 1908, Grant and Higgins surveyed the base of Bainbridge Glacier. At that time a hundred-foot-tall ice cliff reached tidewater. The geologists believed the glacier was at or near its maximum Little Ice Age advance.

Kayaking, Camping, and Hiking:
Beach landings are feasible on the partially protected waterfront at the south end of the glacier moraine. A kayaker may also paddle up the glacial stream during higher stages of the tide. On the ebb, however, the swift current creates hazardous rapids in the stream.

Hikers craving a close encounter with the glacier can scramble over the churned-up moraine to reach the glacier lake. Optional camping spots lie along the moraine beach.

Looking south over the calm waters of Puffin Cove at the head of Port Bainbridge.

Anchorage:
> A weather dependent anchorage for vessels lies near the south end of Bain-
> bridge Glacial moraine where the beach terminates and the steep, rocky
> shore begins. Drop anchor in 8 fathoms, 100 yards offshore.
> An unnamed, steeply walled cove, 1.5 nm south of Bainbridge Glacier, pro-
> vides a tentative anchorage in 8–10 fathoms of water near the cove's head.
> A scenic waterfall stands out on the rocky cliffs high above the cove.

Half-mile Beach

A wetland area occupies the sunken valley floor behind the half-mile-
long beach berm immediately north of Bainbridge Glacier. A slender ribbon
of ice clings to a cirque gouged into the mountainside directly above the
valley. Midway along the beach, less than a quarter-mile offshore, watch
out for a potentially dangerous reef hidden during higher stages of the tide.

Camping:
> An unreliable landing beach and camping location lie in the first tiny cove
> at the north end of Half-mile Beach. A stream exits the low-lying valley and
> enters the cove at the west end of the beach.

Puffin Cove

Puffin Cove occupies the head of Port Bainbridge. A vessel must cross
over a 1.5-fathom-deep glacial sill at Northwest Arm's mouth to reach the
cove. Mariners should steer a course slightly favoring the east shore headland
when approaching the sill. A gravel shelf (partially bare at low water) with
offshore rocks protrudes approximately 0.25 nm from the west shore into the

arm's entrance channel. Thinly scattered patches of bull kelp grow in the channel area. When across the sill, mariners can steer northward, mid-channel, until the arm opens to the west into Puffin Cove. A collection of picturesque, tree-covered islets and islands occupy the cove's western corner. Gravel ledges extend beneath the water's surface connecting the islets.

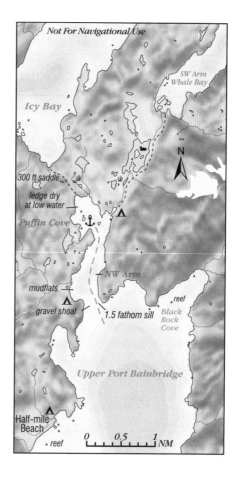

Thick mats of eelgrass grow in the cove's tidal areas, especially in the mouths of the streams and shallow inlets. Unobstructed waters lie in the center of the cove. In summer, Puffin Cove can be flat calm and windless, a situation which can precipitate severe mosquito infestations for visitors.

Sea otters, black bears, and migrating flocks of Canada geese and ducks inhabit the cove and wetland area.

Kayaking, Camping and Hiking:

The easily accessible terrain on the northern shore of Puffin Cove invites hiking and camping, especially in May and June before lush vegetation and insects take over. Two unique wilderness portages exist at the head of the cove. The first, crosses a 1.75-mile-wide isthmus that separates the head of Port Bainbridge from the southwest arm of Whale Bay in Prince William Sound. Here, the portage begins at the finger inlet in the cove's northeast corner. The rugged route follows the east side of a salmon-spawning stream to a large lake (stream not connected to lake). The low rolling terrain requires bushwhacking. After encountering the lake, hike its east shore until the shoreline veers in a westerly direction. At that point, follow the lake's exit stream in a northeasterly direction one-half mile to the head of Whale Bay. The isthmus area is wild country, so hikers should be wary of bears!

The other portage is about a mile in length, but much more strenuous. It begins at tidewater in the northwest corner of Puffin Cove and immediately climbs a rather steep, 300-foot high, thickly wooded saddle and then descends to a cove on the south shore of Icy Bay. Here, marooned icebergs from Tiger Glacier occasionally lay grounded along the waterfront.

For a less demanding exploration, try the north-facing alcove on the south side of Puffin Cove. Begin by hiking alongside the stream at the bight's head. Here, the wooded hillside provides a scenic view overlooking the Icy Bay isthmus.

Anchorage:
Enter Puffin Cove in a westerly direction by passing between the vertical, rock-walled headland and the first lone islet encountered at the cove's entrance. Anchor in 6 fathoms at the mouth of the north-facing alcove, immediately southeast of the wooded island, or vessels can continue another 200 yards westward and anchor in the center of the western bight in 5 fathoms, muddy bottom.

Black Rock Cove

Immediately east of the Northwest Arm and its glacial sill lies a pair of ragged looking, south-facing coves. The western cove is steep with a waterfall at the head.

In Black Rock Cove, a reef (bare at low water) lies 200 yards off the west shore near the mouth. Nearby, a waterfall drops 70 feet into the cove. Ominous looking peaks connected by jagged razor-back ridges encase the cove. Glacial cirques burrow into the upper valley slopes, and avalanche chutes run from the cove's eastern ridgeline to the water's surface. Even in calm weather, an ever-present swell off the gulf crashes along the tattered beach at the cove's head.

Bainbridge Passage

Bainbridge Passage, 10 nm long, separates the Kenai Peninsula mainland from Bainbridge Island. Vessel traffic traveling between western Prince William Sound and the Kenai Peninsula outer coast regularly ply the sheltered waters of Bainbridge Passage. The tidal velocity in the passage ranges between 2 and 3.5 knots.

The bold, craggy face of Point Waters stands prominently on the mainland as vessels approach Bainbridge Passage. At Point Waters, patches of bull kelp sway amongst the nearshore rocks and a pair of offshore boulders located 150 yards southwest of the point.

Kayaking and Camping:
Directly across Bainbridge Passage from Point Waters, on the western tip of the passage's southern shoreline, stands a prominent cobble beach easily accessible to beach landings. This strategic area is not only a perfect location for waiting to catch the flood tide for the paddle up the passage, but it also presents a spectacular view of Bainbridge Glacier and the southern portion of Port Bainbridge.

This refuge site is a good place to stop and assess weather and sea conditions, especially if proceeding to the outer coast. From Bainbridge Passage, the incoming swell from the gulf only increases in height as one proceeds southward down Port Bainbridge.

North shore lagoon, Hogg Bay.

BAINBRIDGE ISLAND

Hogg Bay

At the western end of Bainbridge Island sits Hogg Bay. At the bay's north entrance point rests Hogg Point, a striking 1,375-foot-high headland scarred by a massive talus slide. For mariners, the most hazardous navigational obstruction inside the bay is a rock pile located 1 nm east of Hogg Point along the north shore. This foul area, surrounded by deep water, lies 350 yards offshore and is covered by a 3-foot or higher tide. Another rock, awash at low water, sits inside the 10-fathom curve, 180 yards off the southern shore and 1.7 nm east of Swanson Point.

The Hogg Bay shoreline is intriguing because of its numerous beaches and sheltered areas, including a well-protected anchorage in the bay's northeast arm. Here, in the 1920s, a prospector named Domonic Vietti worked a mining claim at the arm's head. Moss-covered ruins of the Vietti cabin lie on the west side of the stream.

Kayaking and Camping:

Touring kayakers will find Hogg Bay's northern shoreline an inviting place to explore and set up a campsite. Perhaps the bay's most scenic and certainly the most convenient camping area is on a barrier beach 0.6 nm east of Hogg Point. A narrow stream slices through the gravel beach berm to a peaceful lagoon surrounded by rye grass and wetlands. This lagoon attracts an assortment of waterfowl including flocks of merganser, harlequin and goldeneye ducks. Several dead-fall trees partially obstruct the stream's channel, which, at high water can be navigated by kayakers to reach the lagoon.

Anchorage:
    Depending on the weather and wind direction, a selection of alternative anchorages lies within Hogg Bay. At the head of the bay's northeast arm, the water rapidly shallows. Tidal mudflats extend more than a quarter mile from the stream's mouth, so allow for sufficient swing room. Drop anchor in 8–10 fathoms, muddy bottom.
    Small craft can find anchorage along the east shore at the mouth of the northeast arm. Here a 7-fathom spot lies north of the two conspicuous wooded islets. The water east of the islets, toward the beach, is shallow. Another option for anchoring lies along the bay's southern shore near the head. Here, a prominent 90-foot-tall islet marks the general area. Anchor in 8-fathoms midway between the islet and the south shore. The bottom is a mixture of soft mud and gravel.

Swanson Bay

Swanson Bay is similar to Hogg Bay, although not as scenic or hospitable. The bay's shoreline is thickly wooded and in places, extremely steep. Swanson Bay is mostly clear of obstructions except for a foul area, 200 yards off the north shore, 1.2 nm east of Swanson Point.

Kayaking, Camping, and Anchorage:
    On Swanson Bay's south shore, immediately eastward from Point Pyke, a mile-long chain of thin, gravel beaches provides indifferent camping. Mariners seeking anchorage can drop anchor in 9–10 fathoms along the bay's south shoreline, 1.5 nm east of Point Pyke.

Procession Rocks

Rocky islets and a cluster of jagged, wave-washed boulders encompass Procession Rocks. This hazardous area lies less than a mile from the southwest shore of Bainbridge Island and 1.5 nm southeast of Point Pyke.

The largest and highest islet in this group measures 70 feet high. Patches of bull kelp grow close around the perimeter of the islets and rocks. A shallow shelf with a depth of 1.5 fathoms extends 200 yards off the north end of the island group. In light seas and good visibility, small craft can safely pass on the north side of Procession Rocks by favoring the Bainbridge Island shoreline.

From a distance, the grim profile of Procession Rocks resembles the teeth of a crosscut saw jutting from the water's surface. Procession Rocks could undoubtedly be a nightmarish sight to any unsuspecting mariners crossing their path in foul weather and poor visibility.

The Procession Rocks area hosts harbor seals and sea lions that endure the relentless surf by climbing high on the rocks. Vessel traffic in this area is light, which is an added incentive to the dozens of skittish harbor seals that traditionally gather here during low water. Sea lions and harbor seals do not intermingle though they inhabit the same waters. Seals are wary of sea lions and they avoid them by using different haulout spots.

Procession Rocks.

EVANS ISLAND

Squirrel Bay

Squirrel Bay at the southwest end of Evans Island marks the southern entrance of Prince of Wales Passage. Salmon seine vessels and others fishing in the Elrington Passage area sometimes use the bay as an alternative anchorage to Fox Farm Bay. Squirrel Bay offers a convenient hold-over place to wait for the flood tide before proceeding up Prince of Wales Passage.

Anchorage:
In most weather, except westerly winds, the bay provides suitable anchorage along the southern shore in 8–10 fathoms, sand and mud bottom.

ELRINGTON ISLAND

Fox Farm Bay

South of Port Bainbridge and 1 nm east of the Lonetree Point navigational light, at the western entrance to Elrington Passage, sits Fox Farm Bay. This sheltered bay is a traditional refuge for vessels waiting for traveling weather before proceeding to points along the North Gulf Coast.

Fox Farm Bay is familiar not only with scores of halibut longliners, salmon seiners, and fish tenders, but also every vessel operator in western Prince William Sound. The bay's location allows easy access to abundant fishing opportunities, especially for halibut and salmon.

Kayaking, Camping, and Hiking:
A 200-yard wide spruce and moss covered isthmus, crisscrossed by game trails, separates Fox Farm Bay from the surf-worn boulder beach at the head of North Twin Bay. Set up a campsite high on the beach or in the woods on the Fox Farm Bay side of the isthmus. This easily accessible isthmus with its sandy beach is no stranger to human foot traffic, especially to summer beachcombers and autumn deer hunters.

Another camping choice rests in the bay's east corner. Here, a cobble spit and submerged gravel bar (mostly dry at lower stages of the tide) connect Elrington Island to an adjacent conical-shaped island that partially obscures the bay from Elrington Passage. Choose a campsite on the gravel spit.

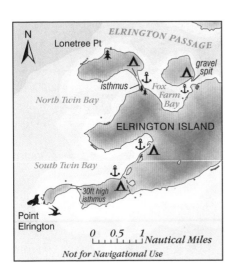

Anchorage:
Mariners intending to check out the Fox Farm Bay isthmus can drop anchor in 4 fathoms approximately 150-yards off the isthmus beach. Another popular anchorage lies in the east corner. Drop anchor in 4–10 fathoms southwest of the prominent gravel spit that lies between the large island and Elrington Island's east shoreline. This anchorage catches northeasterly winds blowing down Elrington Passage, but the fetch is minor, except at high water. Small boats can find anchorage at many locations within Fox Farm Bay.

South Twin Bay

South Twin Bay sits exposed to the westerly weather and oceanic ambiance issuing from the Gulf of Alaska. Thick alder patches line the waterfront where wide-terraced beaches reveal uplift from the 1964 Alaska earthquake. At the bay's southwestern entrance point, dome-shaped Point Elrington stands alone, connected to the island by a thin isthmus of boulders and gravel aggregate.

Camping and Hiking:
The beachfront along South Twin Bay's southern shore offers a range of potential landing options and campsites areas, with the bay's head being the obvious choice. Here, a fast-flowing stream descends the hillside. Set up camp along the waterfront east of the stream.

The Point Elrington isthmus is an interesting physical feature. By carefully scrambling up the steep, crumbling slope of the 30-foot-high isthmus, an awesome view awaits. Atop the narrow isthmus, a hard-packed footpath lies covered with colorful lichen and moss. On the outer beach, beachcombers can search among piles of boulders for unusual flotsam and debris deposited by

Outer boulder beach, Point Elrington isthmus.

the relentless surf. Eager climbers can continue exploring the unique pillow lava formations along the adjacent hillside.

Another bushwhacking opportunity exists one mile east of the isthmus, mid-way along the bay's southern shore. Here, a half-mile trek crosses over a for-ested neck of land to a vantage point overlooking Latouche Passage.

Anchorage:
In fair weather, small craft can anchor in 10 fathoms of water almost anywhere along the bay's southern shore from the Point Elrington isthmus to the bay's head. In easterly weather, drop anchor in 8–10 fathoms at the head.

Point Elrington

Point Elrington is geologically similar to Cape Resurrection, 31 nm to the west, in that molten lava from beneath the sea created the two prominent headlands. The Coast Guard maintains a navigational light on Point Elrington. Here a cluster of wave-washed rocks provides haulout ledges for dozens of Steller sea lions. In summer, the vibrant waters at the western entrance of Prince William Sound teem with salmon, halibut, marine mammals, and seabirds.

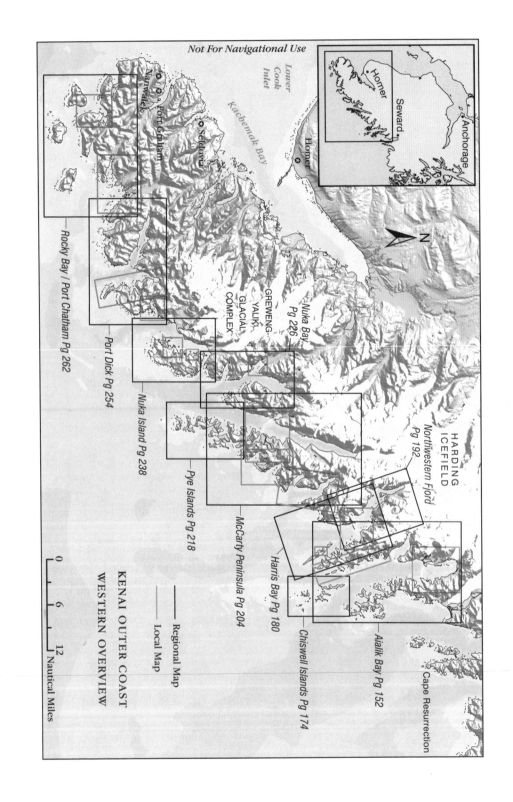

Not For Navigational Use

Lower
Cook
Inlet

Kachemak Bay

Homer

Seward

Homer

Anchorage

N

Cape St. Elias
Nanwalek

Port Graham

Seldovia

—— Rocky Bay / Port Chatham Pg 262

—— Port Dick Pg 254

GREWENG-
YALIK
GLACIAL
COMPLEX

Nuka Bay
Pg 226

HARDING
ICEFIELD

Northwestern Fjord
Pg 192

Nuka Island Pg 238

Pye Islands Pg 218

McCarty Peninsula Pg 204

Harris Bay Pg 180

Chiswell Islands Pg 174

Alalik Bay Pg 152

Cape Resurrection

0   6   12
                Nautical Miles

KENAI OUTER COAST
WESTERN OVERVIEW

—— Regional Map
—— Local Map

Section 2

Heading Westward
from
Resurrection Bay

Verdant Cove, Aialik Bay.

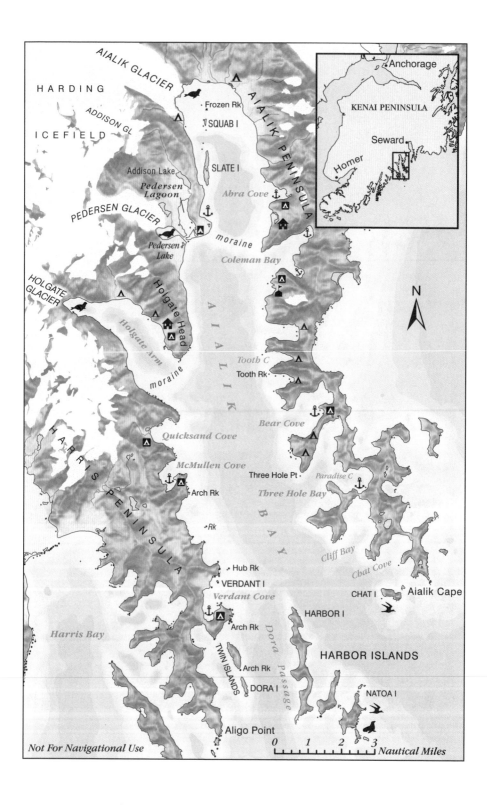

HARDING

ICEFIELD

AIALIK GLACIER

ADDISON GL

ADDISON GL

Frozen Rk

SQUAB I

SLATE I

Addison Lake

Pedersen Lagoon

PEDERSEN GLACIER

Pedersen Lake

moraine

Abra Cove

Coleman Bay

AIALIK PENINSULA

HOLGATE GLACIER

Holgate Head

Holgate Arm

moraine

HARRIS PENINSULA

Quicksand Cove

McMullen Cove

Arch Rk

•Rk

A I A L I K

Tooth C

Tooth Rk

Bear Cove

B A Y

Three Hole Pt

Paradise C

Three Hole Bay

Cliff Bay

Chat Cove

CHAT I

Aialik Cape

Hub Rk

VERDANT I

Verdant Cove

Arch Rk

TWIN ISLANDS

Arch Rk

DORA I

Aligo Point

Harris Bay

Dora Passage

HARBOR I

HARBOR ISLANDS

NATOA I

N

KENAI PENINSULA

Anchorage

Seward

Homer

Not For Navigational Use

0   1   2   3
Nautical Miles

14

Aialik Bay

AIALIK CAPE TO ALIGO POINT

Wildlife Viewing:
Aialik Bay supports a diverse range of marine birds and mammals. In June during harbor seal pupping, hundreds of seals ride atop drifting icebergs in Aialik Glacial Basin. Also in June, red salmon begin to invade Pedersen Lagoon from Aialik Bay. Summer flocks of shorebirds and waterfowl gather and nest around the wetlands surrounding the lagoons. Scores of Marbled and Kittlitz's murrelets occupy Aialik Bay with Kittlitz's concentrated north of the moraine, in the glacial basin.

Kayaking:
Reliable landing beaches are limited in lower Aialik Bay. The best landing spots are in Verdant, Bear, McMullen, and Quicksand coves, and at a tiny pocket beach near Three Hole Point. The sheltered waters of upper Aialik Bay are perfect for kayaking but expect to encounter brash ice and growlers if you visit Holgate Arm, Pedersen Lake, or Aialik Glacial Basin.

Camping and Hiking:
The north shore of Holgate Arm, the Pedersen Lagoon area, and Aialik Glacial Basin provide miles of beaches and lowland terrain to hike and camp.

Fishing:
The rocky bottom adjacent to Aialik Cape is renowned for lingcod, rockfish, and halibut. Silver salmon concentrate along the lower Aialik Peninsula from mid-June through early-August. Troll the waters along the scenic headlands of Chat Cove and Cliff Bay. In upper Aialik Bay, try fishing for halibut south of Aialik's glacial moraine, near the outer mouth of Coleman Bay.

Anchorages:
Most coves and bays in Aialik Bay are extremely deep except near shore. All are susceptible to williwaws in heavy weather. In the glacial basin, anchored vessels are at risk of roaming ice packs. Best anchorages: Coleman Bay, Abra Cove, Bear Cove, McMullen Cove, Pederson Bight, Verdant Cove, Paradise Cove.

A ialik Bay is a 17 nm long glacial fjord flanked by high mountain peaks, hanging glacial valleys, and three major glaciers — Aialik, Holgate, and Pedersen. Aialik and Holgate glaciers terminate at tidewater. The fjord is crammed with drowned cirques and valleys, creating coves and multi-arm bays. In fact, nowhere on the Kenai Peninsula mainland is the

Aialik Cape.

shore as twisted and irregular as along Aialik Peninsula. As for the name Aialik, the Russians traders who visited the area acquired the bay's name from the local Sugpiaq. The Sugpiaq term *aya* means "a special surprise" and *lik* means "place."

In summer, high-pressure atmospheric conditions above the Harding Icefield typically spill cold air into the fjord, generating localized breezes. By mid-morning, the fjord acts as a funnel as the opposing "day breeze" invades the bay from the gulf. Glacial ice from the tidewater glaciers infrequently drift south of Bear Cove. Slow your vessel down when encountering ice and give a wide berth to bergy bits and larger ice. Also, avoid hard surface ice in the glacial basin that can be encountered in winter and early spring and can severely damage the hull and prop.

Razorback ridges, waterfalls, sea arches, and steeply wooded coves characterize the east and west shores of Aialik's lower bay. Land subsidence has been a major force in shaping the region. As a result of the 1964 earthquake, parts of the outer coast subsided up to six feet. The evidence is most noticeable in Verdant, McMullen, and Quicksand coves (on Aialik's western shore). Here, barrier beaches and ghostly hulks of spruce and hemlock trees, killed by saltwater, dominate the low-lying landscape.

The lower bay attracts wildlife tour vessels that loop around the Chiswell and Harbor islands. The vessels intercept pods of humpback and gray whales during their annual migrations. Transient killer whale pods are known to prey on the local seal and sea lion populations along lower Aialik Bay and the offshore islands. Resident killer whales move in family pods along the Kenai Peninsula coast and feed on fish.

Aialik Cape

The expanse of open water that lies between Aialik Cape and Pilot Rock can be as calm as a pond or as wild as a washing machine. When a brisk wind is blowing from the east or southeast, mariners should stay a mile or more offshore from Aialik Cape. The convergence of tidal currents with winds over the irregular bottom tends to amplify sea conditions around the cape.

Mariners new to this area should give a wide berth to the bare rock islets and submerged boulders that lie at the jagged tip of Aialik Cape. In calm seas, charter vessels and fishing boats frequently use "Chicken Pass," a shortcut between granite boulders inside Aialik Cape. Do not attempt passage without local knowledge.

Chat Island, Chat Cove, and Cliff Bay

Marine bird enthusiasts should note that the steep talus slopes of Chat Island are the summer home of a colony of storm petrels. This is the northern-most colony of this species known to exist on the outer coast.

Powerboats entering Aialik Bay usually transit between Chat Island and Aialik Cape. However, mariners should favor the mainland shore as

Rock-bound shoreline, Cliff Bay.

rocks and low-lying islets extend eastward from Chat Island. Southerly weather directly influences both Chat Cove and Cliff Bay. Their rock-bound shoreline comprised of broken boulders and vertical ledges lack any convenient landing beaches.

In Cliff Bay, the shore is rugged and mostly inaccessible. Beneath the crumbling ridge are scattered piles of bus-sized boulders resting on the steeply angled slope. A light-colored granite headland lies along the west entrance point. Glaucous-winged gulls nest on the cliffs.

Anchorages:
On occasion, commercial fishing vessels and sport boats temporarily anchor in the northeast corner of Chat Cove in 11 fathoms of water; however, swells from the gulf surge into the cove and also into Cliff Bay. Avoid use as an over-night anchorage. Vessels seeking an anchorage in Aialik's lower bay can steer a course for Three Hole Bay.

Three Hole Bay

A unique collection of eroded rock arches lies at the tip of Three Hole Point. The arches, a traditional stop for charter vessels and first-time visitors to the bay, are among the most photographed features in Aialik Bay.

Three Hole Point was captured on film by Grant and Higgins more than a century ago. Since then, the image of these natural arches has repeatedly appeared in magazines, articles, and travel blogs. In Three Hole Bay, points of interest include the secluded head of the north arm and Paradise Cove located in the bay's east corner.

Kayaking and Camping:
In Paradise Cove, a primitive campsite awaits in the southern corner, near the top of the steeply sloped saddle. Here, the low saddle offers an alluring view of Cliff Bay and beyond to the Harbor Islands. It also serves as a place to assess sea conditions in the lower bay. The landing beach is calm, but the shoreline lies broken and rocky and lacks a water source.
A better beach and campsite option, especially for traveling kayakers, lies in the south-facing bight, one-half mile north of Three Hole Point. Here, a small pocket beach (accessible in light sea conditions) provides camping space and a cascading stream.

Anchorage:
In light weather, Three Hole Bay is a handy anchorage though quite deep. Mariners can anchor in Paradise Cove in the south corner adjacent to the low-lying saddle in 9–15 fathoms. In foul southeasterly weather, williwaws are known to sweep across Paradise Cove creating havoc on anchored vessels. During windy conditions, re-anchoring between Paradise Cove and the north arm may become necessary.
At the head of the north arm is a tiny funnel-shaped alcove. In northerly winds, small boats can find some protection by anchoring outside the alcove in 10–12 fathoms on a rock bottom. A southerly groundswell from the gulf can make the north arm uncomfortable for overnight anchoring.

Waterfront islet at the inner Bear Cove camping beach.

Bear Cove and Tooth Cove

Midway along Aialik's eastern shore is a series of west-facing indentions with steep shorelines and bold headlands. Here, the taller peaks of the Aialik Peninsula measure up to 3,000 feet altitude or more. Gravel pocket beaches periodically punctuate the shoreline. Otherwise, the shoreline is rockbound. In spring, piles of snow lie at the base of avalanche chutes, barely above the reach of high water. Brash ice pushed by westerly winds and an ebbing current occasionally escape the confines of Holgate Arm and enter into lower Aialik Bay.

Oral history, collected from Port Graham chronicles past generations of Sugpiaq people that seasonally occupied Bear Cove. An archaeological study discovered fish-bone evidence suggesting the Bear Cove inhabitants ate an abundance of gray cod, with some fish weighing more than 20 pounds.

Kayaking, Camping, and Hiking:

In Bear Cove, setup camp at one of a pair of pocket beaches situated along the cove's southern shore. The outer pocket beach is more primitive and has a view of Holgate Glacier. Behind the cobble beach rests several CMTs.

The inner pocket beach, one mile from the cove's south entrance point and once used by the Sugpiaq, is the best camping spot in lower Aialik Bay. A KFNP bear-proof food locker stands atop the berm on the north end of the beach adjacent to a level campsite. Other cleared campsites are on the south end. Behind the berm, a wetland stretches to the brushy hillside. Neither pocket beach has a convenient water source. The head of Tooth Cove has a wilderness camp area that has a water source but lacks a food locker.

Anchorage:
> Bear Cove is a suitable anchorage, though deep and exposed to westerlies. Anchor off the inner pocket beach. Here, the bottom contour is moderately steep and extends offshore for a short distance before rapidly dropping off to more than 20 fathoms. Try anchoring 60 yards northwest of the conspicuous rock islet in 5–7 fathoms on a rocky bottom with some kelp. Mariners will quickly discover that Tooth Cove has little to offer as an anchorage.

Coleman Bay

Coleman Bay reveals two steeply-walled indentions. Cruising boats and commercial fishing vessels almost exclusively use Coleman Bay when anchoring in upper Aialik Bay. The bay's scenic southeast arm provides a secure base camp for mariners exploring Aialik's glacial basin.

Impressive waterfalls tumble from the steep cliffs surrounding the terminus of both arms. The sound of falling water is everywhere. In summer, as the sun sinks over the Harding Icefield, the sun's dying rays floods the southeast arm with dazzling light.

Be sure and visit the picturesque north arm. The mineral-stained headwall reaches more than 2,000 feet above the water's surface.

The Kenai Fjords National Park maintains a ranger cabin along the shore immediately south of Coleman Bay.

Camping:
> The only pocket beach lies in the SE arm. The beach is primitive, and the camping is challenging, but the location is impressive. Several water sources exist at the head. Another camp area with a stream and KFNP food locker lies near the south entrance to Coleman Bay, north of the ranger station.

Anchorage:
> Coleman Bay's spectacular southeast arm is the best anchorage in Aialik Bay during heavy southeast weather. The bottom is deep and clear except near the head where sunken rocks do exist. Vessels have several options for mooring. Small craft can anchor with a view of Pedersen Glacier in 5–10 fathoms. To catch a firmer grip, move offshore and anchor in 14–16 fathoms, in mud.

AIALIK GLACIAL BASIN

A glacial sill (moraine bar) 1.6 nm long stretches across upper Aialik Bay from the northern point of Coleman Bay to the gravel outwash plain fronting Pedersen Lagoon. Aialik Glacial Basin occupies the area north of the moraine bar. Safe crossing for small crafts lies anywhere around mid-channel with a minimum depth of 3 fathoms.

The moraine bar marks the farthest advance of Aialik Glacier during the Little Ice Age. The glacier likely retreated from the moraine by the late 1600s. Rafts of brash ice and growlers can be encountered anywhere north of the moraine bar. Strong northwest winds in the glacial basin greatly influence the movement of the ice pack by dispersing it around the basin.

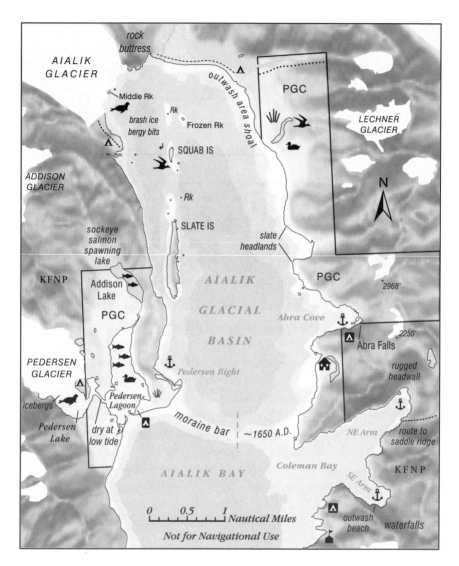

AIALIK GLACIER

rock buttress

outwash area shoal

Middle Rk

brash ice bergy bits

Rk

Frozen Rk

PGC

LECHNER GLACIER

ADDISON GLACIER

SQUAB IS

Rk

sockeye salmon spawning lake

SLATE IS

slate headlands

N

KFNP

Addison Lake

PGC

AIALIK

GLACIAL

BASIN

PGC

2968'

Abra Cove

2250'

Abra Falls

PEDERSEN GLACIER

Pedersen Bight

rugged headwall

icebergs

Pedersen Lagoon

Pedersen Lake

dry at low tide

moraine bar

~1650 A.D.

NE Arm

route to saddle ridge

AIALIK BAY

Coleman Bay

SE Arm

KFNP

0   0.5   1
Nautical Miles

outwash beach

waterfalls

Not for Navigational Use

Aialik Glacier

The tidewater face of Aialik Glacier presently terminates 4.5 nm from its former moraine. The glacier has been relatively stable for more than 100 years but has undergone considerable thinning. Aialik Glacier calves most actively in late spring and early summer. At times, icebergs and packed ice may restrict boat traffic in the upper basin. Glacier watchers should note that fragments of ice continuously slough off from the glacier's steep face. When massive seracs fall, they displace a large volume of water near the face. This water, in turn, creates waves that slosh around the basin. Resembling miniature tidal waves, they are relatively harmless in deep

Aialik Glacier viewed from the south moraine at low water.

water. However, these waves crest and break over shallow areas, and can sweep over sand bars and exposed beaches more than a mile away. Never approach the face of a tidewater glacier, and avoid being jammed among ice, as random waves can throw heavy bergs against your vessel.

Aialik Glacier's long, sloping ice tongue lacks medial moraines. This conformation gives the glacier an exceptionally clean appearance with a baby-blue reflection. Not that Aialik Glacier doesn't produce silt — in fact, the three main glaciers at the bay's head, Aialik, Skee, and Lechner, continuously dump glacial flour into the basin through their outwash streams. Glaciologists estimate the floor of the glacial basin accumulates about a foot of new silt each year.

For decades, Aialik Bay, Harris Bay, and McCarty Fjord were the focal centers of large-scale seal harvesting. The Territory of Alaska initiated a two-dollar bounty on harbor seals in 1927 for each seal scalp turned in. Also, the hunters could sell the hide and liver separately, which were usually worth more than the bounty. Between 1964 and 1966, when seal harvest numbers peaked, thousands of seals were taken in the Kenai Fjords. However, this "take" was only a fraction of the 150,000 seals harvested statewide in the same period.

The legal harvest of harbor seals continued until 1972 when Congress passed the Marine Mammal Protection Act and the Endangered Species Act. The federal legislation banned marine mammal hunting for non-Alaska

Natives. Ironically, the harbor seal population in the Kenai Fjords during the decades of unlimited bounty hunting was higher than the current seal population. Seal numbers began dropping soon after hunting was banned. Today, harbor seals have undergone more than four decades of limited harvest by Alaska Natives as well as increased protective management by the state and federal governments. Some scientists suggest the decrease in the harbor seals population may reflect marked ecological changes seen in the Gulf of Alaska since the mid-1970s.

In Aialik Bay, the month of June is the peak of harbor seal pupping. A visitor to the glacial basin in June of 1980

Harbor seal hauled out on ice.

could observe as many as 1,600 seals riding atop ice floes in the basin. In 2003, daily counts were about 200 seals during peak pupping. Since then, seal numbers have increased and now exceed 700 seals divided between Pedersen Glacier Lake and Aialik Glacier.

A few sea otters also traverse through the basin and may be seen swimming among the icebergs or curled up on pieces of brash ice. Marine mammals such as humpback and killer whales and harbor porpoises sporadically surface near the thick ice pack, but are more frequently seen feeding elsewhere in the fjords.

When fog or low clouds sweep in from Blying Sound, the lower bay is more affected than the upper bay. Patches of blue sky often persist over the glaciers and icefield even when the lower bay is entirely socked in.

A long, low-lying, gravel shoreline stretches from Abra Cove to the northern flank of Aialik Glacier. Mariners should be aware that shallow water (less than five-fathoms deep) extend one-quarter mile offshore along the entire length of the basin's northeastern shore. Along this shore are several outwash deltas, streams, and thick alder groves. A series of tidal lagoons and waterways meander behind the waterfront.

Kayaking, Camping, and Hiking:

In late spring, an ice-free lead usually opens between Slate Island and the mainland. Paddlers can generally approach Aialik Glacier when this passage is available. The level of glacial calving activity, time of year, tidal conditions, and wind direction affect accessibility to the upper glacial basin, especially in May and early June. At times, drifting ice clog the waters between Aialik Glacier and Squab Island. However, a clear lead often runs along the basin's northeastern shoreline all the way from Abra Cove to near the glacier's icy face.

A pair of streams, a large delta area, and a lagoon mark the basin's northeast corner. Pink salmon spawn in the tidal delta while chum salmon try to reach the lagoon. Private landholdings, owned by the Port Graham Corporation, dominate the eastern shore. (See Map)

The southern portion of Aialik Glacier is land-based and rapidly thinning. Land by kayak or inflatable toward the southeast end of the moraine, away from glacier-wave influence.

Caution: The raging stream issuing from the glacier's southern ice terminus is susceptible to massive blowouts from pressurized water trapped under the glacier. Do not land watercraft in the direct path of glacial waves and pack equipment high on the beach to avoid it from being trashed by waves or stolen by the tide.

Slate Island

Slate Island, a mile-long slate ridge running parallel to the mainland shore, lies immediately north of Pedersen Bight. Centuries of ice-scouring has smoothed its perimeter. Lush alder growth and stunted spruce trees cling to the thin soil atop the island.

A small colony of mew gulls nest on the north end while horned puffins may nest in rocky crevices along the island's west side. Occasionally, an observer will spy a black bear on the island or swimming in the channel. A submerged rock lies 0.3 nm north of Slate Island.

Squab Island

Squab Island, measuring one-quarter mile in length and 125 feet high, rests one-mile from Aialik Glacier's ice face. At times, a thick ice pack engulfs the island while clouds of screeching gulls swirl overhead. More than 1,000 glaucous-winged gulls have nested during the summer in the patchy vegetation atop the treeless island. One notable, tagged gull born on Squab Island later turned up at a landfill site in San Francisco Bay!

Mariners exploring the area around Squab Island should note that Frozen Rock, hidden by high water, lies 0.35 nm north of Squab Island. Another sunken rock lurks 0.2 nm west of Frozen Rock and only shows during very low water. The outflow of meltwater escaping from beneath Aialik Glacier tends to push boats that are drifting in front the glacier toward Frozen Rock. Glacier waves sometimes crest as they pass over the shallow area.

Abra Cove

A "diamond in the rough" describes Abra Cove, considered among the most picturesque locations in Aialik Bay. This precipitous indentation, gouged into the glacial basin's eastern flank, sits 1.5 nm north of the moraine bar. Abra Cove is the best summer anchorage in the glacial basin, although it is sometimes prone to drifting ice and local winds. The cove is an excellent choice as a base camp for field trips to explore the basin.

A sizable boulder ledge (submerged at higher stages of the tide) protrudes from the north shore near the headwall. Shallow water and rocks extend well off the

Abra Falls.

ledge. Additional boulders obstruct access to the cove's head for vessels, but not for kayaks or inflatable dinghies, except at very low water.

The real prize for visitors is Abra Falls, a remarkable water and mineral-stained, nearly vertical, granite headwall. Atop the colorful, 1,000-foot high headwall, an ice-filled cirque discharges a continuous stream of meltwater that cascades into a calm basin stretching the length of the headwall. Birdwatchers may spot black oystercatchers and semipalmated plovers that nest on the rocky ledge beyond the reach of high water.

Black bears, wolverines, and mountain goats are a few of the commonly seen resident land mammals in the basin. A KFNP public use cabin (PUC) is located one-half mile south of Abra Cove. The cabin looks out on Aialik Glacier and the frozen heights of the Harding Icefield.

Kayaking and Camping:

Abra Falls awaits visitors at the granite headwall. A short paddle tour of the base of the wall is a must. A shallow channel runs alongside the headwall as volleys of water tumble down the colorful granite face.

A well-used camping area with late afternoon sun exposure lies west of the food locker on the south shore of Abra Cove. Make camp atop the beach berm. A reliable water source resides in the SE corner of the headwall.

Caution:
  Do not camp next to the Abra Cove headwall even though it may look inviting. Massive avalanches are known to sweep down the steep slope in the corner of the cove causing blocks of ice and boulders to smash along the waterfront or careen into the water.

Anchorage:
  Drop anchor in the middle of Abra Cove, 8–10 fathoms, silt bottom. The drifting ice pack in the basin occasionally invades Abra Cove so keep an eye out. The cove's head is foul with boulders.

Pedersen Lagoon

As recently as 1896, Pedersen Glacier may have reached tidewater. Grant and Higgins named the feature, during their excursion to the area in 1908, for the Reverend H. L. Pedersen, a Seward resident. Nearby Addison Glacier was named after Grant's son.

During the past century, Pedersen Glacier has slowly pulled back, exposing Pedersen Spit, Lagoon and Lake. The glacier now rests 2 miles from tidewater. An ice-clogged lake rests at the glacier's base. Pedersen Glacier Lake is a secluded haven for harbor seals that gather on the drifting ice floes during the summer. The terrain surrounding Pedersen Lagoon and shoreline includes the best bird watching areas in Aialik Bay. Birdwatchers can spy a variety of marine associated birds, including Arctic terns, mew gulls, semipalmated plovers, spotted sandpipers. Black oystercatchers nest on the grassy spit beyond the reach of high water. Patient wildlife observers

Pedersen Lagoon with Pedersen Glacier in background.

can sometimes see both sea otters and playful river otters swimming in the lagoon. Harbor seals regularly cruise the silt-laden waters hunting sockeye salmon and other fish. Mountain goats browse the hillsides adjacent to the lake. Small pieces of ice often ride the ebbing current out the lagoon's channel into the bay.

In summer, salmon seiners traditionally fish at the entrance to Pedersen Lagoon for milling schools of sockeye. At the north end of the lagoon, a stream leads to Addison Lake, where the salmon spawn. The shallow-draft pocket seine boats sometimes enter and depart the lagoon at high water, but mariners without local knowledge should not attempt entering the lagoon. The channel is shallow in spots, and breakers can partially or entirely seal off the entrance in stormy weather.

The Port Graham Corporation owns the uplands surrounding the Pedersen Lagoon area and has designated 1700 acres, as the Pedersen Lagoon Wildlife Sanctuary. Alaska Wildland Adventures (in partnership with PGC) operate the Kenai Fjords Glacier Lodge located on Pedersen Lagoon's east shore. The lodge provides guided hiking and canoe tours of Pedersen Lagoon and glacial lake area as well as kayaking tours of Aialik Glacial Basin.

Kayaking:

At high tide, during calm sea conditions, a kayaker can paddle up the lagoon channel or haul out on Pedersen Spit, east of the stream entrance. The spit is a handy portage to the lagoon if the entrance is not navigable. From the lagoon, a kayaker can paddle to the glacial lake at the base of Pedersen Glacier via the stream located on the west shore of the lagoon. Consult the tide table because tides have a strong influence on the lagoon and lake. Also, the glacier stream goes nearly dry during low water.

A paddler starting in the lagoon will need the upper end of high water and possibly a short portage or two across a sandbar to reach the glacial lake 0.75 miles away. Expect to see brash ice and bergy bits grounded high and dry along the glacier stream.

Use caution!

On the incoming flood tide, the water level in the lake may be significantly lower than in the stream. At such times, the stream can transform into a rushing river as it descends to the glacier lake. Before entering the lake by kayak, haul out on a sand bar and check for dangers.

After entering the glacier lake, avoid the dense ice pack and floating icebergs. Stick to open leads. During lower tidal stages, ice in the lake may lie aground or be trapped in the tide zone. Harbor seals in the lake are very skittish and are easily disturbed by aircraft, kayaks, and canoes.

Note:

Before exiting Pedersen Lagoon into Aialik Bay, check the entrance for sea and wave conditions. The worst time to exit through the channel is during a strong ebb tide, especially with a southerly swell and brisk south wind (typical in the afternoons). Breakers can completely obstruct the channel's entrance.

Hiker's overlook, Pedersen Glacier and ice-filled lake.

There may be up to a 2-hour lag (from the tide table estimate) for low water in the lagoon. Also, the lagoon's channel entrance begins to ebb 30 minutes to more than an hour before the glacier lake starts to ebb. About an hour after high water at the lagoon's entrance, the ebbing tidal current may make exiting the channel unsafe.

Hiking:

The Pedersen Spit tidelands are among the more attractive hiking areas on the entire Kenai coast. A hike along the shore from Pedersen Bight to the lagoon's channel entrance is wild and refreshing. Keep an eye out for semipalmated plovers and black oystercatchers along the beach.

Camping:

The upland area around Pedersen Lagoon is owned by the Port Graham Corporation. The PGC does not require a permit for campers staying less than 24 hours at designated easement campsites. The public campsite easement for the Kenai Fjords National Park is on the eastern shore of the lagoon, just inside the channel entrance.

Campers can set up their tents and tarps on the ground in the southern most stand of spruce trees. The woods tend to buffer the bay's southerly day breeze that strikes the spit in the afternoon. Drinking water is lacking. A bear-proof food locker is located near the camping area.

Anchorage:

Pedersen Bight provides partial protection from southerly winds but is susceptible to drifting ice packs. Keep an eye on the depth sounder when approaching Pedersen Bight. A black sand beach extends well offshore. Small craft can anchor in the bight's west corner in 6 fathoms.

Holgate Arm

Holgate Arm is a prominent, 4 nm long fjord recessed in the western shore of Aialik Bay. The arm was named by Grant and Higgins in 1911 for Thomas Franklin Holgate (1859-1945), Dean of the College of Liberal Arts of Northwestern University.

Holgate Arm terminates at the steep, icy face of Holgate Glacier. The glacier is thought to have reached its Little Ice Age maximum at the mouth of Holgate Arm by the 1600s. Remnants of the shallow terminal moraine sill extend 0.5 nm off Holgate Head and also off the shallow area, inside the south entrance point. Occasionally, the ice pack completely clogs the fjord. However, ice-free leads generally allow vessels and kayaks into the upper portions of the arm.

Once inside Holgate Arm, the towering walls echo with the sounds of primal ice age groans. Atop the arm's rugged southern flank, a series of alpine glaciers can direct an icy stream of katabatic wind, down into the fjord and across the water's surface.

A former tributary glacier approximately 0.3 nm east of Holgate Glacier (on the south shore) has recently withdrawn from tidewater. Adjacent the glacier stands a prominent islet 30 feet high. The islet provides a handy,

Tour vessels, Holgate Glacier.

elevated perch from which to view the icy terminus of Holgate Glacier. Beware of random waves created by ice calving from Holgate Glacier, as well as wakes from tour vessels, lapping upon the beach.

Holgate Glacier is presently a tidewater glacier, but it appears to be ever so slowly pulling back onto land, particularly when viewed during low water. The ice face does fluctuate back and forth, but for now, its powerful ice calving activity continues to shock and awe visitors.

Sand beach, Quicksand Cove.

Kayaking, Camping, and Hiking:

An ice-free lead typically runs alongside the arm's north shore west of Holgate Head. Bergy bits and thick brash ice often clog the area directly in front of Holgate Glacier.

The northern shoreline of Holgate Arm provides several sites for landing, camping, and beachcombing. A Park Service public use cabin and food storage locker are located 1 nm from Holgate Head on the first long beach on the north shore. The spot is an excellent camping area with a great view of Holgate Glacier and is safe from glacial waves.

Hiking opportunities are best along the arm's north shore where a prominent beach and valley stand out along the shoreline. A robust stream marks the area about two miles from the tidewater glacier. Here, glacier waves and vessel wakes occasionally affect the waterfront, so carry watercraft high up the beach.

Anchorage:

Holgate Arm should not be used as an overnight anchorage because of drifting ice. However, small craft can find a temporary anchorage midway along the arm's north shore between Holgate Head and the glacier. Drop anchor on the shelf in 7–10 fathoms. Because of the risk of glacier-generated waves, always anchor an extra safe distance offshore in depths more than 6 fathoms deep.

Small vessels can also temporarily anchor near the tributary glacier on the south shore, when ice conditions allow. Drop anchor east of the rock islet in 8–10 fathoms. Here, a powerful stream outwash exits from beneath the glacier and provides an offshore current that whisks away drifting icebergs.

Quicksand Cove

"Stunning" describes the expansive setting of the wetlands behind the beach in Quicksand Cove. Here, a stream slowly meanders across the sunken valley floor, through grasslands and decayed trees killed by saltwater from land subsidence. A cluster of granite glacial cirques and deglaciated cliffs stretch across the cove's head, resembling a Swiss painting.

The beach has a layer of soft dark sand with yellow flakes of fool's gold. At low water, the waterfront provides a firm highway along the south shore and head. Small flocks of bald eagles, ravens, and glaucous-winged gulls congregate like vultures at the stream mouth in autumn.

Even in mild weather, a swell from the gulf reaches into the cove to cause uncomfortable conditions while on anchor.

Kayaking, Camping, and Hiking:
Quicksand Cove's constant wave action can make beach landings messy. Accessing the head is easier along the south shore.

Choose a camping spot atop the wide beach berm. The KFNP has installed bear-proof food locker at the south end of the beach. Nearby a cascading stream presents a water source. The cove's head screams out to be investigated, though trekking in the lowlands areas is hampered by swampy terrain.

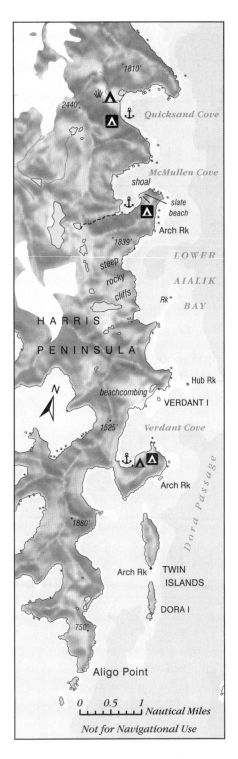

Avalanche chutes, driftwood, and dead snags, McMullen Cove.

McMullen Cove

A notable, often photographed, 70-foot tall sea arch stands out, one-half mile south of McMullen Cove. The mouth of the cove appears deep and harmless, but do not be fooled. A submerged slate ledge nearly obstructs the entire mouth. Mariners, especially with deep-keeled vessels, should enter and exit by steering a course parallel to the northwestern shoreline. Here, a 20-fathom-deep channel leads around the slate ledge.

A steep bulwark of razorback ridges and peaks wraps around the cove's headwall. Along the tide line, exposed tree roots cling to the bare rock while piles of talus jut at steep angles.

Low water exposes an extensive slate spit inside the south entrance point. Here, like at many locations along the drowning Kenai coast, decaying stands of bleached, lifeless trees hug the waterfront. The McMullen spit is a rock hound's delight. On a minus tide, hordes of prime slate saucers pepper the shore. Slate fragments range in sizes from an inch to over four feet in diameter.

McMullen Cove was named for Captain McMullen one of many who skippered the steamship *Dora* during the dawn of the 20th century. In 1896, the *Dora* began a legendary career carrying mail from Port Townsend, Washington, to coastal Alaska and the Aleutian Islands. During her distinguished service, the *Dora* was a familiar and welcomed sight in coastal towns and villages. Crowds of people, summer or winter, would line the dock to await the ship's arrival.

The *Dora* and her crew were involved in many heroic rescues at sea, but she also had her share of misadventures. She was wrecked at Unimak Pass in 1910, Cook Inlet in 1911, and ran aground in Resurrection Bay in 1912, but survived. The *Dora* was sold in 1918 by the Alaska Steamship Company. Shortly after that, she met her fate along the rocky coast of Vancouver Island, where she ran aground at Alert Bay in the winter of 1920.

Kayaking and Camping:

McMullen Cove's southeastern shore is a reliable landing destination for kayakers. The cobble beach berm atop the slate spit is the best camping area. A bear-proof food locker is located on the north end of the beach and is easily located. Please give a wide berth to the pair of well-known black oystercatchers that annually nest on the cobbles above the high-water mark at the south tip of the spit.

McMullen Spit has a magnificent view of the towering cliffs encircling the cove's head. Finding a water source in the cove for drinking and cooking is problematic. The best chance for collecting water is early in the year or during periods of rain, when water flows everywhere.

Hiking:

In summer, after the avalanche threat is gone, a scenic but rugged hike up through the rocky notch at the head leads to several alpine lakes.

Anchorages:

A small vessel can drop anchor atop the narrow, rocky, 6-fathom ledge (marked on marine charts), which protrudes from a wooded point of land along the western shore.

A more secure anchorage is located nearby in the south-facing bight adjacent the slate spit. However, the funnel-shaped notch tapers down and provides only limited swing room. A small craft can anchor in the bight in 8–15 fathoms, and larger vessels can drop anchor at the bight's mouth in 20 fathoms onto a sticky mud bottom.

During spring tides, the spit and a significant portion of the slate ledge go dry. This low water situation tends to seal off the cove from heavy seas that can boil in lower Aialik Bay. In southeasterly storms, however, high water causes waves to wrap around the end of the spit and surge into the small anchorage, making conditions very sloppy.

Verdant Cove

Verdant Cove is a northeast-facing bight with a dependable landing beach along the eastern shore. A ghost forest stands out along the beach.

At the head of Verdant Cove is a low, tree-covered saddle. The saddle area is private property. Here, the ruins of a Quonset hut lie partially hidden in the thick woods. The hut was built on a 40-acre homestead by Alma Dodge and her husband Jack in the 1960s. A nearby landing beach consists of broken rocks and boulders. An abandoned mooring lies tethered near the shore. The uplands behind the prominent beach west of Verdant Island are also private property, but the waterfront is good for beachcombing.

Sunken cobble beach, Verdant Cove.

Mariners entering or leaving Verdant Cove to the north should be aware that Hub Rock is a hazardous reef covered at high water. Hub Rock lurks 0.25 nm offshore from the cove's north point. Another rocky area covered at high water, and 0.5 nm offshore is located 1.2 nm NW of Hub Rock.

A prominent sea arch shoots through the middle of a rock islet south of and around the corner from Verdant Cove. The scenic arch marks a good fishing area for silver salmon, rockfish, and lingcod.

Historical documents and oral history from Native elders in Nanwalek indicate that Verdant Cove was among the last occupied Sugpiaq villages on the outer coast. The village was abandoned sometime after 1880 when its residents relocated to Nanwalek (then called English Bay.)

Kayaking and Camping:
The cobble beach on the east shore of Verdant Cove is a reliable landing and camping spot. At the beach's north end sits a KFNP bear-proof food locker. A couple of cleared and level campsites sit behind the berm in the alder, near the shoreline's bend. The beach lacks a convenient water source.
A sunken swamp lies between the beach berm and the forested hillside. Ghost trees haunt the area.

Anchorage:
Verdant Cove is exposed to northeast winds but provides protection from moderate southeast weather. During gale conditions, however, the cove becomes sloppy from the excessive water movement generated in the gulf. Anchor at the south end of the east shore beach (about 0.2 nm from the head) in 8–15 fathoms on a sloping mud bottom.

Twin Islands

At the mouth of Aialik Bay, northeast of Aligo Point, lies two heavily forested islands known as the Twin Islands. The northern island has a hollowed sea arch on its southern end. The smaller island carries the name of Dora. Both Dora Island and Dora Passage refer to the steamship *Dora*. In the early 1900s, Seward and Valdez were the ship's home ports.

Aligo Point

At the western entrance to Aialik Bay, where the rocky headland of Harris Peninsula terminates, rests Aligo Point. Orth's Dictionary of Alaska Place Names states Aligo Point was named by surveyors working for the U. S. Coastal & Geodetic Survey in 1929. The name was derived from the Native word meaning "quartz," in reference to the geological formation at the point.

Adjacent to Aligo Point is a pair of 100-foot-tall spruce-crowned islands, surrounded by a handful of rock islets that extend southward into the entrance of Granite Passage. The steep rock shoreline of Harris Peninsula and relentless swell in this area prevent reliable access to the shore.

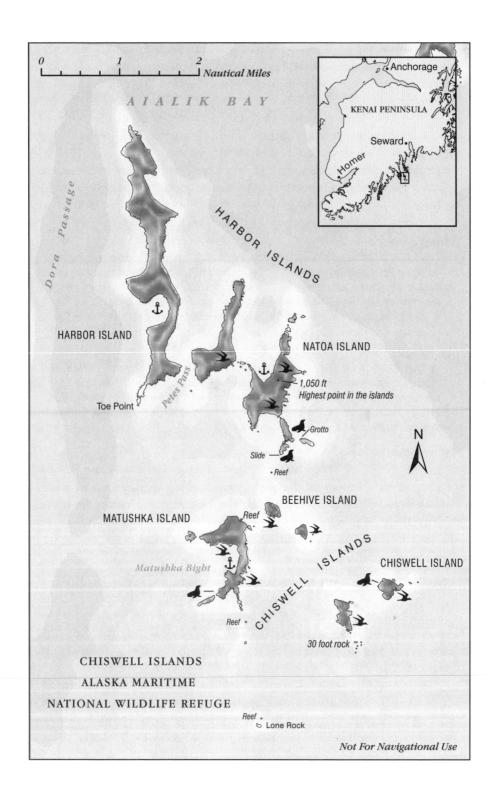

0　　　1　　　2
Nautical Miles

Anchorage
KENAI PENINSULA
Seward
Homer

A I A L I K　B A Y

Dora Passage

HARBOR ISLANDS

HARBOR ISLAND

NATOA ISLAND

Petes Pass

Toe Point

1,050 ft
Highest point in the islands

Grotto

Slide

Reef

N

BEEHIVE ISLAND

MATUSHKA ISLAND

Reef

CHISWELL ISLANDS

CHISWELL ISLAND

Matushka Bight

Reef

30 foot rock

CHISWELL ISLANDS

ALASKA MARITIME

NATIONAL WILDLIFE REFUGE

Reef
Lone Rock

Not For Navigational Use

Chiswell & Harbor Islands
CIRCUMNAVIGATING THE ISLANDS

Special Wildlife Viewing:
   The Chiswell Islands, part of Alaska's Maritime National Wildlife Refuge, reign as the premiere viewing location for marine life on the outer coast. In summer, the islands come alive with more than 75,000 marine birds, the largest seabird concentration on the Kenai Peninsula. Large numbers of Steller sea lions inhabit the rock ledges of Chiswell and Natoa islands. Pods of humpback and killer whales are drawn to the area to forage in the bountiful waters.

Kayaking and Camping:
   The islands' steep, rock-bound shores are inhospitable to humans. A few pocket beaches exist, but they are washed by heavy surf and are undependable for landing a kayak. The nearest reliable landing beach is in Verdant Cove, in lower Aialik Bay, 7 nm from Matushka Island. The crossing of Dora Passage can be difficult on an ebbing tide during windy conditions. The rocky head of Matushka Bight and the northeastern tip of Matushka Island only are accessible in ideal weather. All locations have limited room on shore with no guarantee of a safe or timely departure. Usually, kayakers avoid spending extended time in the islands, which are better to visit by boat.

Fishing:
   A fertile halibut ground exists on the shelf lying between Harbor and Matushka island at 30 to 40 fathoms. The strong tidal currents can limit bottom fishing to periods of neap tides or slack water. Silver salmon fishing is best in the island passages, in tidal eddies, and near points of land.

Anchorages:
   Overnight anchorages in the Chiswell and Harbor islands provide little protection from gulf weather. Check the latest weather forecast before dropping anchor. The best anchorage in the Chiswells is at Matushka Bight.

More than a dozen windswept islands and monolithic sea stacks comprise two distinct groupings, the Chiswell Islands, and Harbor Islands. The islands collectively were once an important hunting and gathering area for local Native inhabitants. Summer foraging trips to the islands were often in pursuit of seabird eggs for food as well as feathers for clothing. Today, most visitors witness the vast wealth of marine life from the deck of a wildlife tour vessel or a sport fishing boat.

Toe Point at the southern tip of Harbor Island.

Small boat mariners unfamiliar with the area should pay close attention to the navigational chart. Numerous offshore reefs and rocks lie scattered throughout the Chiswell Island area. A notable reef located midway between Natoa and Beehive islands will appear at lower low water and is often difficult to spot. Another reef to watch out for lies 0.3 nm southeast of Matushka Island. Besides the gulf swell, active water movement is normal throughout both island groups, particularly when tidal currents and winds periodically clash with the Alaska Coastal Current. Upwelling occurs where water currents confront the relatively shallow waters surrounding the Chiswell Islands. Mixing of water and nutrients is enhanced as currents funnel between islands, over shoals, or around capes or headlands. The wind accentuates water mixing. All these conditions augment food production for seabirds but invigorate the water for mariners.

HARBOR ISLANDS

The Harbor Islands are a collection of heavily wooded, predominantly granite islands and islets located within the mouth of Aialik Bay, and north of the Chiswell Islands group.

Harbor Island

The largest island in the group, Harbor Island, flanks the east side of Dora Passage. The island, formed by a series of narrow peaks is linked together with a crumbling ridgeline. This ridge stretches more than three miles, terminating on the island's south end at Toe Point, a cream-colored, wave-washed granite islet. Pods of killer and humpback whales frequently visit the area.

Pete's Pass, a narrow waterway that separates Harbor Island and the unnamed island to the east is the main thoroughfare for vessels cruising the inshore waters between Resurrection Bay and McArthur Pass. Pete's Pass usually provides calmer cruising conditions than the route through or outside of the Chiswell Islands. The pass is named for "Herring" Pete Sather, a commercial fisherman, fox farmer, miner, and local legend. Sather regularly plied this island passage on his sea journeys between Seward and his home on Nuka Island.

Natoa Island

Natoa Island, named by the local Sugpiaq, means "the highest island in the vicinity." It also is among the steepest. Along Natoa Island's precipitous eastern shore, a remarkable 1,000-foot high cliff descends vertically to the water's edge. Hundreds of auklets, puffins, murres, and kittiwakes nest on the sea cliffs.

The three small islets adjacent to Natoa's southeast point are traditional haulout areas for mainly juvenile sea lions. What appears to be a narrow passage between the west side of Natoa Island and the neighboring island is obstructed with small islets and submerged rocks and should not be used.

Anchorages:
A tentative fair-weather anchorage is located on the western lee shore of Natoa Island, just southeast of the rock obstructed pass. The bottom is deep and steeply sloped.
Another fair-weather anchorage is in the small, deep cove along Harbor Island's western shore. The cove, however, receives an annoying gulf swell but can be used in calm weather. Mariners in need of a more secure anchorage should steer a course for Verdant Cove or Three Hole Bay.

CHISWELL ISLANDS

Chiswell Island

Visitors wishing to view a Steller sea lion rookery should head for the sloping west shore of Chiswell Island. The size of the Chiswell Island rookery is small compared to those located further to the west. Nevertheless, any mariner who drifts downwind will quickly notice the rookery's distinctive odor, which can overpower a sensitive nose.

Do not approach the Chiswell Island rookery too close. Frightened sea lions may stampede into the water and crush young pups. Kayak and small boat operators should be cautious of sea lions, especially sub-adult males, who may harass those who ventures too close to a haulout area. Be wary of

Slide Rock (foreground) with Beehive (left) and Matushka Island (right).

dangling your hand in the water or over the side of a boat. Juvenile sea lions can be intimidating, especially when they swim around in gangs.

Around the turn of this century, the Steller sea lion population from the Kenai Peninsula westward to Russia was in steep decline. Recently, their numbers appear to have stabilized and are even increasing in some areas. In order to better understand the local sea lion population, marine mammal biologists are studying the rookery located on Chiswell Island.

Beehive Island

Thousands of tufted puffins cloud the sky around the honeycombed rock monolith of Beehive Island and the neighboring unnamed island. These two 500-foot tall sea stacks provide ideal nesting habitat for more than 30,000 tufted puffins: the largest nesting population of tufted puffins on the entire Kenai Peninsula. Each evening, the sky darkens as thousands of puffins take wing and encircle the sea stacks.

Matushka Island

Another marine bird nesting area is on Matushka Island. The Russian name *matushka* means "mother," and aptly describes the loveliest of the Chiswell Islands. Visit Matushka Bight, a wooded cove on the island's west side. In the evening the bight comes alive with seabirds. Observe the nesting routine of horned puffins as they swoop down from their rocky crevices to gather fish and exchange incubation chores with their mate.

Matushka Bight also attracts flocks of rhinoceros auklets that parade around the cove. Watch for a peregrine falcon that lurks on the sea cliffs and may dine on nearby auklets.

The steep rocky shoreline in Matushka Bight makes kayak or raft landings tough, at best. Even if you can climb ashore, there is little ground among the boulders and sea cliffs to find an adequate camping spot.

Anchorages:
Matushka Bight is only partially protected from easterly weather and should be considered only a fair-weather anchorage. A lively gulf swell circulates around the bight. Commercial halibut boats use this anchorage when baiting up or while waiting to haul gear from the offshore waters. Drop anchor near the bight's head in 10–15 fathoms onto a rocky bottom, and be prepared to spend a restless night, especially if sea conditions are anything other than calm.

Beehive Island, Chiswell Islands.

Enthusiastic marine bird watchers can venture out to 3-acre Lone Rock, home of the only known northern fulmar colony on the Kenai Fjords coast. At Seal Rocks, the outermost island in the Chiswell Island group, a remarkable sea arch bores through the large island. In 1916 Seal Rocks became one of the earliest offshore hazards on the outer coast to be crowned with a navigation light.

The Chiswell Islands were among the first prominent physical features to be named on the Kenai outer coast. Captain Portlock noted the rocky offshore island cluster on his track chart of the Kenai Peninsula in 1786. According to statements by Captain Vancouver, the islands were named for Trench Chiswell, a wealthy Englishman, and friend of Captain Portlock.

On early Russian navigational charts, the island group was called the Aialik Islands. The name acquired from the Sugpiaq, who hunted the offshore island area for marine mammals and birds.

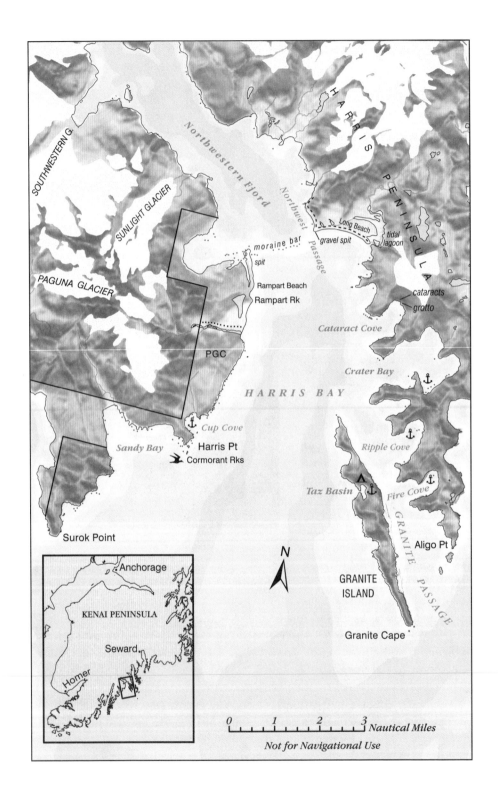

SOUTHWESTERN G.

SUNLIGHT GLACIER

PAGUNA GLACIER

Northwestern Fjord

Northwest Passage

HARRIS PENINSULA

moraine bar

spit

Long Beach

gravel spit

tidal
lagoon

Rampart Beach

Rampart Rk

cataracts

grotto

PGC

Cataract Cove

Crater Bay

HARRIS BAY

Cup Cove

Sandy Bay

Harris Pt

Cormorant Rks

Ripple Cove

Taz Basin

Fire Cove

Surok Point

Aligo Pt

GRANITE PASSAGE

N

GRANITE
ISLAND

Granite Cape

Anchorage

KENAI PENINSULA

Seward

Homer

0   1   2   3 *Nautical Miles*

Not for Navigational Use

16

Harris Bay

ALIGO POINT TO SUROK POINT

Wildlife and Scenic Viewing:
  The picturesque waters of Granite Passage are renowned for viewing pods of
  humpback whales that feed in the nearby coves. On a seacoast crammed with
  magnificent scenery, two coves stand out from the others: Cataract Cove,
  known for its majestic waterfalls and Taz Basin, a partially landlocked
  anchorage, surrounded by spectacular granite cliffs.

Kayaking and Camping:
  Ocean kayakers should explore the exposed waters of Harris Bay with caution,
  as protected landing spots are limited. Be assured, however, the partially
  sheltered waters of Granite Passage with its coves and bays provides a scenic
  place to paddle. Granite Passage is flanked on the west by Granite Island and
  on the east by the steeply-sloped and heavily-wooded Harris Peninsula. A
  particular attraction is the cascading falls in Cataract Cove. Unfortunately, the
  rocky shoreline of Granite Passage lacks an adequate landing beach. On
  Granite Island, Taz Basin provides a landing area and camp spot, although
  landing on the rock ledges at the north point can be tricky when a significant
  swell is running. In a calm sea, Rampart Beach, at the western head of Harris
  Bay, can be safely landed on.

Anchorages:
  In general, the vessel anchorages in Harris Bay are deep with steeply sloped
  shorelines and rocky bottoms. The best all-purpose vessel anchorage is in
  Crater Bay. Taz Basin is secure, but its narrow entrance should be avoided
  during rough sea conditions. Mild-weather anchorage options include Fire,
  Ripple, Cataract, and Cup coves.

Harris Peninsula sculpts the meandering eastern shore of Harris Bay.
Geologists define the peninsula as a granite intrusive. It formed
during the Tertiary Period, 60-million years ago. Between Aligo
Point and the head of Harris Bay is a contiguous series of southwest-facing
coves and bays. Stands of spruce and hemlock grow along the water's edge,
their roots often immersed in salt water by storm tides. Granite Island, long
and straight, runs parallel to Harris Peninsula. Granite Passage, a narrow,
scenic waterway, slices between the mainland coves and the precipitous
shore of Granite Island.

Western shore, Granite Island.

A rock-littered, 1.5 nm long, glacial moraine partially obstructs North-western Fjord at the head of Harris Bay. Abandoned in 1894 by the retreat of Northwestern Glacier, the moraine bar is composed of large boulders and sand bars that are most obvious at low water. At the eastern head of Harris Bay is Long Beach, a gravel outwash plain. The outwash has created a beautiful crescent-shaped barrier beach with an extensive wetland area behind its surf-battered waterfront. Northwest Passage, a narrow channel that leads across the moraine bar into Northwestern Fjord, lies adjacent to the gravel spit at the western end of Long Beach. See Chapter 17, *North-western Fjord* for information on entering Northwest Passage.

GRANITE ISLAND

Granite Island's towering profile is the most prominent physical feature at the mouth of Harris Bay. Part of Alaska's Maritime National Wildlife Refuge, this long, tall, narrow island resembles a granite slab tilted on end. The shore is a series of gray cliffs, eroded avalanche chutes, and slender, spruce-covered ledges. The island is surrounded by deep, unobstructed water, except at Granite Cape where a pair of dangerous rocks lies 150-yards offshore. On the sloped northern tip is an active bald eagle nest, easily seen in the branches of a tall spruce tree.

Concealed along the towering sea cliffs of Granite Island's western shore is one of the most scenic and secluded small boat anchorages on the outer coast. Known to local fishers as "the hole in the wall" and on nautical charts as Taz Basin, this little cliff-lined shelter is a geological oddity worth exploring. During rain squalls, this basin erupts with dozens of cascading waterfalls.

Taz Basin

Only enter or depart Taz Basin during safe sea conditions. In the center of the narrow entrance into Taz Basin lies a large flat-top boulder. Vessels can pass into the basin by navigating mid-channel between the boulder and the north entrance point. Patches of kelp grow in the channel and around the obstructing boulder. Minimum depth is two fathoms.

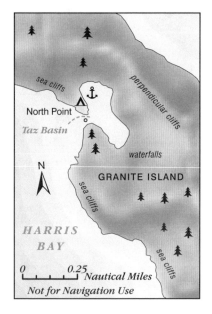

Small craft mariners should not be overly nervous about negotiating Taz Basin's narrow entrance; occasionally monohull vessels, nearly 90 feet in length, wedge their way through the entrance into the basin.

Kayaking:

Even an experienced ocean kayaker must use caution and common sense when paddling along the exposed western shore of Granite Island. If a large swell is present, it can make landing an awkward situation even in the usually tranquil waters of Taz Basin. The only decent landing area is among granite boulders and ledges inside the basin's north entrance point. Once firmly on shore, you've got it made.

Camping and Hiking:

Visitors to Taz Basin should take time to explore the northern entrance point where water erosion has engraved the granite ledges with potholes and spillways. The north point peninsula is about 150-yards wide. The exposed shore of the peninsula is comprised of wave-worn boulders with numerous, rainfilled ponds that can provide a source of cooking water, if necessary.

A collection of spongy moss, colorful lichen, and twisted, windswept hemlock trees that resemble a Japanese watercolor grow on the rocky hillside. An 8x8-foot squared-off, flat-topped granite block stands out prominently atop the north point's highest knoll.

The relatively gentle terrain on the point has a textured surface, which invites foot traffic. Hikers can pick their way over rock ledges that are a stone's throw from the sea or climb to areas atop the north point that display a breathtaking view of the Kenai Mountains and the outstretched headlands ranging from Harris Point to McArthur Pass and the Pye Islands. There are few places on the outer coast as exhilarating as the north point of Taz Basin.

Calm water reflections in Taz Basin, Granite Island.

Anchorage:
>A handful of small boats can find adequate room to anchor in the deep basin. Vessels can drop anchor near the northwest corner, 60-yards from shore, in approximately 8–10 fathoms on a sloping rock bottom. However, most boats prefer to anchor in the center of the basin at 14–18 fathoms. Here, the sticky bottom is an anaerobic-smelling, black mud.

Granite Passage

Vessels traveling to Harris Bay from the east, enter the bay by cruising through Granite Passage, a narrow 4.5 nm long channel between Granite Island and the mainland of Harris Peninsula. This picturesque island passage is deep and clear of obstructions, except for a 6-fathom shelf that extends more than midway into the passage from the northwest entrance point of Fire Cove.

In summer, Granite Island's 1,600-foot-high, perpendicular shoreline is a vivid display of lichen-covered, charcoal-gray cliffs with florescent green vegetation. Keep your eyes open for marine life in the passage. The small coves along Granite Passage, not unlike many island passages in the Kenai Fjords, attract a remarkable number of marine mammals, including humpback whales, that spend extended periods of time feeding in the area. Roving pods of resident killer whales frequently cruise the passage as well as Dall's porpoises. The passage also attracts a resident and migratory collection of waterfowl including mergansers, marbled murrelets, pigeon guillemots, black legged kittiwakes, and both horned and tufted puffins.

Looking across a foggy Granite Passage to Granite Island.

Fire Cove

Fire Cove's ragged shore is steep and rocky with scant landing sites for either a raft or kayak. Vessels sometimes use Fire Cove as an anchorage, especially in mild weather.

Fishing:

A handy fishing spot lies atop the 6-fathom ledge extending from Fire Cove's northwest entrance point. Try anchoring on the shelf, or try several drifts across it during the flood tide. Bait up for halibut, but expect anything from a juvenile pollock to a large-mouth lingcod, or even a feisty coho.

Ripple Cove

In Ripple Cove, thick stands of spruce reach up from the water's edge to about 1,200 feet. Above the spruce trees, barren sea cliffs stretch upward to the ridge. Below the summit, massive granite blocks rest scattered along the steep slope.

The shoreline is abrupt and alternates between mounds of loose talus and stacks of boulders. Beyond the reach of high water, the ragged shore lies covered in a moss blanket, entwined with alder and devil's club roots. There is no easy way to access the ragged shore within Ripple Cove, and certainly no space for camping.

At the cove's head sits a reef littered with jagged rocks. The reef is hidden during periods of high water. Nearby, a steep avalanche chute scars the hillside. A mound of snow and talus is piled at its base.

Granite shoreline, Granite Island.

Anchorage:
> A small vessel can anchor at the head of Ripple Cove, west of the reef that protrudes from the northeast shore. Here, the water is 12 to 15 fathoms deep with a sloped bottom.

Crater Bay

Crater Bay is the largest embayment within Harris Bay and the place where most mariners prefer to drop anchor. The shoreline rises abruptly from the water. There are no pocket beaches, campsites, or reasonable landing areas in this bay.

Anchorage:
> A secure anchorage during easterly weather is located in the bay's easternmost bight of the south corner, and is marked 16-fathoms on the marine chart. Here, the recessed head, partially fouled with rocks, is best avoided by anchoring in 6–8 fathoms at the mouth, on a rock bottom. Further offshore, in 16–20 fathoms, the bottom turns to mud. Rock ledges protrude offshore along the southeastern shore of this bight.

Cataract Cove

Cataract Cove is a remarkable place and a positively must-see location for anyone visiting Harris Bay. The cove is a drowned glacial cirque, and as its name suggests, a series of waterfalls perpetually tumble down the vertical, water-stained granite walls. The water source, for the waterfalls, is an alpine glacier straddling the ridge of Harris Peninsula, more than 2,500 feet in altitude.

Hidden in a rocky crevice immediately east of the waterfalls is Twin Falls Grotto, a notch gouged into the headwall. The grotto is deep enough for a small vessel or kayak to nose into the entrance and capture a misty photo of the falls.

Kayaking:
Cataract Cove is a popular destination for paddlers traveling the western shore of Harris Peninsula. Breathtaking cataracts unleash a magical atmosphere as plumes of water vapor, blown by an icy down draft, fill the grotto with mist. At times, the roar of water and the occasional thunderclap issuing from Northwestern Fjord creates a surreal ambiance for visitors.

Cascading water, Cataract Cove.

Anchorage:
The wakes from vessel traffic and an uneasy exposure make Cataract Cove a poor choice as an overnight anchorage. However, small boats can temporarily anchor adjacent to the grotto, in 4–6 fathoms, approximately 75 yards from the steep granite headwall, weather permitting.

EASTERN HEAD OF HARRIS BAY

Between Cataract Cove and the eastern head of Harris Bay are several small indentations that afford neither a reliable landing beach nor a secure, overnight anchorage.

Expansive outwash areas, tidal lagoons, and beaches lie at each end of the moraine bar at the head of Harris Bay. The outwash areas provide ideal hiking and wildlife viewing opportunities. River otters are abundant as are eagles, assorted waterfowl, and black bears.

At the bay's head is Long Beach, a sandy, crescent-shaped, 1.5 nm long barrier beach with shallow water extending well offshore. A large tidal lagoon is located at the east end of the beach with an outlet stream into Harris Bay. The lagoon has two arms — one arm runs semi-parallel to Long Beach, the other arm extends inland along the hillside to a waterfall system.

Rye grass, Long Beach.

Kayaking:
Even in light weather, a constant swell rolls in from the gulf and crashes onto Long Beach. Kayak or raft landings on the beach are nearly impossible without getting wet. The channel entrance to the tidal lagoon is on the east end of Long Beach.

Note:
The stream entrance into the Long Beach lagoon should only be navigated by a kayak at high water slack during neap tide cycles. A smooth sea is essential. At the tide-change, when the stream's flow starts to ebb, waves immediately begin to break across the channel mouth. If you do enter, quickly depart or plan to stay awhile. Immediately haul out inside the entrance and check the tidal channel before proceeding. A significant elevation drop takes place as the fast moving tide rushes to fill the low-lying tidal lagoon. Another way to access Long Beach and the head of Harris Bay is to enter Northwest Passage, which crosses over the moraine bar into the protection of Northwestern Fjord.

WESTERN HEAD OF HARRIS BAY

Rampart Beach and Northwestern Glacier Moraine

Rampart Beach lies along the western shore, adjacent to the moraine bar at the head of Harris Bay. The uplands from mean high water are private property owned by the Port Graham Corporation. Rampart Rock is a prominent 70-foot-tall rock monolith that stands out midway along the contiguous, 2-mile-long beachfront.

The low-lying area north of Rampart Rock terminates on a wooded spit near the former Northwestern Glacier moraine bar. A mossy stand of stately spruce trees, hundreds of years old and four to six feet in diameter, grows at the northern tip of the wooded spit. These old trees mark the maximum Little Ice Age position of Northwestern Glacier in 1894. A trim line of young and old-growth trees is etched across the hillside above Otter Cove in Northwestern Lagoon.

Looking southward from the Northwestern Glacier moraine to Granite Island.

Immediately south of Rampart Rock, a small stream channel cuts through the gravel berm and drains a primitive looking lagoon surrounded by a moss-laden forest. In Beards Hollow, the meltwaters from three alpine glaciers merge to create a roaring stream that enters Harris Bay at the southern end of Rampart Beach.

Kayaking, Camping, and Hiking:
> The Rampart Beach waterfront is accessible to beach landings from the head of Harris Bay only when calm sea conditions are present. The waterfront around the moraine bar is wilderness beachcombing at its best. An unmarked public easement trail, across PGC land, follows the Beard Hollow stream to KFNP lands.

Note:
> In foul weather or poor visibility, mariners should give a wide berth to the exposed western shoreline and moraine bar area at the head of Harris Bay. Strong tidal currents combined with uncharted rocks and sand bars along the moraine bar can pose hazardous conditions to underpowered boats and kayaks. Only use Northwest Passage. Do not attempt to cross the moraine bar at any other location.

Heading southwest from Rampart Beach, a 2-mile-long stretch of inaccessible sea cliffs culminates at the thousand-foot-tall outcropping of Harris Point. At the crumbling base of Harris Point sits a picturesque collection of wave-washed islets and rock pinnacles (Cormorant Rocks). Beach landing are possible at Cup Cove, weather permitting.

Rampart Rock along the western shore of Harris Bay.

Cup Cove

Immediately north of Harris Point, rests Cup Cove nestled in a sea cliff setting. The cove's exposure to the ocean makes this a tenuous place, but one worth checking out.

Inside Cup Cove are two pocket beaches separated by a rock outcropping that is surrounded by patches of kelp. The west beach is a mixture of gravel and sand with a stream exiting on the northern end. The north beach is very short and steeply cut. A small stream drains an alluring valley that lies behind the beach berm and wooded waterfront. In calm sea conditions, Cup Cove holds good beachcombing potential and is a rarely visited location to explore.

The upland areas (above mean high water) in Cup Cove and Sandy Bay are private property owned by the Port Graham Corporation and there are no public campsite or trail easements in this area. Advance permission is needed from the corporation to camp or hike on their land. See Chapter 2, *Kenai Fjords Land Issues* for information on PGC land use permits.

Anchorage:

Southeast-facing Cup Cove provides limited protection from gulf weather and only should be used in northerly or westerly weather conditions. Anchor near the center of the cove in 4–6 fathoms. The bottom is rocky and gently sloped. A rolling swell enters the cove from the gulf, and the loud noise of surf slamming the beach renders this anchorage as a poor choice for sleepy mariners. A better, more comfortable anchorage lies 4 nm away in Taz Basin.

Sandy Bay

A relentless gulf swell funnels into Sandy Bay and washes high up on the beach. The bay is directly influenced by gulf weather and is relatively shallow, which tends to amplify the incoming swell. The area bestows an uncomfortable, exposed feeling when hanging on anchor.

A wild looking, rarely visited valley, overgrown with thick clumps of alder and spruce, occupy the bay's head. This unforgiving indentation is not a place to be when southeast weather threatens. Beachcombers will need nearly ideal sea conditions to land or depart the wave-washed sandy beach.

A rocky shore with rugged sea cliffs wraps around Sandy Bay and continues southwestward along the seacoast to Surok Point. There are no landing beaches between Sandy Bay and Surok Point, however in Paguna Arm, a short distance away, a mariner can find a good selection of anchorages, landing beaches, and camping areas with suitable water sources.

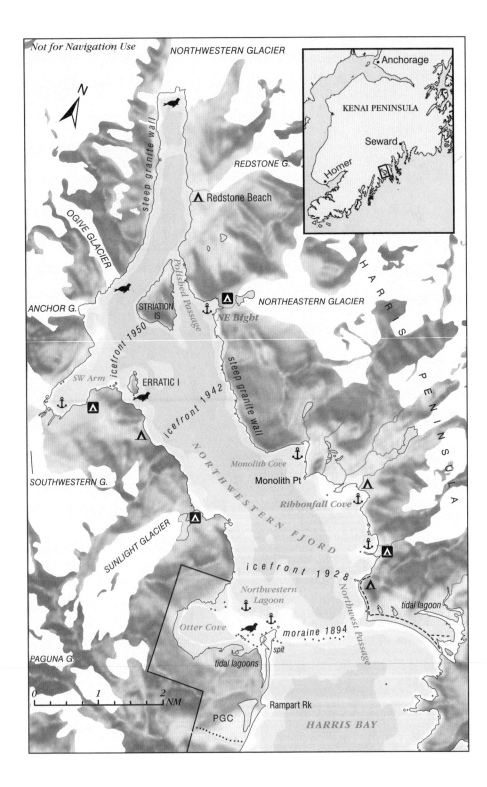

Not for Navigation Use

NORTHWESTERN GLACIER

N

OGIVE GLACIER

steep granite wall

REDSTONE G.

⛺ Redstone Beach

ANCHOR G.

Polished Passage

icefront 1950

STRIATION IS

⚓ 🏕 NORTHEASTERN GLACIER

NE Bight

HARRIS

SW Arm

ERRATIC I

steep granite wall

⚓

🏕

icefront 1942

NORTHWESTERN FJORD

Monolith Cove

⚓

SOUTHWESTERN G.

Monolith Pt

🏕

Ribbonfall Cove

⚓

🏕

SUNLIGHT GLACIER

🏕

⚓

🏕

icefront 1928

Northwest Passage

tidal lagoon

Northwestern Lagoon

⚓

⚓

moraine 1894

PAGUNA G.

Otter Cove

spit

tidal lagoons

0   1   2
NM

Rampart Rk

PGC

HARRIS BAY

KENAI PENINSULA

Anchorage

Seward

Homer

Northwestern Fjord

NORTHWEST PASSAGE TO NORTHWESTERN GLACIER

Wildlife Viewing:
Rafts of sea otters feed in the shallow waters around the moraine bar and throughout the Northwestern Lagoon area. In summer, hundreds of harbor seals haul out on bergy bits floating in upper Northwestern Fjord. Marbled and Kittlitz's murrelets seasonally inhabit the icy waters. These diving birds can show up in small numbers or in rafts containing several dozen paired individuals. A variety of birds and mammals including Arctic terns, mergansers, parakeet auklets, rhinoceros auklets, river otters, and black bears inhabit the extensive outwash areas around the moraine bar, Long Beach, Otter Cove, and Ribbonfall Cove.

Kayaking, Camping, and Hiking:
The traditional drop-off, staging, and camping area for kayak tour groups and others is located one-mile north of Northwest Passage. A protruding, gravel spit along the east shore identifies the location. A bear-proof food locker and water source are nearby. Remember, the further north one travels into the fjord, the cooler the temperatures. Other camping destinations are at Redstone Beach, Southwestern Glacier, and Ribbonfall Cove.

Anchorages:
Drifting ice is not usually a problem for vessels anchored in the lower glacial basin, but mariners should always be aware of the wind direction, tidal current, and movement of the ice pack when lying at anchor. Anchorage choices include the Northeastern Bight, Monolith Cove, Ribbonfall Cove, Northwestern Lagoon, and the Southwestern Arm.

Perhaps the best-kept secret on Alaska's coast is the spell-binding glacial enclave of Northwestern Fjord. In 1894, Northwestern Glacier rested on its terminal moraine at the head of Harris Bay. The glacier was at the maximum extent of its Little Ice Age advance. In 1909, Grant and Higgins reported the glacier had pulled back 400 yards from the moraine into deep water. The report added that the two-mile-wide tidewater glacier, with six medial moraines, was the most striking physical feature on Alaska's North Gulf Coast.

Northwestern Glacier has retreated more than 10 miles in the past century and continues to retreat. Even though the receding glacier is only a shadow of its former self, the newly uncovered glacial basin with spectacular islands and miles of polished granite walls more than makes up for its diminished size.

In total, eight major glaciers flow from the mile-high Harding Icefield into the tributary arms of this steeply walled embayment. When you visit Northwestern Fjord, you enter a micro ice age environment that heightens your senses. The cold seeps into your bones as if you stepped into a freezer. The light appears more blue and gray. Noises are harsh and brittle with an amphitheater-like effect. At first, one hears only a dull hiss. After a while, you realize that it is the sound of water: running, falling, crashing, and cascading. Water creates the constant background music of Northwestern Fjord. The music is only periodically drowned out by a sudden thunderclap or a primal groan radiating from the bowels of the glaciers. At other times, the air is thick, wet, and muffled like the inside of a cloud.

Northwestern Glacier, c. 1980.

Northwestern Fjord is a physical place where the forces of nature are omnipresent. It continues to be a place of constant change and one of the wildest seascapes on the Kenai Fjords coast.

Since the early 1900s, icebergs and strong tidal currents have slowly eroded portions of the moraine bar that once blocked vessels from entering Northwestern Fjord from the head of Harris Bay. Significant land subsidence (6.7 feet) resulting from the 1964 earthquake hastened the breakdown of the moraine bar and widened a narrow channel on the east end, now called Northwest Passage.

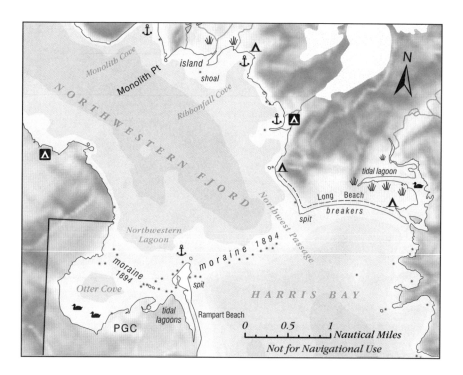

Northwest Passage

Northwest Passage is wedged between the glacial moraine bar and the low-lying sand spit, which protrudes from the western end of Long Beach. Shallow sand bars and submerged rocks pinch the Northwest Passage from both sides. Mid-channel lies one-quarter mile (measured by radar) from the high-water mark on the mainland sand spit. The glacial moraine bar encroaches into the passage from the southwest and is discernible by boulders, sand bars, and crashing surf. In clear weather, the mid-channel approach can be identified by sighting south down Granite Passage and lining up the headland tips of Crater Bay and Fire Cove with Seal Rocks. The channel has a maximum depth of approximately 5 fathoms at mean lower low water (MLLW). Be cautious; only enter and depart Northwestern Fjord via Northwest Passage and only when sea conditions are favorable, preferably around slack water.

Dangerously swift tidal currents and rough seas can converge on the Harris Bay side of Northwest Passage. These conditions can be treacherous for small boats and kayaks. Strong tidal currents can suck a kayak or an underpowered boat into the passage and possibly into danger. Plan ahead and check out the sea conditions in the passage before proceeding. If necessary, wait for slack water. Do not attempt to travel, into or out of Northwest Passage during the middle or bottom stage of an ebbing spring tide, espe-

Looking northwest across the moraine bar into Northwestern Fjord.

cially when a significant swell from the gulf is present. Those mariners without local knowledge of Northwest Passage may want to follow another vessel over the sill. Be prepared to wait out unfavorable tidal or sea conditions when trying to depart Northwestern Fjord.

LOWER NORTHWESTERN FJORD

The hanging glaciers in the lower fjord are deeply fissured and radiate a luminescent glow with shades of turquoise. Energetic glaciologists will have a field day hiking across the glacial till to any one of a half-dozen accessible, land-based glaciers. Alder and willow thrive on the recently deglaciated moraines. Several land-based glaciers like Northeastern, Southwestern, and Sunlight have retreated from tidewater within the past half century.

Although the maximum depth of the glacial basin exceeds 1,000 feet, known hazards include shallow water and rocks located throughout the northern portion of Ribbonfall Cove, especially around its small, low-lying offshore island/peninsula.

Additional offshore rocks and a shallow moraine bar obstruct the mouth of Otter Cove and along the southern shore of Northwestern Lagoon. Rocks and shallow water lie adjacent to the south tip of Erratic Island. Numerous alluvial fans exist around stream mouths and at the heads of arms and bays. Care must be taken when traveling close to glacial moraines and shorelines because of uncharted offshore rocks and boulders.

Northwestern Lagoon

Northwestern Lagoon is a large, oval-shaped bight in the lower south-western corner of Northwestern Fjord. Mariners should note that North-western Lagoon has an outer and inner basin separated by a shallow moraine bar that goes mostly dry on minus tides. A scattering of jagged rocks and boulders lie atop the moraine bar.

The inner portion of Northwestern Lagoon is known as Otter Cove due to the cove's high concentration of sea otters. Because of the shallow moraine bar, only kayaks and very shallow draft boats should cross the bar into Otter Cove. Other vessels are limited to the outer portion of the lagoon. Extensive mudflats and boulders also range along the lagoon's southern shore.

Kayaking and Hiking:
A one-quarter mile long, unnamed tidal lagoon, which goes dry at low water, lies on the south side of Northwestern Lagoon adjacent to the moraine bar. At higher stages of the tide, the lagoon's waterfront offers a convenient beach landing area, without having to hike over extensive mudflats. Hike along the tidelands. The uplands from mean high water are private property owned by the Port Graham Corporation. A trek along the state-owned tidal waterfront leads to the spit area, moraine bar, and Rampart Beach, a 2-mile long beach at the western head of Harris Bay.

Anchorage:
Vessels can anchor in the center of the outer portion of Northwestern Lagoon in 5–7 fathoms. The bottom is a mixture of gravel, silt, and patches of kelp. In summer, Northwestern Lagoon is generally free of drifting ice.

Sunlight Glacier

This land-based glacier is wedged into the steep valley behind the waterfront. Sunlight Glacier last reached tidewater in the 1940s. Today, alder and willow grow along the shore once covered by blankets of ice.

Camping and Hiking:
The Sunlight Glacier waterfront is a reliable landing and camping location. The gently sloped valley invites hikes over the glacial till to the retreating ice front. A bear-proof food locker is located behind the beach berm in the alder growth mid-way along the waterfront. Water is available from several streams that exit the valley floor.

Anchorage:
A 5–6 fathom deep ledge toward the north end of the Sunlight Glacier beach offers a convenient spot to anchor in fair weather.

Ribbonfall Cove

Vessels should avoid the entire northern portion of Ribbonfall Cove. Boulders and shallow mudflats dominate an extensive area around the low-lying island to Monolith Point. In the cove's east corner a ribbon-thin waterfall cascades over a sheer rock headwall.

Waterfront, Ribbonfall Cove.

Camping and Hiking:
> The inviting cream-colored beach of Ribbonfall Cove is comprised of a gritty granite powder. The cove's hospitable shoreline is a terrific place to roam on foot or to camp. In summer, shorebirds often flit about the tidal zone. A collection of hanging glaciers stands out above the cove's head. Several streams meander down from the valley to the beach and provide a water source for campers.

Anchorage:
> Small boats can anchor in the east corner of Ribbonfall Cove, just slightly west of the stream mouth in 8–10 fathoms. The entire northwest portion of the cove is shallow, and mudflats extend well offshore. On summer afternoons, the anchorage is often exposed to an obnoxious, southwesterly breeze that sends a chop into the cove.

Monolith Cove

Vessels seeking a secure, ice-free anchorage generally use this south-facing cove. An 80-foot tall rock monolith stands at the east entrance. Mariners can easily pick out Monolith Point from anywhere in the lower fjord. Kayakers tend to pass by the nondescript cove without stopping, although the beach at the head provides a suitable landing spot.

Anchorage:
> Drop anchor in 10–15 fathoms offshore from the head. Allow enough swing room to stay off the shoal that extends out from the beach. In summer, this anchorage is usually ice free and shielded from harsh winds, except for southerly gales.

Erratic Island

Erratic Island is the largest of a pair of prominent, boulders near the eastern entrance to Southwestern Arm. The colorful granite island and its smaller neighbor have been repeatedly scoured by glacial ice. The island is layered with bands of quartz and encrusted with patches of orange, green, and brown lichens and algae.

A collection of harbor seals often haulout on the rocks that extend into the passage from Erratic Island's southern end. This spot is important during pupping and their molt, especially when ice is light. Deep draft sailboats may want to avoid the shallow and narrow passage on the island's south end. Visitors can land on the island's north end, which has a commanding view.

Nearly all the placenames and features located in Northwestern Fjord were christened by USGS glaciologist Austin Post during his glacial and bathymetry work in the late 1970s.

Anchorage:

During neap tides and light ice conditions, a small boat can temporarily drop anchor along the western shore of Erratic Island. Enjoy the view. The anchorage is midway along the island's shoreline, approximately 40 yards offshore in 6–8 fathoms.

Do not anchor in the bottleneck passage between Erratic Island and the mainland shore. Swift tidal currents sometimes accompanied by icebergs funnel through the passage during the ebb tide.

Erratic Island (left) and Ogive Glacier.

Looking southward into the Southwestern Arm.

UPPER NORTHWESTERN FJORD

Southwestern Glacier

In 1950, the entire Southwestern Arm was drowned by glacial ice. Today, Southwestern Glacier winds down from the Harding Icefield and terminates in the gently sloped valley at the arm's head, approximately a mile from tidewater. The Southwest Arm is deep except near the head, where the water rapidly shallows onto the tidal flats. Silt, gravel, and boulders extend offshore. In the upland valley, several streams exit from beneath Southwestern Glacier's wide terminus and then cut their way through the gravel outwash to tidewater.

A prominent unnamed glacier rests near tidewater on the western shore of the arm's head. The raw-looking moraine is littered with broken fragments of granite, and the icy terminus is darkened by glacial till. Above the glacier's base, thick ice sheets cling to the top of a vertical 1,000-foot-high headwall. At the silt-laden high-water mark, a torrent of water escapes from beneath the moraine.

Camping and Hiking:
Choose a camping spot along the Southwestern Arm's rough-and-tumble east shore. Two pocket beaches standout mid-way along the waterfront. The first beach (west facing) has a stream, several cleared campsites, and a bear-proof food locker. The food locker is hidden toward the south end of the beach where a dry creek bed and trail leads to its location.

The arm's head is a raw landscape comprised of scantly-vegetated glacial till and silty outwash from the robust stream at the west end of the beach. Hikers have the option to check-out the deglaciated valley and gritty ice terminus of Southwestern Glacier.

Anchorage:
Small craft can drop anchor in 10 fathoms or deeper about mid-way along the shore at the head of the Southwestern Arm. Stay away from the stream out-wash, and give yourself sufficient swing room from shore, as the silt-clogged head rapidly shallows.

Anchor & Ogive Glaciers

Anchor and Ogive glaciers calve into the frigid waters west of Striation Island. A bold rock face separates the two glaciers. Both tidal ice fronts are nearly vertical and rise more than 100 feet above the water's surface. At times, large tilted seracs overhang the water just before calving. Brash ice and bergy bits often clog the passage between these two glaciers and Striation Island.

Ogive Glacier is notable for the curving bands of ice alternating from dark to light. High above the ice front are large, suspended ice blocks that routinely plummet over a sheer rock precipice.

Mariners and kayakers should note a potentially dangerous, one-fathom-deep shoal that lies directly in front of Anchor Glacier. Calving ice may cause glacier waves to break across this shoal area. It is wise to stay in deep water when around tidewater glaciers.

Northeastern Bight

Immediately east of Striation Island rests a small indentation known as Northeastern Bight. Above the bight, on the hillside approximately one mile from the water, sits Northeastern Glacier. In 1982, the glacier termi-nated about 0.3 mile from high water. It probably withdrew from tidewater in the early 1960s. Based on carbon-14 dating, tree fragments examined in the streambed below the glacier suggest a forest existed in the valley about 1,600 years ago, before the Little Ice Age advance.

Kayaking, Camping, and Hiking:
The head of Northeastern Bight provides a landing location for camping and exploring the deglaciated valley with its racing outwash stream. Pick your way over the rugged terrain, through the stands of alder and willow, to excellent vantage points looking toward Striation Island, Polished Passage, and Anchor Glacier. Northeastern Bight is a convenient base camp area for extended pad-dle trips around Polished Passage and the upper portion of Northwestern Fjord. A food locker exists midway along the beach in the alders.

Anchorage:
Drop anchor at the head of the Northeastern Bight, north of the outwash stream in 10–12 fathoms on a silty, rock bottom. You may risk the chance of swinging onto the mudflats by anchoring too shallow. At low water, bare tide-

Northwestern Glacier.

lands extend into the bight more than 150 yards from the high-water mark. This anchorage can remain relatively calm even when the outer coast is hit by southeasterly winds. For anchored vessels, a drifting ice pack can present an occasional hull-thumping event. Avoid overnight anchoring when threatening amounts of ice are seen drifting in Polished Passage.

Striation Island

As recently as 1942, thick ice from Northwestern Glacier all but covered this 1,263-foot high, conical island. Today, the island is surrounded by silt-laden water, reaching more than 100-fathoms deep. The entire granite surface of the island has been ground, smoothed, and polished by the scouring action of glacial activity. From any angle, Striation Island is the single most dramatic land feature in Northwestern Fjord.

An eagle nest is located on a rock ledge about 150 feet above the water on the island's northern tip. In summer, vegetation grows in the recessed cracks and fissures formed in the granite rock. Along the island's southwestern shore, a few rock ledges are accessible to a raft or kayak at different stages of the tide. The panoramic view of Anchor and Ogive glaciers from the elevated shore is spectacular.

Nearby, Polished Passage (often choked by ice and resting harbor seals) funnels visitors through an ice-scoured granite channel into the upper reaches of Northwestern Fjord.

Redstone Glacier

Redstone Glacier hangs on the glacier-carved slope of the fjord wall. Composed of grit-filled ice, the leading edge of the glacier is about 0.4 miles from tidewater. A roaring stream tumbles down a steep, boulder-filled streambed. Redstone Glacier reached tidewater as recently as 1964. Wood fragments taken from a buried tree in the streambed suggest that a forest grew here about 1,400 years ago.

Less than two decades ago, as many as a thousand seals spent the pupping season in the upper fjord between Redstone and Northwestern glaciers. Recent seal surveys indicate a seal population in the mid-hundreds.

Kayaking, Camping, and Hiking:
Redstone Beach, an outwash area, is the closest camping spot to Northwestern Glacier. It is an excellent camping location in dry weather. Pitch a tent wherever you can find some level terrain. Hikers can trudge up the rugged stream or climb to panoramic vistas along the fjord wall. Willow and alder grow to about the 1,000-foot elevation, and boulders litter the steeply sloped terrain. During periods of heavy rain, do not camp here, as Redstone Beach is subject to severe flooding.

Northwestern Glacier

At the fjord's head, Northwestern Glacier plunges into the sea. The eastern portion of its ice face has withdrawn onto land. Along the lateral edges are recent signs of deglaciation, evident by the sparkling bright, newly exposed granite. At times, Northwestern Glacier calves sufficiently to clog the fjord with floating ice and to wash the nearby shoreline with powerful waves. Dangerous icefalls can occur at any time from (hidden) seracs located along the rock ledges high above the glacier's main terminus.

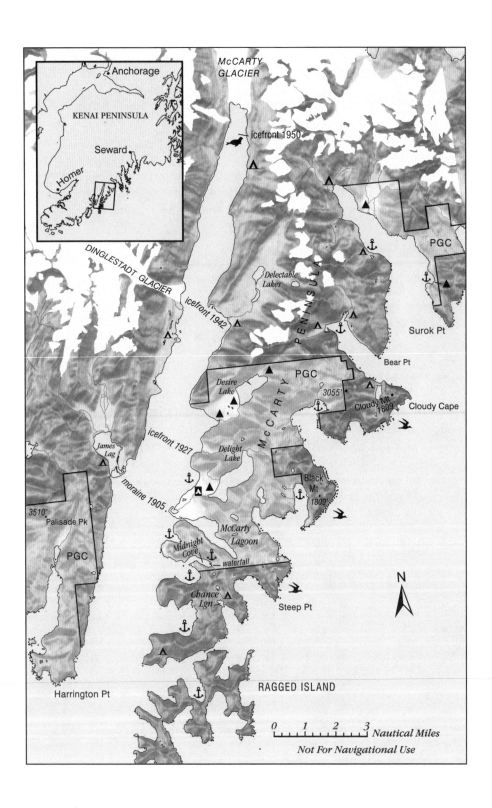

McCARTY
GLACIER

Anchorage

KENAI PENINSULA

Seward

Homer

icefront 1950

DINGLESTADT GLACIER

icefront 1942

Delectable
Lakes

PENINSULA

PGC

Surok Pt

Bear Pt

Desire
Lake

McCARTY

PGC

3055'

Cloudy Mt
1809'

Cloudy Cape

icefront 1927

James
Lag

Delight
Lake

Black
Mt
1809'

moraine 1905

3510'

Palisade Pk

PGC

Midnight
Cove

McCarty
Lagoon

waterfall

Chance
Lgn

Steep Pt

N

Harrington Pt

RAGGED ISLAND

0   1   2   3 Nautical Miles

Not For Navigational Use

18

McCarty Peninsula

SUROK POINT TO HARRINGTON POINT

Wildlife Viewing:
> Surok Point, Cloudy Cape, Black Mountain, and Steep Point attract scores of nesting marine birds including murres, puffins, kittiwakes, and auklets. Migrating gray whales appear alone or in small groups in spring. Pods of resident and transient killer whales routinely hunt in the McArthur Pass area. The low-lying outwash deltas and wetland areas around McCarty and James lagoons provide ideal bird watching habitats.

Kayaking:
> Only well-equipped, seasoned ocean kayakers should attempt to paddle the exposed seacoast from Harris Bay to McArthur Pass. This region requires detailed planning and skill. In locations like Two Arm Bay, Thunder Bay, and Chance Lagoon, a person can spend days without seeing human activity.

Camping and Hiking:
> Two Arm Bay and Thunder Bay have choice camping areas with plenty of wild terrain to explore. McCarty Fjord exhibits miles of rarely visited waterfront with secluded lagoons, and salmon-filled streams and lakes.

Fishing:
> Excellent bottom fishing is found within a mile of the exposed headlands of Granite Cape, Surok Point, and Cloudy Cape. The 25- to 40-fathom rocky areas at the entrances to Thunder and Black bays are popular halibut grounds. In McCarty Fjord, beginning in late June, red salmon can be snagged along the gravel spits in front of Desire and Delight creeks.

Anchorages:
> An excellent selection of anchorages is scattered along this region. Two inviting places to drop anchor are Two Arm Bay and Thunder Bay. In McCarty Fjord, a host of good anchorages include Square Bay, Moonlight Bay, Midnight Cove, and Repose Cove.

A long string of bold, storm-beaten capes and ice-free fjords range between Surok Point and the McArthur Pass entrance. Here, the seacoast is as rugged and unyielding as any shoreline on the Kenai Fjords coast. The handful of fjords in this region affords sea travelers a place to wait out foul weather as well as an opportunity to behold breathtaking seascapes.

Two Arm Bay

Two Arm Bay encompasses two modest fjords known as Paguna and Taroka arms. The name *taroka* is derived from the Sugpiaq word for brown bear. The bold headland separating the two fjords is known as Bear Point.

Visitors to out-of-the-way places like Two Arm Bay usually peek into the mouth, but seldom explore the head of either arm. Be assured that Paguna and Taroka exhibit more than just scenic mountains. They are endowed with enough beaches and accessible terrain to keep the curious exploring for days.

Paguna Arm

Kayaking, Camping, and Hiking:

The first northwest facing cove tucked inside Surok Point has a little of every-thing for the traveling mariner: a suitable anchorage, a reliable landing beach, and an excellent water source. Behind the barrier beach, a cascading stream spills down the hillside into a pool. This small alcove is a handy refuge from foul weather in the gulf. Several CMTs stand out behind the beach. In upper Paguna Arm, visitors will find two welcoming beaches. The first is located on the west shore approximately 2.5 nm from the head. Behind this long, pebbled beach are football-sized fields of storm-washed cobble, scattered driftwood logs, and eerie lowlands complete with a swamp, lagoon, and ghost forest. An iron bulldozer chassis from the mid-20th cen-tury rests in a shallow grave on the beach.

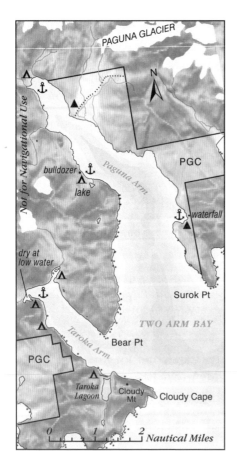

Paguna Arm's east shore beach (1.4 nm from the head) is actually an expansive, alder-covered out-wash plain. A stream drains a wide, low-lying, partially glaciated valley. This picturesque valley has grand hiking potential. The PGC owns the uplands in this area. Paguna Glacier hangs prominently above the valley floor. At the low-lying head is a delta area with a network of streams.

Anchorages:

The most convenient anchorage lies in the first cove on the east side of Paguna Arm, just 1.7 nm northwest of Surok Point. This tiny cove, with an irregular bottom, affords only mediocre protection. A rocky ledge rests along the bight's south shore, marked by kelp. Anchor in 10–15 fathoms in the center of the bight.

In upper Paguna Arm, alternative anchorages lie off the mudflats at the head and alongside the upper west and east shore beaches.

Taroka Arm

Along the arm's southern shore and approximately one-mile from Cloudy Cape is a conspicuous cobble beach and wooded area. A narrow valley occupied by Taroka Lagoon sits behind the berm. The lagoon drains into the arm on the east end of the beach.

A Sugpiaq village called Kanilik (meaning "two bays") is thought to have been located in the area. In the woods behind the waterfront, adjacent the lagoon, lies a quiet secluded area where a dozen Culturally Modified Trees (CMT) still stand.

Taroka Lagoon, Two Arm Bay.

Camping and Hiking:
Taroka Arm, 3.3 nm long, has a camping and hiking area at the head. Here, a tidal lagoon, barrier beach, and narrow valley sit in the arm's west corner. The tidal lagoon goes nearly dry at low water, so it is only accessible during higher stages of the tide and only by kayak, skiff, or raft.

An accessible, cobble beach runs the length of Taroka Arm's north shore. Here, visitors can choose to beachcomb or camp anywhere along more than a mile of waterfront.

Anchorage:
At the head of Taroka Arm, in the northwest corner, a vessel can drop anchor in 6–8 fathoms onto a muddy shelf. Avoid the shallow water at the mouth of the tidal lagoon.

Likewise, in the arm's northeast corner lies a narrow inlet. Small craft can anchor at the inlet's mouth in 6–8 fathoms or tuck slightly inside the mouth and anchor in 4–6 fathoms on a mud bottom with limited swing room.

Waterfall, Thunder Bay.

Thunder Bay

Storm-weary sailors riding a tempest wind should steer for this walled-in shelter. Thunder Bay is a compact fjord, 2.5 nm long and 0.5 nm wide. A spectacular line of cliffs and boulders flank the entrance, which leads to a right-hand dogleg and a cirque-shaped basin at the bay's terminus. One glimpse to the bay's north corner reveals a distant but nevertheless thundering waterfall. The waterfall's reservoir is a large alpine lake formed in a valley cirque at the 500-foot elevation.

Thunder Bay is a familiar destination for a handful of offshore fishing vessels and cruising mariners. Ask people who have anchored there, and they will tell you that Thunder Bay is one of the most spectacular bays on the outer coast. The shore exhibits plenty of beach hiking terrain and towering waterfalls. CMTs can be found in many locations. Thunder Bay is an ideal place to drop anchor for an entire weekend. The VHF weather reception from Homer is only fair.

The property upland from mean high water in Thunder Bay belongs to the PGC, but there are tidal lands and beaches the public can explore.

Kayaking, Camping and Hiking:

Beachcombing and wilderness camping options lie in bay's west corner. Here, three notable beaches scream out to be explored, weather permitting. Of particular interest is the middle barrier beach where, behind the berm, a waterfall cascades down a fern covered stream bed. This is a handy spot to collect water. At times, the middle beach can be loaded with flotsam.

Anchorage:

> The area at the eastern head is an all-weather anchorage but is susceptible to occasional williwaw floggings in strong southeasterly weather. Anchor in 10–12 fathoms. Larger vessels can range further offshore and anchor in 15 fathoms onto a sandy mud bottom. A snow bowl clings to a cirque at the basin's head. Be sure to stay away from the entrance to the finger inlet because rocks foul the mouth.

Black Bay

A collection of outstretched capes, shoreline palisades, and a strong southwesterly current combine to create a series of catch basins between Black Bay and McArthur Pass. A dramatic granite headland at the south entrance to Black Bay conjures an image of a walled fortress from Tolkien's Two Towers. Four peaks, each 2,000 feet high, surround the north arm with Black Mountain at 2,075 feet

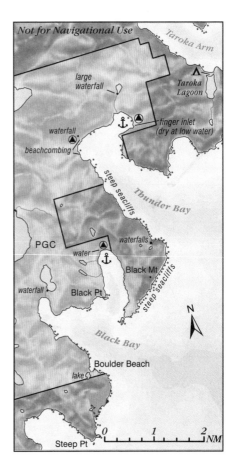

forming the east flank of the north arm. The cliffs range, in color from orange to black, making the bay unique from other outer coast locations.

Kayaking and Beachcombing:

> Boulder Beach lies 0.5 nm west of Black Bay's southwest entrance point. This short barrier beach cannot help but catch your eye. Beach landings are weather dependent. A terrific beachcombing site, Boulder Beach is comprised of cream-colored, oval, granite boulders ranging in size from a baseball to a beach ball. An earthy noise resonates from the rocks grinding together in the surf. Atop the beach rests a massive driftwood sea wall. A pond sits in a sunken valley on the other side, which qualifies as bear country.
> Both arms of Black Bay exhibit a granite shoreline worth a closer look. Miles of weather-dependent landing beaches, tiny islets, and rocky nooks offer great paddling for visitors. In Black Bay, most upland areas are owned by the PGC.

Anchorages:

> The best anchorage is located at the head of the north arm. A pocket beach, a football field in length, marks the area. Several streams tumble down the hillside surrounding the head. Anchor in 10–18 fathoms, mud bottom.

Chance Cove and Chance Lagoon

The best feature of Chance Cove is the gouged-out granite basin at the cove's head, known as Chance Lagoon. In summer the basin reflects an alpine lake-like environment. The vivid green, gently sloped terraces contrast with the smooth, cream-colored granite boulders that wrap around the water's edge. A bay breeze funnels into the cove in the afternoon.

Entering Chance Lagoon:

The narrow entrance to Chance Lagoon lies west of the low-lying islet partially obstructing the lagoon's mouth. Pass into the channel during the upper stage of the tide or during periods of slack water. Approach mid-channel between the islet and the rocky ledge that protrudes from the west shore. The channel has a minimum depth of 2.5 fathoms.

Kayaking, Hiking, Camping:

The lagoon's waterfront is lined with bleached, lifeless spruce trees. Smooth, granite ledges provide a relatively easy landing spot for a kayak or raft. At the head, the sloping alpine terrain invites an elevated perspective of the oval-shaped lagoon and McArthur Pass. A fast-moving stream located on the lagoon's north shore descends from a lake, one-quarter mile up the rocky hillside.

Anchorages:

Chance Lagoon should be considered a fair-weather anchorage. Drop anchor in 12 fathoms in the middle of the basin. Southeast winds, day-breezes, and a lively swell funnel into Chance Cove and the lagoon, which can cause uncomfortable mooring conditions.

The granite waterfront of Chance Lagoon.

McArthur Pass

McArthur Pass knifes between the Kenai Peninsula mainland and the Pye Islands. The symmetrically sloped profile of the passage stands out when approaching from east or west. Fish boats, sailboats, and powerboats (including the Alaska State Ferries) use this convenient, well-marked channel as a shortcut route to Nuka Bay and Nuka Passage.

Sea cliffs near Steep Point.

Small vessel and kayak operators should pay close attention when tidal currents and winds converge, especially in the east entrance of McArthur Pass where tide rips may develop.

The island passage was named after the steamship *McArthur* that conducted coastal survey work along the Kenai Peninsula outer coast in 1906-07. The original navigational light was installed at McArthur Pass in 1934. See Chapter 19 *Pye Islands*, for additional information on the McArthur Pass area.

During the 1989 *Exxon Valdez* oil spill, a team of archaeologist discovered a Sugpiaq refuge site in a west-facing bight on the north shore of McArthur Pass, approximately 1.2 nm west of the McArthur Pass navigation light. This refuge site is a strategic place for kayakers to wait for traveling weather, if necessary.

Kayaking and Camping:
The refuge site is marked by an eye-catching CMT that stands out along the fractured granite waterfront. The CMT also signals the landing area. A wooded hillside affords harsh wilderness camping among spruce trees and moss covered boulders. Nearby, a creek trickles down the steep hillside and offers the only flowing water source in the area.

Anchorage:
The nearest anchorages are in McArthur Cove and Morning Cove on Ragged Island. See Chapter 19, Pye Islands. Another nearby anchorage is located in Square Bay at the mouth of McCarty Fjord.

Square Bay, McCarty Fjord.

McCarty Fjord

McCarty Fjord (Nuka Bay's East Arm) is a deep, ice-scoured embayment, more than 20 nm in length. The fjord is the longest glacial fjord on the outer coast. The steep, scantily-vegetated walls rise more than 4,000 feet and are crammed with snow bowls, cirques, and tributary glaciers. Thick stands of Sitka alder and mountain willow thrive on the deglaciated shoreline and on the gravel outwash beaches. A series of waterfalls stretch mile after mile in testament to the ongoing glacial withdrawal.

McCarty Fjord is an out-of-the-way destination and probably the least visited fjord on the outer coast, except during salmon season. Salmon seiners towing small pocket seiners usually invade the lower fjord in search of sockeye and chum salmon by mid-summer when the activity peaks.

Square Bay

This squarish enclosure (also ambiguously known as Roaring Cove) is the first potential anchorage along the east shore of McCarty Fjord. The bay affords a convenient anchorage for cruising vessels.

Anchorage:
A narrow alcove surrounded by tall granite cliffs lies in the northeast corner of Square Bay. For small boats, the area provides a good place to drop a lunch hook. A giant boulder (covered by high water) partially obstructs the head. Anchor in 5–6 fathoms just inside the mouth. Scenic location!
A suitable anchorage during southeast weather is located in the bay's southeast corner. Drop anchor in 8–15 fathoms, rocky bottom.

Moonlight Bay

Stay well off the south entrance point when entering the bay. Also, avoid a 5-foot-deep rocky area 300-yards south of the west entrance point to Midnight Cove (a thumb-shaped indentation that lies along on the north shore).

Anchorage:
Moonlight Bay is a reliable anchorage with a good holding bottom. Drop anchor at the bay's head in 15 fathoms, sticky mud.

Midnight Cove

In Midnight Cove, a serene waterfall tumbles down a moss-covered rock staircase. The waterfall is recessed into a small grotto at the cove's head and is only accessible by kayak or dinghy.

Anchorage:
Midnight Cove affords a secluded anchorage for small craft. Anchor near the right-hand dogleg where the shoreline turns eastward, in 9–10 fathoms, or in the middle, in 16 fathoms, with a yielding mud bottom. A rocky spit, bare at low water extends into the cove 150 yards from the head.
Contrary to its appearance, Midnight Cove is a poor location during south-easterly gales. At such times, holding anchor may become impossible. If necessary, re-anchor at the head of Moonlight Bay.

Repose Cove

Anchorage:
Repose Cove is a steeply-walled cirque with a gently-sloped bottom. Drop anchor mid-way into the cove in 7 fathoms, mud bottom. A rock-strewn spit uncovers during low water and extends outward 75 yards from the cove's head. The anchorage provides a convenient base camp from which to explore James and McCarty lagoons by inflatable, kayak or skiff.

McCarty Fjord Moraine Bar

A 2.5 nm wide submerged moraine bar, a remnant from McCarty Glacier's Little Ice Age advance, crosses the fjord between McCarty and James lagoons. Deep water lies on either side of the sill. Mariners attempting to cross the moraine bar into the long glacial basin should use caution, especially during periods of low-water or minus tides.

Water depth over the moraine bar ranges from 2 feet (0.5 nm west of the south entrance point to McCarty Lagoon) to less than 3 fathoms elsewhere in the area. To safely cross the moraine bar, steer a course slightly east of mid-channel where a 5-fathom deep channel is located.

Sailboats and other deep-draft vessels should avoid the shallow water around the moraine bar, especially the areas near the mouths of James and McCarty lagoons.

Caution: an uncharted rocky shoal uncovers at low water, 1.25 nm north of the moraine bar, a quarter-mile off the east shore.

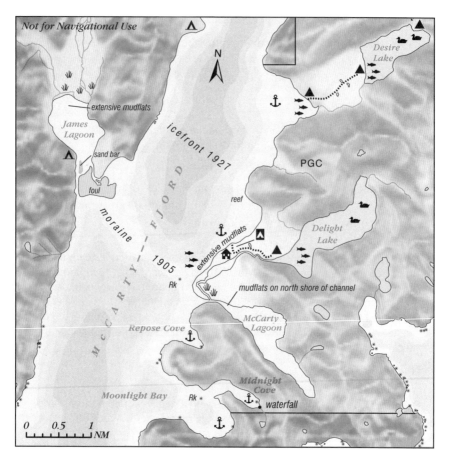

McCarty Lagoon

In summer, salmon tenders and seine boats work the shallow waters around McCarty Lagoon and Delight Creek. At times, hundreds of hungry glaucous-winged gulls and dozens of eagles congregate along the low-lying outwash plain between the mouth of the lagoon and Delight Creek.

Shallow-draft vessels should only enter or depart McCarty Lagoon during brief periods of high slack water. A slender channel runs along the south shore of the lagoon entrance. Tidal mudflats on the north side pinch into the channel just inside the entrance. An estimated 8- to 12-knot tidal current runs in the entrance channel during peak flow. Mariners without local knowledge should avoid entering McCarty Lagoon.

In the early 1930s, Bob Evans, a World War I veteran, seal hunter, photographer, and prospector lived alone in a small cabin near the north shore of McCarty Lagoon. At the time, the terminus of McCarty Glacier was only a short distance from his cabin door. The rapid retreat and frequent calving of McCarty Glacier often choked the fjord with drifting ice making navigation in the fjord impossible. The severe ice conditions left Bob isolated at his homestead for extended periods of time and visitors were rare. In summer, Bob occasionally made supply runs to Seward in his vessel *Nuka Bay Comet*. The *Seward Gateway* described the *Comet* as a speed boat.

Bob was good friends with his distant neighbors "Herring" Pete and Josephine Sather on Nuka Island. They would sometimes visit, share local information, and hunt seals together. Bob was also known to be a talented photographer. Some of his photographs accompanied magazine articles that Josephine wrote about fox farming and the rugged lifestyle of living on Nuka Island.

Bob spent his final years at McCarty Lagoon in declining health. He had throat cancer and bad lungs from being gassed during the war, but he continued to hunt seals at the lagoon and prospect for gold around Nuka Bay. Josephine, aware of Bob's pain and depression over his fading health, encouraged Pete to check on him.

On a visit to Bob's cabin in May 1941, Pete discovered that Bob had taken matters into his own hands and shot himself. After making arrangements and notifying the coroner, Pete brought Bob's body back to Seward where he was buried at the local cemetery.

James Lagoon

A broad spit with a notable 90-foot-tall dirt monolith lies along the outer mouth of James Lagoon. Inside the lagoon, extensive mudflats wrap around the north shore.

Kayaking and Camping:
Kayakers should wait for periods of slack water to enter James Lagoon. Low tide can be messy due to the extensive mudflats, especially in the inner lagoon and outer spit areas. Setting up camp on the wooded portion of the spit or a west shore pocket beach just inside the mouth may render the mudflats less of an issue. Several water sources drain into the lagoon.

Anchorage:
The James Lagoon entrance channel is 0.8 mile long and runs alongside the west shore. Extensive sand bars and rocks project south and west of the spit, nearly blocking the entrance channel. The minimum depth mid-channel is 3 feet at mean low water. A 6- to 10-knot tidal current runs during peak flow. Only shallow-draft vessels, during high slack water, should attempt to enter the lagoon. Mariners without local knowledge should avoid James Lagoon.

Delight Lake

In the 1960s, a commercial sockeye salmon fishery developed at the mouths of Delight and Desire creeks. Today, this region is one of the top producing red salmon fisheries on the outer coast.

Waterfront near Delight Creek.

The upland areas from the north shore of Moonlight Bay to Desire Lake, including McCarty Lagoon and Delight Lake, are private property owned by the Port Graham Corporation. The approximate location of public trail and campsite easements are shown on the map. The PGC maintains a cabin, one-quarter mile, north of the mouth of Delight Creek.

Camping and Hiking:
The outwash delta and tidal lands in front of McCarty Lagoon and Delight Creek are an ideal area to explore on foot. Approximately one-mile north of the moraine bar that fronts McCarty Lagoon is the designated landing beach for the Delight Lake trail and camping area. Look for a yellow PGC easement signpost which stands about 75 feet behind the beach. A bear-proof food locker sits nearby. This is the beginning of the one-mile-long easement trail to Delight Lake. Several other hiking trails crisscross in the woods. A PGC owned cabin (hidden in the spruce forest behind the beach) is located less than a quarter-mile south of the signpost marker.

Desire Lake

In the 1940s, the rapid withdrawal of McCarty Glacier opened up access to Desire Lake, just three miles north of Delight Lake. Today, Desire Creek is a red salmon stronghold. Beware, mosquitoes and flies are more abundant than fish, so bring bug protection. Harlequin ducks, mergansers, murrelets, and oystercatchers are abundant in the fjord and scores of Arctic terns nest along the low-lying beach frontage.

Camping and Hiking:
The lands surrounding Desire Lake are owned by the PGC. A public trail easement, approximately one mile long, begins at the mouth of Desire Creek and gradually climbs to the lake. Public campsite easements are located at both ends of the trail. An alternative public campsite easement lies on the north end of Desire Lake.

Dinglestadt Glacier

As one travels up McCarty Fjord, the air and water temperatures drop as well as the snow level. Land-terminating Dinglestadt Glacier lies along the western shoreline. This 13-mile-long glacier borders the Kenai National Wildlife Refuge and stretches from McCarty Fjord across the peninsula to Sheep Creek, located at the head of Kachemak Bay. The abandoned moraine is overgrown with thick stands of alder and willow. The glacier is accessible to ice climbers.

McCarty Glacier

In 1860, McCarty Glacier was at the maximum extent of its Little Ice Age advance. It is estimated that at that time the glacier began a slow but steady retreat from its terminal moraine between James and McCarty lagoons. As the massive tidewater glacier began to withdraw from its moraine, it withdrew only one mile during the first 65 years. Then, in 1925 the glacier reached deep water, and a catastrophic retreat began. For decades, the relentless ice calving clogged the entire lower portion of McCarty Fjord. Often the ice pack made vessel navigation in the fjord impossible. During the dark winter months, drifting icebergs reached the mouth of Nuka Bay, which created hazardous conditions for boats using McArthur Pass.

Today, the McCarty Glacier terminus rests at the extreme head of the fjord, 13 nm north of the moraine bar. Large pieces of drifting ice seldom reach south of the moraine bar, and many of the smaller tributary glaciers that once fed the main trunk are greatly diminished and have vanished from sight.

The remoteness of McCarty Glacier and the lack of vessel traffic in the upper fjord help attract scores of harbor seals to the area. Presently the fjord maintains one of the largest concentration of harbor seals on the Kenai Peninsula.

On the southbound run down McCarty Fjord, slow vessels and kayaks may want to ride the ebb tide to Harrington Point. The rocky headland was named for Otis Harrington, one of the early mining pioneers who success-fully discovered gold at the head of the West Arm of Nuka Bay.

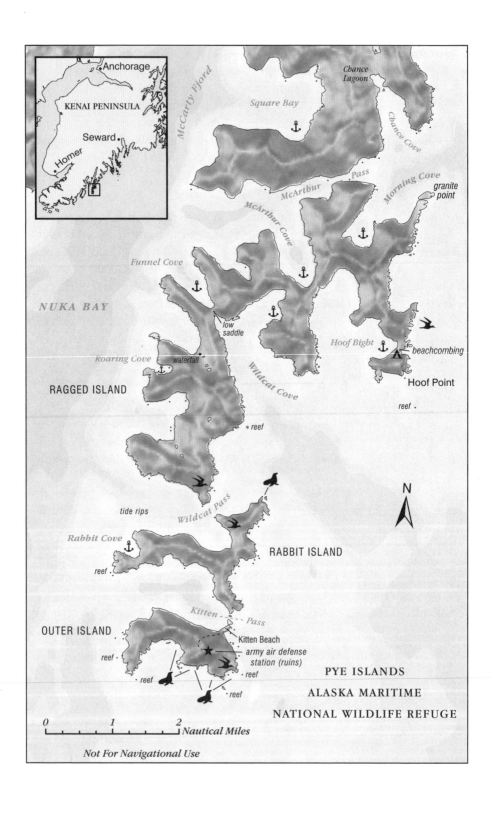

Anchorage

KENAI PENINSULA

Seward

Homer

McCarty Fjord

Square Bay

Chance
Lagoon

Chance Cove

Pass

Morning Cove

granite
point

McArthur

McArthur Cove

Funnel Cove

NUKA BAY

low
saddle

Hoof Bight

beachcombing

Hoof Point

Roaring Cove

waterfall

Wildcat Cove

RAGGED ISLAND

reef

reef

tide rips

Wildcat Pass

Rabbit Cove

RABBIT ISLAND

reef

N

Kitten — Pass

OUTER ISLAND

Kitten Beach

army air defense
station (ruins)

reef

reef

reef

PYE ISLANDS

reef

ALASKA MARITIME

NATIONAL WILDLIFE REFUGE

0   1   2
                        Nautical Miles

Not For Navigational Use

19

Pye Islands

EXPLORING RAGGED, RABBIT, AND OUTER ISLANDS

Special Wildlife Viewing:
> The Pye Islands, a part of Alaska Maritime National Wildlife Refuge, are a designated critical habitat for marine birds and mammals. Outer Island attracts thousands of nesting marine birds in addition to hosting the largest Steller sea lion rookery on the Kenai Peninsula.

Kayaking:
> The islands partially obstruct the flow of the Alaska Coastal Current. This bottleneck tends to amplify tidal currents in the passages, near points of land, and over shoals. Only an experienced, well-conditioned, ocean kayaker should attempt visiting the Pye Islands. There are only a few, weather-dependent, landing beaches.

Camping, Hiking, and Fishing:
> Camping and hiking areas are limited, and access is poor. To protect the Steller sea lion rookery located on Outer Island, the National Marine Fishery Service restricts vessel traffic within a three nautical mile radius of the island's southern tip. Only Ragged Island is available as an anchorage and for camping. In the event restrictions are lifted, this chapter includes presently closed camping locations. The two accessible areas in the Pye Islands include rugged beaches at Hoof Bight (open) and Kitten Pass Bight (closed). Both areas possess terrific hiking and beachcombing opportunities.

Anchorages:
> Anchorages in the Pye Islands tend to be extremely deep with a rock or mud bottom depending on depth. Morning and McArthur coves standout as the most secure anchorages in the islands. Other anchorages include Roaring and Wildcat coves, as well as Hoof Bight, all of which are weather dependent.

The Pye Islands sit at the mouth of Nuka Bay, 60 nm, by boat, southwest of Seward. The remote and seldom explored Pye Islands (Ragged, Rabbit, and Outer) represent the tip of a drowning mountain range. The islands are easily distinguished by their gracefully curved ridgelines and cone-shaped peaks. The cream-colored granite shoreline binds the islands into a dramatic seascape. With respect to con-

Gulls along foggy, rock-bound shore, Wildcat Cove.

trasting colors and symmetry, the Pye Islands stand distinctly from the remainder of the Kenai Peninsula outer coast.

The outer extent of the Pye Islands lies 7 nm from the peninsula's mainland coast and is often the first landfall sighted by offshore vessels. Captain Portlock observed and named the islands in 1786.

For sailors, these outstretched islands afford protection and a potential anchorage at the mouth of Nuka Bay. Nearshore vessels plying the lower outer coast primarily use McArthur Pass, located between the mainland and the north end of Ragged Island. Navigating through the other island passages is weather dependent.

Cruising sailboats, halibut longliners, salmon tenders, and sea travelers from time to time hold up and overnight near McArthur Pass in either Morning or McArthur coves. Small boats may briefly anchor, and then catch a timely tide to quicken the passage around Gore Point and through the Chugach Passage into Cook Inlet. Other mariners may stop to wait for daylight or for the fog to lift before proceeding.

For planning purposes consider the weather as a limiting factor for visiting the Pye Islands. The remoteness also presents logistic and safety concerns to contemplate. The Pye Islands are as spectacular and exhilarating as any physical feature along the Kenai Fjords seacoast when viewed during mild weather, but remember, the islands are desolate and harsh when the elements rage.

RAGGED ISLAND

Ragged Island is crammed with secluded indentations, especially along the western shore. Many of the nameless enclosures display low-sweeping saddles at the head. In calm weather, a mariner has a choice of anchorages and scenic vistas that encompass miles of spectacular scenery.

McArthur Pass

McArthur Pass is 120 yards wide and 0.3 nm long. It is straight and easy to navigate. Patches of kelp grow along the shoreline and in mid-channel. The passage holds a minimum depth of 6 fathoms. At its narrowest width, the channel is about 60 yards wide. A navigational light stands on the north shore adjacent to the narrowest part of the passage. Tidal currents can run at an estimated 3–4 knots and are strongest on the flood. In summer, the passage can be relatively calm, but tide rips can form on the eastern approach to the pass.

Anchorage:
> The small indentation on Ragged Island's north shore, across from the McArthur Pass navigational light, is used by fishing vessels as a convenient, temporary anchorage in mild weather. Anchor in 6–10 fathoms, mud bottom. A more secure anchorage is available in either Morning or McArthur coves.

Kayaking and Camping:
> See Chapter 18, McCarty Peninsula, for information on the McArthur Pass refuge camp site, which is located 1.2 nm west of the navigation light.

Morning Cove

A prominent low-lying granite island stands out at the northeast entrance to Morning Cove. Morning Cove functions as a catch basin for all kinds of flotsam, including an endless supply of driftwood and plastic containers that circulate within the cove. After the 1989 *Exxon Valdez* oil spill, Morning Cove became one of the worst oiled locations on the outer coast and the site of a major cleanup operation. Evidence of the oil spill remains buried on the beach in the southwest corner. The unwelcoming waterfront lacks camping potential. However, beach landings are feasible and the beachcombing intriguing, to say the least.

Anchorage:
> Small craft anchor in the cove's oval-shaped south corner in 9 fathoms, rocky bottom. Others, anchor in the middle in 20 fathoms. The anchorage becomes sloppy in easterly weather.

McArthur Cove

Kayaking and Camping:
> McArthur Cove is ringed by a cream-colored granite shoreline that offers little in the way of an easy landing or camping beach, except for short stretch of weather dependent rock ledges at the cove's east entrance point.

Anchorage:
> Large vessels prefer to anchor toward the head of McArthur Cove in 15–20 fathoms, muddy bottom. Small boats generally drop anchor in 7–10 fathoms near the saddle. Not surprisingly, during southeasterly gales, the cove is known for careening winds that blast over the saddle.

Roaring Cove

Roaring Cove is a rock enclosure used mainly by small boats hunting for a convenient anchorage in good weather. The cove is surrounded on three sides by steeply wooded terrain and a 1,350-foot tall headwall that gives protection from easterly breezes. The basin lacks a practical landing beach and is more of a curiosity than a secure anchorage.

Anchorage:
> Small craft can anchor in the middle in 5–7 fathoms. Avoid the cove's head where the swing room is limited and boulders lurk near shore.

Wildcat Cove

Wildcat Cove is a steeply contoured basin with a semi-sheltered, recessed arm. A noticeable gulf swell washes around the perimeter. In the northwest corner lies a small, tapered, indentation which functions as a catchall for lost trawl gear, tangled crab line, and deflated buoys. Check it out in light weather.

In the northeast arm, on the east hillside, a noticeable column of felled trees lie like dominoes on the ground — victims of a williwaw.

Anchorage:
> Anchor in the northeast arm. The area is marked 4.5 fathoms on the NOAA marine chart. Drop anchor in 8–10 fathoms. Alternatively anchor nearby in the north corner, 150 yards off the rock-bound shore in 11 fathoms, muddy bottom. Wildcat Cove should only be used as an overnight anchorage during light and favorable weather.

Hoof Point and Hoof Bight

Hoof Bight is a dramatic place. It lies around the corner from Hoof Point, which is an impressive 100-foot high granite pillar, surrounded by a collection of alabaster-colored islets. A reef, generally marked by cresting waves and surf, but covered at high water in calm seas, lies 0.5 nm southeast of Hoof Point.

Hoof Bight has a perceptible oceanic character — a restless swell and roaring surf. A prominent, 70-foot-high grass covered saddle stands out at the head. The alpine terrain atop the saddle is wild and raw, similar to the bight's spectacular location.

A close inspection of the hillside area with binoculars reveals windswept stands of spruce trees lying prone on the ground. An ominous reminder that Hoof Bight gets blasted by severe winds.

Rock-covered hillside above landing beach, Hoof Bight, Ragged Island.

Camping and Hiking:

Slightly north of the grass saddle lies a ragged pocket beach, comprised of basketball-sized granite boulders. In light weather, it is possible to land a kayak or raft on shore. Primitive camping lies behind the berm.

A short traverse over and around a rocky terrain leads to the saddle and terrific alpine hiking. The high ground is packed with panoramic vistas. A crescent-shaped ridgeline climbs from the saddle to the 650-foot-high headland above Hoof Point.

Hikers and recyclers of beach trash will find a remarkable, cliff-lined catch basin by hiking across the saddle to the island's exposed shore. Here, a 30-yard-long recessed beach is stocked with piles of driftwood and commercial fishing gear. The last time I visited this beach, it held a cruise ship fender and enough discarded plastic to fill a railroad car.

Anchorage:

Hoof Bight is a fair-weather anchorage that should be abandoned when foul weather threatens. Anchor in 8 fathoms in the bight's easternmost corner, about 250 yards from the landing beach.

RABBIT ISLAND

Currently, Rabbit and Outer islands are off-limits to camping and vessel traffic. To protect endangered Steller sea lions, the National Marine Fisheries Service restricts access and vessel traffic within three nautical miles of the southern tip of Outer Island (No-Entry Zone). In the event restrictions are lifted, this chapter includes information about presently closed locations.

EXPLORING ALASKA'S KENAI FJORDS

Rabbit Island is bordered to the north by Wildcat Pass and to the south by Kitten Pass. The Rabbit Island waterfront offers little in the way of a beach or camp area. Lofty sea cliffs stretch the length of the island's east coast, while spruce trees grow within feet of water on the west coast. A persistent groundswell makes beach landings difficult.

Wildcat Pass (open to continuous transit only)

Wildcat Pass is 400 yards wide. An 8-fathom-deep ledge extends from the north shore of the passage into the middle of the passageway. Here, a 20-fathom-deep channel lies 100 yards off the south point. A solid rock islet and a submerged rock also lie close to the south entrance point. The tidal velocity in the passage is estimated at 4–5 knots on the flood.

At the eastern approach to the pass, a spectacular series of wave-beaten cliffs guide the southwesterly coastal current into the funnel-shaped entrance. Along the north shore, upwelling and eddies boil to the surface moments before the water is squeezed through the bottleneck passage. On the western approach, 1.5 nm from Wildcat Pass, lies a 6-fathom area marked by patches of bull kelp. Turbulent water or tide-rips routinely occur in the area, especially on spring tides.

Anchorages: (closed area)
Vessels can find deep anchorage in the northwest-facing bight just south of Wildcat Pass. Small boats also can conveniently anchor in 10 fathoms in Rabbit Cove on the island's west end.

OUTER ISLAND

The southern shoreline of Outer Island supports the largest breeding population of Steller sea lions on the Kenai Peninsula. At one time, an estimated 4,000 sea lions inhabited the area. Today, sea lion numbers hover around 300 to 400 adults and pups.

The inshore waters east and south of Outer Island have several shoals and reefs to consider. A 2.5-fathom shoal surrounded by deep water lies 0.4 nm east of the island's southeast end. Breakers generally mark the shoal. The largest reef in the area is Pye Reef, awash at high water and distinguished by exploding breakers that can be seen a mile away. Pye Reef rests 1.5 nm southeast of Outer Island.

Kitten Pass (closed to vessel traffic)

Kitten Pass, 65 yards wide, has been mainly used by fishing boats. The combination of slack tide with calm wind and sea are required for an uneventful passage. A prominent, tree-crowned islet sits in the middle of Kitten Pass. On the north shore, three granite boulders lie off the entrance point. A clear channel cuts between the tree-crowned islet and the granite boulders. Minimum depth (slightly south of mid-channel) is 14 feet but

RABBIT ISLAND   224

reaches 30 feet by favoring the rocks. Even in light seas, tidal currents in the passage are likely to swirl and boil with noticeable waterfalls. During foul weather, the passage should be avoided.

Kitten Pass Beach lies on the northeast tip of Outer Island. The beach is actually part of a boulder-covered isthmus. Atop the isthmus, resides a mountain of driftwood dumped by storm waves. A rugged beachcombing experience awaits on the outer beach.

In World War II, after the Japanese attacked Pearl Harbor and invaded Attu and Kiska islands, the Army hastily built an air defense station atop the southeastern part of Outer Island. Kitten Beach became the main access point on and off the island. Ironically, the station was abandoned shortly after it was rushed to completion.

Beachcombers take a break from gathering buoys at Kitten Pass, Outer Island.

Camping and Hiking: (closed)
Kitten Pass Beach is the most friendly landing beach on Outer Island, which isn't saying much. An inflatable can access the beach in light weather. Landing with a kayak is more difficult. At the base of the hillside, explorers will discover the mossy remains of a log staircase. Nearby, the ruins of a steel-railed tram ascend the hill to a primitive road that traverses the slope to where the air station was constructed. The ruins of barracks and Quonset huts are all that remain. To fully explore the area requires hours of strenuous hiking and bushwhacking. May and early-June are the best times for unencumbered hiking.

Anchorage: (closed area)
Kitten Pass Bight is only a calm-weather anchorage. It receives a modest wave surge even in light weather. Anchor off the beach in 12 fathoms on a sloped, rock bottom. Sporadic sea breezes can influence the anchorage.

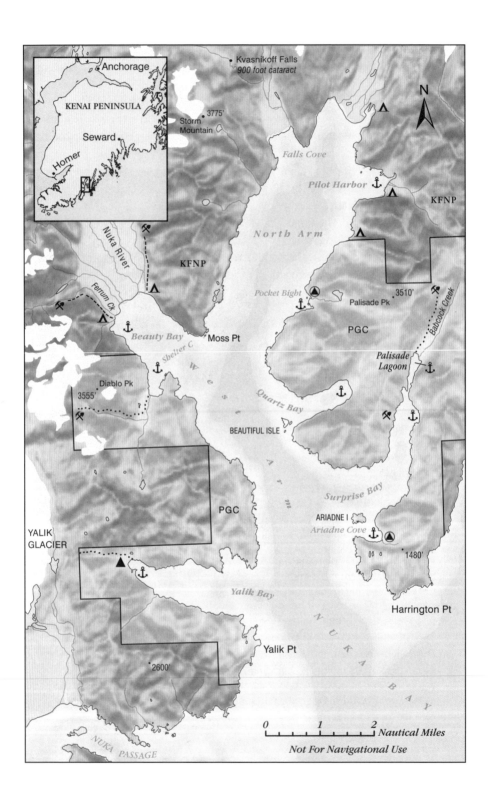

Anchorage

KENAI PENINSULA

Seward

Homer

Kvasnikoff Falls
900 foot cataract

Storm
Mountain • 3775'

N

Falls Cove

Pilot Harbor

KFNP

North Arm

Nuka River

KFNP

Pocket Bight

3510'

Palisade Pk

Beauty Bay

Ferrum Ck

Moss Pt

PGC

Shelter C.

Babcock Creek

*Palisade
Lagoon*

Diablo Pk

3555'

Quartz Bay

W e s t   A r m

BEAUTIFUL ISLE

Surprise Bay

E a s t   A r m

ARIADNE I

Ariadne Cove

YALIK
GLACIER

PGC

1480'

Yalik Bay

Harrington Pt

Yalik Pt

2600'

N U K A   B A Y

*NUKA
PASSAGE*

0   1   2 *Nautical Miles*

Not For Navigational Use

20

Nuka Bay

HARRINGTON POINT TO YALIK POINT

Special Wildlife Viewing:
  Humpback and killer whales frequently tour the mouth of Nuka Bay. Large flocks of common mergansers and shorebirds migrate through wetland areas near Palisade Lagoon, Shelter Cove, Yalik Bay, and Beauty Bay.

Kayaking:
  A remote blend of sheltered, seldom-visited coves, lagoons, and bays, as well as scores of reliable landing beaches, provide Nuka Bay with a marine environment tailor-made for a kayak or small boat.

Camping and Hiking:
  Nuka Bay's extensive seacoast hosts ideal wilderness camping opportunities. The West Arm comprises a gold mining "museum" representing a half-century of sporadic gold mining activity, now abandoned. In the 1920s and 1930s, prospectors combed every inch of Nuka Bay for quartz outcroppings and veins that would yield enough gold to pay for the time and effort to remove it. Today, overgrown cat roads and rough trails, some with public trail easements, lead to abandoned tunnels and mill sites in Nuka Bay.

Anchorages:
  Nuka Bay's assortment of secluded coves and bays provides wild and scenic locations to visit. Secure anchorages are located at Shelter Cove, Surprise Bay, Palisade Lagoon, Quartz Bay, Pilot Harbor, and Yalik Bay.

Nuka Bay is a multi-armed fjord with diverse, glacial landscapes of mountainous terrain interspersed with spacious valleys and river systems. Lieutenant Gavrila Sarychev visited Nuka Bay with Captain Joseph Billings in the summer of 1790. In his 1826 *Atlas of the North Pacific Ocean*, Sarychev recorded the Native name as *Nuka* meaning "young bull caribou" as told to him by the Sugpiaq residents living there. The reference to caribou reflected the time before 1883 when large numbers of caribou ranged on the Kenai Peninsula. The Nuka Bay region boasts a long history of Sugpiaq settlement activity and a short-lived gold mining era during the early 20th-century prior to its inclusion into the Kenai Fjords National Park. Fully exploring Nuka Bay would take weeks. The lack of any refueling stations or grocery stores within 70 nm requires advance planning. A good way to visit Nuka Bay is to concentrate on a small portion of the area. Nuka Bay provides some of the most idyllic camp site locations found on the outer coast. The VHF radio receives weather information transmitted from Homer on WX-2, in open areas such as the West Arm.

WEST ARM, NUKA BAY

A part of Nuka Bay's intrigue arises from its colorful place names originating during the gold mining era. Names like Quartz, Surprise, and Beauty bays, as well as Beautiful Isle, paint a timely description of the hopes and dreams of hard-working miners. Other descriptive place names reveal a sober reality. Storm Mountain and Diablo (devil) Peak stand vigil over abandoned gold claims along Nuka River and Ferrum Creek.

At the beginning of World War II, the federal government temporarily halted all mining activity in this region. Since then, the area has never regained productivity, except for a brief period in the mid-1960s.

Ariadne Island and Ariadne Cove

The thickly wooded, 90-foot tall Ariadne Island sits at the outer mouth of Ariadne Cove, 2 nm northwest of Harrington Point. The waters in and around Ariadne Cove and Island are less than 10 fathoms deep with a scattering of offshore rocks and reefs.

The lands between Ariadne Cove and Quartz Bay are private property owned by the Port Graham Corporation. Camping above mean high water requires a PGC land use permit.

Kayaking and Camping:
A suitable landing beach and camp area lie on the north side of the stream. The water flows down the wooded valley along the base of a sheer headwall, more than 1,300 feet high.

Anchorage:
A popular anchorage for small boats lies in the southeasterly portion of the Ariadne Cove. Drop anchor in 7–9 fathoms, muddy bottom. The presence of Ariadne Island at the cove's mouth requires vessels to approach the anchorage from either the north or west. If approaching from the north, favor the mainland shore to avoid a rock that uncovers during periods of low water in mid-channel.

If approaching from the west, a 2.5-fathom shoal area, and a reef which bares at low water lies inside the cove's southwest entrance point approximately 125 yards from the mainland shore. Steer a mid-channel course to the anchorage by slightly favoring the island, but take note that a reef awash at high water lies 60 yards south of the island's second point.

At times, Ariadne Cove is susceptible to strong northwesterly winds and steep chop issuing from the West Arm and the Nuka River Valley.

Gravel pocket beach, Surprise Bay.

Surprise Bay

By steering past the rock-riddled shorelines of Ariadne Island and Cove, a turn to starboard points the bow toward Surprise Bay. Palisade Peak (3,510 feet) looms like the Matterhorn above the bay's head. About midway along the western shoreline, watch for a tall, log-crib platform anchored to a large spruce tree beneath a rusted, aerial cable. This is the mine site of the "Golden Horn" prospect, initially staked in 1929 by Charles Goyne. Goyne, who lived and worked at the site, developed several tunnels. The aerial tram, still intact, ascends 1,000 feet up the mountainside to the entrance of the upper mine tunnel. A semi-collapsed shop and cabin are camouflaged in thick alder near the stream. The area also serves as a burial ground for heavy equipment and bent rigging.

Two lower tunnels, each at the 25 and 135-foot elevation, lie respectively, on the hill near the cabin ruins. Also, at the 500-foot elevation, shallow trenching on a quartz vein took place around 1970. A stripped, industrial air compressor collects rust on the beach. Hidden in the thick growth of alders, an old bulldozer melts into the landscape.

Anchorage:

In NW weather, the head can be relatively calm, although an occasional williwaw may careen across the water's surface. In fair weather, small boats can temporarily anchor off either one of the shale beaches along the W shore in 8–10 fathoms, steeply sloped bottom. Another option lies 0.4 nm SE of the lagoon entrance at the mouth of the nook. Anchor in 6–8 fathoms.

Looking north into the entrance channel leading to Palisade Lagoon.

Palisade Lagoon

Palisade Lagoon occupies the valley beyond the narrow channel at the head of Surprise Bay. A 700-foot-high rock wall flanks the eastern shore. Mudflats and eelgrass choke the head where Babcock Creek meanders through a low, swampy tideland. The wildly beautiful, mile-long valley is surrounded by towering peaks more than 2,000 feet high.

At the lagoon's head, one-mile north of tidewater, are the remnants of the Sonny Fox Mine. This mine, which operated from 1928 to 1940, was one of the most active and profitable gold operations in the Nuka Bay Region. After World War II, inconsistent mining activity, changes in mine ownership, and the closing of the operation in the mid-1980s led to the National Park Service acquiring the mine site in the mid-1990s. Babcock Creek was named for Tom Babcock, the miner who initially staked and developed several claims at the head of the lagoon. A public trail easement runs from the tidal flats to the Sonny Fox Mine on the hillside. Miners drilled more than a thousand feet of tunnels, installed several aerial trams, and constructed a rock and wood trestle that connected the mine portal to the mill. The camp once included a log bunkhouse, cook house, and outbuildings.

Entering into Palisades Lagoon:

The *U.S. Coast Pilot #9* describes the entrance to Palisade Lagoon as having "a narrow entrance 40-yards wide and 350-yards long that is too narrow and crooked to be navigated by any except very small vessels. A depth of 4 fathoms can be carried by favoring the east side of the entrance until past the point on the west side, to avoid a rock lying east of this point, thence favor the west shore into the lagoon. A large sand spit, with boulders, is on the east side of the entrance at the inner end."

Hiking:

The former Sonny Fox camp and mine site rests about a mile up the valley. A portion of an obscure, overgrown trail becomes visible behind the beach. This trail is on a public easement to the mining claim. Today, the mining claim is owned by the Kenai Fjords National Park. The lands surrounding Palisade Lagoon and Surprise Bay are the property of the PGC.

Anchorage:

Flanked by high mountain ridges, the lagoon appears impervious to the wind. A beneficial day breeze funnels into the lagoon and helps to subdue the clouds of flying insects but beware, the lagoon is susceptible to gusty, swirling winds when the weather turns foul. Nevertheless, it is still a secure, deep anchorage. The water rapidly shallows at the head, where a mariner must drop anchor in water 8–10 fathoms or deeper to avoid swinging on to the beach. Gravel outwash from Babcock Creek, in addition to tidal flats, clogs the lagoon's head and extends outward from the stream's mouth for at least 200 yards from the high-water mark. Onshore, keep an eye out for black bears that routinely prowl the tidelands. In winter the lagoon can freeze.

Quartz Bay

Wooded islets, rocks, and fouled ground encircle Beautiful Isle at the south entrance to Quartz Bay. Also, a shoal lies off the north shore, in the middle of the bay. The shoal is reported to have a rock lurking 3 feet from the surface. A long, secluded beach wraps around the head. Tidal mudflats extend well offshore.

In the late 1920s, a pair of miners from Seward, Fred Johnston and Mike Deegan, built a cabin and developed foot trails to various quartz veins at the bay's head. The pair worked several years on gold claims that saddled the 1,600-foot ridge overlooking Palisades Lagoon. In 1931, Johnston accidentally fell while working and died that winter from his injuries. Shortly thereafter, work at the mine ceased.

Beach Landings:
> Two water sources drain from the valley at the head of Quartz Bay. The beach frontage is ripe with landing spots although the waterfront is muddy during low water. All upland areas are owned by the PGC.

Anchorage:
> Small boats can anchor in 10–12 fathoms in the northeastern portion of the bay toward the head. Extensive tidal flats lie exposed for more than 300 yards from the high-water mark at the head. Avoid swinging onto the mudflats; the water rapidly shallows once inside the 10-fathom curve.

North Arm, Nuka Bay

Pocket Bight

A pair of steeply wooded valleys descend from the 2,000-foot-high ridge that surrounds the head of Pocket Bight. A landing beach lies along the north shore. Nearby, a creek meanders down the valley from a lake located high on the hillside. This secluded bight is a scenic spot with another stream draining the south valley. Be aware that boulders, rock ledges, and a gravel outwash foul the head.

Anchorage:
> Drop anchor along the south shoreline in 7–10 fathoms, muddy bottom. Stay away from the hazards at the head.

Pilot Harbor

Pilot Harbor is recessed into the eastern shore 1 nm from the arm's head. Enter Pilot Harbor in mid-channel. A 3-foot-high rock lies 275 yards off the south entrance point. This rock marks a shoal with another submerged rock 100 yards immediately to the northeast. Extensive mudflats and eelgrass beds extend out from the beach at the low-lying head. Here, land subsidence is acutely apparent with stands of dead trees lining the shore.

Kayaking, Camping, and Hiking:
> The water at the head is usually flat calm and provides easy access to the beach. At high water, a kayak can enter into the tidal inlet that invades the low-lying valley on the north end of the beach. Fresh water is plentiful. The harbor is an excellent jump-off spot for exploring the entire head of the North Arm. Beware, Pilot Harbor has major mosquito and no-see-um populations that are most active in calm conditions.

Anchorage:
> Pilot Harbor is the most secure anchorage in Nuka Bay, especially when foul, gulf coast weather threatens. An extensive eelgrass shoal, 250 yards wide and nearly dry at low water, wraps around the head.
> Small boats can drop anchor 100 yards west of a small wooded islet protruding from the northeast shore. Here, the muddy bottom is 5–8 fathoms deep.
> Vessels also may simply drop anchor in the center of the harbor in 12–16 fathoms onto a muddy bottom.

Tidal mudflats and eelgrass, Pilot Harbor.

Falls Cove

The North Arm of Nuka Bay terminates at the boulder-strewn outwash plain once occupied by Split Glacier. The glacier now rests approximately four miles up the valley.

Spectacular Kvasnikoff Falls stands out in the steep ravine, high above the cove. The 900-foot-tall cataract is fed by melting ice. A torrent of water cascades hundreds of feet into a deep pool worn into solid rock. From this pool, the stream falls several hundred feet more, radiating plumes of fanning mist before forming a stream that empties into the cove.

Falls Cove is too deep to use as a convenient anchorage, especially with a secure anchorage like Pilot Harbor nearby.

BEAUTY BAY, SHELTER COVE, AND THE NUKA RIVER

Beauty Bay

The Seward register of mining claims recorded more than one hundred mining claims located in the Nuka Bay region in the 1930s. The Nuka Bay Mining Company and the Alaska Hills Mining Company toiled at the head of Beauty Bay on the east side of the Nuka River. Most gold mines in the Nuka Region only functioned from the mid-1920s until 1941.

The Alaska Hills Mining camp was located on the hillside about two miles up the Nuka River. This was where Otis Harrington first discovered gold in 1918. The mine continued sporadic activity for nearly 20 years. The difficulty in reaching the mine site was partially solved when the Alaska Road Commission agreed to build a 1.25-mile long, 7-foot-wide trail to the mine site. When the mine finally closed its door, more than 900 feet of tunnels had been excavated. Today, after more than a half-century of neglect, the remains of mill equipment, collapsed structures, tramways, and cabins blend in with the wilderness.

In the late 1920s, another small gold mine owned by the Nuka Bay Mining Company operated on the hillside beneath the southern ridge of

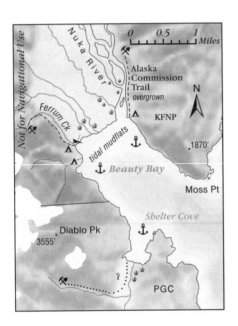

Storm Mountain. The route to the mine portal from the head of Beauty Bay followed along the same Alaska Road Commission trail for three-quarters of a mile, where a log cabin storehouse once stood. The cabin is now reduced to a few rotten logs. From here, a 3,400-foot-long trail leads up the steep hillside toward Storm Mountain, where an upper camp and mill site were located at the 1,200-foot elevation. The Nuka Bay Mining Company changed hands several times but never produced much gold.

The Beauty Bay Mine was originally staked in 1923 by Earl Mount of Seward. It was intermittently active until the 1980s. The mine and campsite were situated on the west side of the Nuka River Valley about one mile from the head of Beauty Bay.

Kayaking and Camping:
During high water, the lower portion of the Nuka River is partially accessible to paddlers. Behind the shallow mudflats that dominate the head of Beauty Bay, young alder and spruce groves now stand where lifeless trees killed by land subsidence once blanketed the Nuka River delta.

On shore, watch for signs of black bear, moose, and river otter. Even the hard-of-hearing will not miss the flocks of squawking ravens and shorebirds that patrol the waterfront.

Near the mouth of Ferrum Creek rests the silt-encrusted hulk of a wooden barge. Mossy patches of level ground lie in the woods adjacent to the stream mouth and provide a good soft carpet for campers. Access to stream water is not an issue in Beauty Bay, but safe drinking water in this former mining area may be of concern.

Ferrum Creek, Nuka River Valley.

Hiking:

> In the northeast corner of Beauty Bay, remnants of the Alaska Road Commission trail are cut into the hillside above the Nuka River Valley. The trail leads to the Alaska Hills Mining Company mill and mine site.
>
> The former Beauty Bay Mine site is reached by first hiking one-half mile up the west side of Ferrum Creek. Watch for a gulch and follow it to the head. The mine is at the 200-foot elevation. Bushwhackers will discover the outline of an overgrown, bulldozed road near a steel-railed supply skid abandoned near the beach. The trail is heavily overgrown with alder and washed away in places.

Anchorage:

> In mild weather, mariners will find suitable anchorage at the northwest head of Beauty Bay. Drop anchor along the western shoreline in 8–10 fathoms, muddy bottom. Avoid anchoring too close to the mudflats that extend more than a quarter-mile from the high-water mark at the head.

Shelter Cove

Shelter Cove sits on the southern shore of Beauty Bay. The cove appears deceptively large, but navigable water is limited to the mouth. Extensive mudflats obstruct the entire head.

The Nukalaska Mine operated at the head of Shelter Cove during the mid-1930s until World War II. This gold mine was one of the last commercially producing mines in the Nuka Bay region. The original, western claim was a bare quartz vein at the 2,200-foot elevation. A 1.25-mile long road was bulldozed from the beach to the main camp and mill located on the southwest side of the cove. Here, a 3,700-foot cable tram stretched up the mountainside to the portal of the western tunnel. By 1940, another 400-yard-long, eastern tunnel was drilled at the 1,300-foot elevation. It was connected to the main camp by a second 2,200-foot-long cable tram. Each winter, persistent snow slides swept away the tram footings at the tunnel entrance and wiped out the road. Every spring, major reconstruction was required before a new mining season could begin.

Hiking:

In Shelter Cove, high-water beach landings are the best time to avoid the extensive mudflats. Along the cove's west shore lies an overgrown trail that climbs the hillside to the former Nukalaska Mine camp and mill site. In summer, the valley is drowned with lush vegetation, which impedes foot traffic. All upland areas are owned by the PGC.

Anchorage:

The sticky, muddy bottom provides a secure anchorage in southerly weather. Drop anchor in 6–12 fathoms, centrally located, immediately inside the cove's mouth. Make sure to allow enough swing room to avoid going dry on the mudflats that clog the head. Occasionally, brisk northerly winds blast into Shelter Cove. At such times, alternative anchorages exist in Quartz or Surprise bays.

Yalik Bay

Yalik Bay was an important Sugpiaq settlement site. The former village was located on the bay's north shore, in a small indention, mid-way into the bay. Today, hardly a trace of the village remains. The land around Yalik Bay is owned by the Port Graham Corporation.

In 1880 Ivan Petrof, an agent for the Federal Census Bureau, recorded 32 natives living on the shores of Yalik Bay. At the time, the settlement was the largest of any kind on the Kenai Peninsula outer coast. Descendants from Yalik Bay now live in Nanwalek and Port Graham.

In general, physical evidence of former settlement and refuge sites along this subsiding portion of seacoast are continually being eroded away by rising sea levels and storm waves. Culturally modified trees are found at many locations along the Kenai Fjords seacoast. Occasionally, a stone tool (adz, seal oil lamp, etc.) is discovered. At such times, the observer should note the artifact's location and report the sighting to the National Park Service. Removing such objects from Park Service land is illegal.

On Yalik Bay's southern shore, 0.75 nm from the bay's head, is a conspicuous outwash plain with a large stream. On the hillside above the east bank of the stream are the ruins of a plank cabin in the woods. The cabin once belonged to "Herring" Pete Sather who worked several gold claims on the nearby hillside about 450 feet east of the cabin.

Two primary streams empty at the bay's head. Extensive mudflats covered with eelgrass line the head of Yalik Bay. Significant land subsidence is visible from the standing rows of dead trees, though many trees have fallen over with the passage of time.

Straddling the ridge high above the bay's head and wooded valley, Yalik Glacier traverses the mountain slope downward to the northern head of Nuka Passage. A cool glacial breeze sweeps down from the ridge into the valley and noticeably lowers the air temperature in the inner bay.

Kayaking, Hiking, and Camping:

Yalik Bay is loaded with beach landing options. At Yalik Point are several black-sand pocket beaches that are interconnected by a series of game trails. The beaches and trails are worth exploring. The unique rock bluffs at Yalik Point provide strategic panoramas of McArthur Pass, the West Arm, and the Pye Islands. A dark colored shale rock comprises the Yalik Point headland. At the head of Yalik Bay, the PGC has established a 24 hr camping easement area. A bear-proof food locker is located midway behind the beach.

Anchorage:

A 4-fathom-deep bight lies 0.5 nm west of the Yalik Bay's north entrance point. This bight is partially protected from northerly weather, although it is susceptible to a bumpy swell from the gulf.

The head of Yalik Bay offers the best all-around anchorage. Drop anchor in 10–14 fathoms onto a mud bottom, in the southwest corner of the bay. A short pocket beach lies nearby. At the bay's head, mudflats and eelgrass extend off-shore a quarter-mile from the high-water mark.

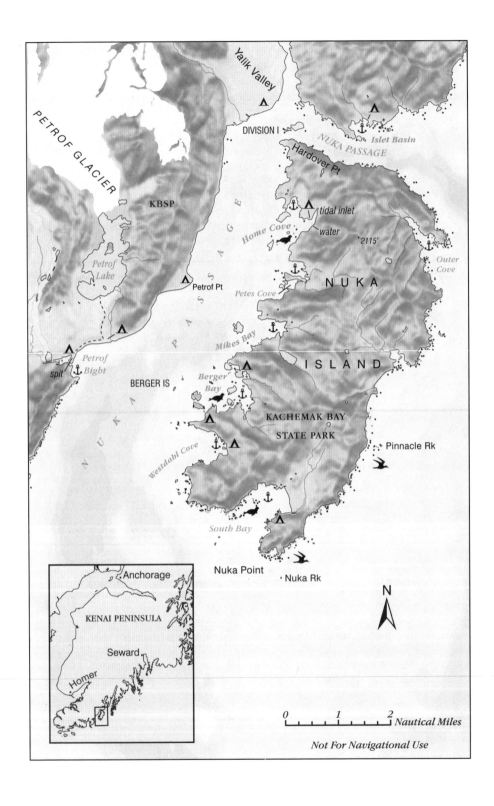

PETROF GLACIER

Yalik Valley

KBSP

DIVISION I

NUKA PASSAGE

Hardover Pt

Islet Basin

Petrof
Lake

tidal inlet

Home Cove

water

2115'

Petrof Pt

Outer
Cove

Petes Cove

N U K A

Mikes Bay

I S L A N D

spit

Petrof
Bight

Berger
Bay

BERGER IS

KACHEMAK BAY

STATE PARK

Westdahl Cove

Pinnacle Rk

South Bay

Nuka Point

Nuka Rk

Anchorage

KENAI PENINSULA

Seward

Homer

N

0   1   2
Nautical Miles

Not For Navigational Use

21

Nuka Island and Nuka Passage

ISLET BASIN TO TONSINA BAY

Wildlife Viewing:
   Harbor seals congregate on the rocky islets and shoreline ledges along Nuka Island's western shore. Scores of river otters, bald eagles, mergansers, and black bears populate the island. Pods of killer and humpback whales routinely travel through Nuka Passage.

Kayaking:
   The sheltered waters in upper Nuka Passage and the western shore of Nuka Island provide some of the best wilderness kayaking in the Kenai Fjords. One scenic paddle route explores the seacoast from Islet Basin to the island's South Bay. The journey follows the mainland shore in upper Nuka Passage then, at Division Island, the route turns southward along the scenic west coast of Nuka Island. Here, a chain of coves and wooded islands stretch all of the way to Nuka Point.

Camping and Hiking:
   A rich bounty of campsites and hiking opportunities awaits visitors to Nuka Island. The best exploring and camping areas include Islet Basin, Home Cove, Pete's Cove, Mike's Bay, Berger Bay, Westdahl Cove, South Bay, and Tonsina Bay.

Anchorages:
   Nuka Island's western shore boasts a wonderful selection of small boat anchorages. Mariners will find Home Cove, Mike's Bay, and Berger Bay excellent all-purpose anchorages.

As mariners enter Nuka Passage from the north, the waterway narrows as the gulf swell fades and pocket beaches and islets appear along the mainland shore. Here, the coastal terrain takes on a different character. The steep headlands and deep bays so familiar on the outer coast abruptly change to gravel beaches and shallow coves with trees growing down to the water line. The western mainland shore of upper Nuka Passage is within the Kachemak Bay State Park.

Islet Basin on the upper mainland shore of Nuka Passage.

MAINLAND SHORE, UPPER NUKA PASSAGE

Islet Basin

The north end of Nuka Passage, 1.5 nm east of Division Island, Islet Basin is tucked into the mainland shore. Here, a series of wooded islets partially protects a pair of pocket beaches. The beaches are inviting and comprised of hard-packed sand. The basin is a convenient and scenic spot to go ashore and explore.

Kayaking, Camping, and Hiking:
Inlet Basin is a refuge area where kayakers can wait for traveling weather when attempting to cross the mouth of Nuka Bay. The recessed, south-west-facing pocket beach is a secluded landing spot. In the woods, several shallow depressions from human activity have been dug into the earth.
A stream flows into the basin at the north end of the beach. Game trails criss-cross the wooded peninsula to an exposed beach with broad mudflats at low tide. Islet Basin is an intriguing place to explore.

Anchorage:
Small boats will find secure anchorage in the basin during light weather. Drop anchor in 4–5 fathoms, 200 yards off the southwest-facing beach. Patches of kelp grow in the shallow areas of the cozy basin.

Division Island

Division Island, 125 feet high, lies in the middle of the north entrance of Nuka Passage. On the north side of Division Island, a rock uncovers in mid-channel during minus tides. Vessel traffic, including ships, use the clear channel south of Division Island. Avoid the rocks and shoals around Division Island by favoring the north shoreline of Nuka Island. Tidal eddies often swirl in the Hardover Point area.

Yalik Valley

Immediately north of Division Island, in the northwest corner of Nuka Passage, Yalik Glacier dominates the skyline as it descends from the upper icefield. Yalik and Petrof glaciers both flow from the Grewingk-Yalik Glacial Complex, which ranges across the Kenai Mountains to the south side of Kachemak Bay. Yalik Glacier rests nearly 4 miles from saltwater and a roaring glacier stream dumps its silty meltwater into the passage at the east end of the moraine beach.

Kayaking, Camping, and Hiking:
A youthful spruce and hemlock forest grows in the deglaciated Yalik Valley. All along the moraine waterfront, the glacial till sprouts patches of dense alder. The moraine beach offers exceptionally wild terrain accessible for kayak landings, beachcombing, and camping.

Petrof Point

Petrof Point prominently stands out along the mainland shore of Nuka Passage. The point consists of a fan-shaped outwash plain with a long, uninterrupted, sand-and-gravel beach.

Kayaking, Camping, and Hiking:
Beach landings and camping areas exist on either side of Petrof Point, depending on weather conditions. The outwash plain is thickly covered with spruce trees and mats of ground moss. This park-like environment offers nearly level terrain to explore by foot.

Petrof Bight

A mile-long sand-and-gravel waterfront wraps around Petrof Bight. Even in calm weather, surf laps the beach. Two streams, one at each end of the beach, flow into Nuka Passage.

The northern stream exits from Petrof Lake while the southern outwash stream drains the 3.5-mile-long Petrof Valley. A pair of unnamed glaciers sit at the valley's head. Float planes have easy access to Petrof Lake from Beluga Lake in Homer or Trail Lake in Moose Pass.

In 1984, the State of Alaska opened the Petrof Valley for land staking. There are approximately 50 private property parcels with several recreation cabins located between the lake and Petrof Beach.

Petrof Glacier is named for Ivan Petrof, who was born in St. Petersburg, Russia, in 1842. In 1861, Ivan Petrof (aka Robert Porter) came to the United States and fought for the Union Army in the Civil War. Shortly after the war, he came to Alaska and lived in Kodiak and Kenai. He traveled

Looking across Home Cove into Nuka Passage.

extensively in Alaska. In the 1870s, Ivan Petrof began writing about Alaska history, geography, and resources. Later hired as a federal agent during the Tenth and the Eleventh United States Census, he was responsible for visiting and enumerating people along coastal Alaska including Prince William Sound and the Kenai Peninsula outer coast.

Petrof also examined and translated Russian documents while working as a researcher for H. H. Bancroft who, in 1886, published the book *History of Alaska*. The original manuscripts now reside at the Bancroft Library, University of California, Berkeley.

Kayaking, Camping, and Hiking:
The Petrof Bight beachfront lies exposed to the ocean swell and is often washed by surf. Access to the beach is dependent on weather and sea conditions. At the south end of Petrof Bight, the stream can be entered around high water by kayak. Land on the sand spit located on the east side of the stream mouth.
At the Petrof Lake outwash stream on the bight's northeast end, a kayaker can gain access to the waterfront by paddling up the stream at high slack water. Camp just inside the stream mouth on the west side. To safely enter or depart either stream by kayak requires the swell to be minimal. Check sea conditions at the channel entrance before proceeding.

Anchorage:
The alcove formed by the wooded peninsula at the south end of Petrof Bight provides an anchorage in light weather. Anchor in 4–6 fathoms. This anchorage is not a place to leave a vessel unattended for an indefinite period.

WESTERN SHORE, NUKA ISLAND

Nuka Island is part of the Kachemak Bay State Park. It encompasses more than 15,000 acres and is the largest island on the Kenai Fjords' coast. The densely-forested island is primarily known for its idyllic coves on the island's western shore. It also boasts scores of eagles, seals, and sea otters as well as a historic fox farm once operated by Pete and Josephine Sather.

When exploring the nooks and crannies along Nuka Island's western shore, the water depth is often less than ten fathoms with many reefs and rock piles to avoid, especially when traveling during high tide. Go slow! Bull kelp marks many rocky shoals and reefs, but not all.

Home Cove

Mariners unfamiliar with this cove should keep a sharp eye on the navigation chart and depth sounder. Low water is a good time to spot potential hazards. The east portion of Home Cove has a water depth of less than six fathoms.

Camping and Hiking:
A secluded camp area lies in Home Cove's east corner. A low-lying spit covered with a ghost forest sits adjacent the west shore of a tidal inlet. The waterfront displays an impressive collection of sandstone rocks. A pair of water sources flows down the mountainside directly across the inlet from the camp area. A dozen CMTs, standing and laying prone, litter the spit. In the spruce forest behind the waterfront resides a lily pond.

Anchorage:
Most vessels anchor in the northwest corner of Home Cove in 9-fathoms, muddy bottom. Enter Home Cove from the south where a 130-foot-tall wooded island forms the cove's north entrance point. Follow the island's east shore northward into the oval-shaped anchorage. The flat terrain surrounding the anchorage leaves the basin susceptible to both southeast and northwest winds, although the fetch is minor. An alternative anchorage for small boats is in the east corner, 300 yards south of the tidal inlet. Favor the east shore, drop anchor in 5 fathoms onto a mud bottom. A nearby reef lies hidden on an 8-foot or higher tide.

Pete's Cove

The former abode of "Herring" Pete and Josephine Sather is situated 1 nm south of Home Cove. The Sather's cabin and outbuildings are located midway along a narrow, wooded peninsula. The area is now owned by the University of Alaska.

A 7-fathom-deep, unnamed cove (marked on the nautical chart) lies adjacent the north side of the wooded peninsula. A collection of rock islets and boulders lie off the west tip of the wooded peninsula.

Pete Sather was born Pete Pederson on May 29, 1895. He emigrated from Norway, probably before 1920. Like many Norwegians, Pete came to Alaska to work in the herring fishery, which was booming on the Cook Inlet side of the Kenai Peninsula. Exactly how he received the nickname of Herring Pete is debatable. One story suggests that while working as a deckhand on a herring tender in Juneau, his crew mates began calling him Herring Pete to distinguish him from all the other fishermen named Pete Pederson.

Another version of the story tells of an incident where Pete fell off a seine boat into a net full of herring. When Pete emerged from the net, covered head to toe in silvery fish scales, a colorful nickname was born. Later, he traded his Pederson surname for Sather to distinguish himself from several men who worked at the cannery with similar names to his own. By 1922, Pete had become the captain of a fishing boat.

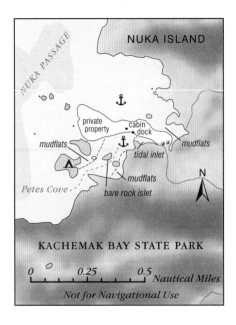

In 1923, while Pete was knocking about the Kenai Peninsula seacoast, he happened to drop anchor along the western shore of Nuka Island, where he met Josephine and her husband, Ed Tuerck. Ed and Josephine had traveled from Cordova to Nuka Island a few years earlier to raise blue foxes. Raising foxes was a lucrative business in the early 1920s, and suitable islands to start a fox farm were in demand. For Josephine, raising foxes became her calling.

At the time of Pete's visit, Ed was gravely ill with stomach cancer. Pete helped Ed by hauling him to Seward to get checked out by a doctor. Josephine stayed on the island to tend to the foxes and hold the homestead together.

After the two men had arrived in Seward, Ed made a trip to Anchorage to consult with doctors, who could do nothing. Ed returned to Seward and died shortly after that. His death left Josephine alone on the island to tend to the foxes and survive the best she could.

In May 1924 Pete married Josephine in Seward, and they returned to Nuka Island. Some say the union was a marriage of convenience, but there is no doubt that they had a great deal in common. They both were self-reliant and chose to live far from civilization.

Looking into Nuka Passage from the landing beach at the mouth of Pete's Cove.

Pete continued to halibut fish and began prospecting for gold in addition to hauling mail and supplies to miners in Nuka Bay. Josephine continued the daily chores of housekeeping, tending her garden, and trying to build the fox farm into a viable business. Protecting the foxes from predators was a task that Josephine took seriously. In an interview, Josephine recalled shooting at least 30 bears and hundreds of eagles, which were natural enemies of the foxes.

To feed the hungry foxes, Pete and friends resorted to shooting sea lions and seals, and gathering large quantities of salmon. He also had the task of hauling heavy sacks of grain and rolled oats from town back to the island.

Pete worked hard and lived hard. Stories describe Pete's physical appearance as "extremely rustic." He was seldom known to change clothes. His various boats had two things in common: they were in poor condition and they smelled like rotten fish. On the other hand, Josephine was known to be fastidiously clean, and she disliked Pete and his foul-smelling fishing friends stinking up her home. Whenever Pete came back from an extended fishing trip, Josephine insisted that Pete and crew take a cold shower outside before stepping across the threshold — a tradition enforced in summer and winter!

Pete had the reputation as a tough character, though he barely weighed 100 pounds soaking wet. He also was known throughout the region for his kind heart, wiry toughness, and great skill as a mariner. He was a jack-of-all-trades and natural-born mechanic, able to fix any engine. During the glory days of gold mining in Nuka Bay, he also worked several gold claims including one in Yalik Bay.

In August 1961, Pete tied up the *Rolfh III* in Seward during the very first silver salmon derby. While in town, he made his rounds gathering the necessary supplies needed for the upcoming winter on the island. He also took time for his customary trip downtown to visit friends in the taverns.

At age 66 with nearly four decades of surviving on the outer coast, Pete cast off the *Rolfh III* for the long run back to the island. He never made it home. After hundreds of round-trip voyages between Nuka Island and Seward, Pete's luck had finally run out. Weather reports, at the time, mentioned poor sea conditions in the gulf, but no one knows what happened. Several weeks after Pete's disappearance, a Seward fisherman reported spotting traces of floating debris, possibly from the *Rolfh III*, in Wildcat Pass, although nothing was confirmed.

With help, Josephine spent the winter on the island, but within a year she decided to return to her native Austria. Josephine died in 1964 at the age of 80.

Today the remnants of Pete and Josephine's handiwork include their cabin, shop, outbuildings, garden, and dock, along with numerous board and batten, 6x8-foot fox-feeding sheds that can be found along the island's western shore.

Kayaking, Camping, and Hiking:

A scenic camping area is on the first wooded island at the entrance channel leading into the Pete's Cove. The landing beach displays a boat engine and shaft partially buried in shale. Once firmly on shore, optional campsites choices present themselves.

At the head of Pete's Cove lies a small tidal inlet. A rusted water pipe that once delivered stream water to the house runs along the shoreline to a creek at the inlet's head. At higher stages of a spring tide, a kayaker can paddle over tidal lands and navigate stream channels to the cove located immediately north of Pete's Cove.

Anchorage:

Pete's Cove is located 1 nm south of Home Cove, and is not presently named on the navigational chart. Approach the channel entrance to the cove from the south end of the islands. A hidden quarter-mile-long, narrow channel runs between the Nuka Island shore and several offshore islets. The small boat route into Pete's Cove is mid-channel. Pass between the last two islets to reach the anchorage near the dock ruins (see map). Here, the remnants of a bulldozer, shop, and cabin stand out along the peninsula's shore. The anchorage in the basin, adjacent to the cabin, is 3 fathoms deep with limited swing room during periods of extreme low water.

An alternative anchorage is in the unnamed 7-fathom-deep cove immediately north of Pete's Cove.

Tree-crowned islets at the head of Mike's Bay.

Mike's Bay

Mike's Bay indents the seacoast 1 nm south of Pete's Cove. At the bay's head, a jagged collection of rocky islets forms a breakwater to a tidal area clogged with eelgrass and mud. The tidal lands go dry on minus tides. Several streams drain into the basin, including one from the lake that occupies a deglaciated cirque at the 200-foot elevation.

Mike's Bay is named for Smokehouse Mike, a homesteader who lived there from 1918-1921. Mike built a warehouse at the bay's head on a grassy knoll and he moored his boat in the adjacent tidal mudflat. During the prohibition years, Mike was an entrepreneur in the business of distilling moonshine whiskey. Smokehouse Mike and an Englishman named George Hogg, along with a friend known only as Jack, spent their days stoking the fire of a thirty-gallon whiskey still. Eventually, at the request of Josephine Sather (a teetotaler), Mike corked the jug and abandoned his island distillery. Today, the property in the bay's northeast corner, adjacent to the tidal inlet, is owned by the University of Alaska.

Camping and Hiking:
  The head of Mike's Bay offers rough camping options. Bight green mats of eelgrass congest the tidal inlet. In the south corner of the inlet, hikers can bushwhack a quarter-mile along the stream to a mountain lake.

Anchorage:
  Drop anchor northwest of the rocky islet chain in 6–8 fathoms, muddy bottom. Take care to avoid the mudflats in the bay's northeast corner.

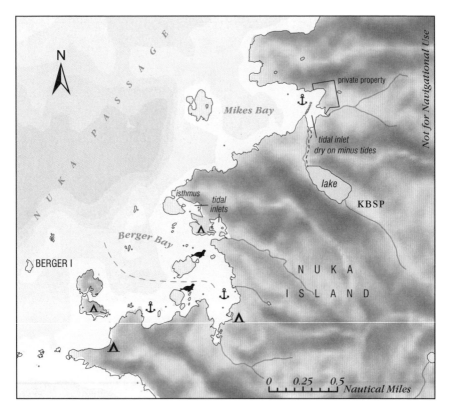

Berger Bay

Certainly, Berger Bay ranks as one of the most alluring bays along Nuka Island's western shore. Wooded islands and rocky islets lie scattered around the picturesque bay, all of which is ideal for exploring by kayak or dinghy. During periods of low water, view dozens of harbor seals perched on the offshore rocks.

Navigating a vessel in reef-infested waters like Berger Bay requires a mariner's vigilant attention to their charts, the shore, the water's surface, and a depth sounder.

Berger Bay was named for Captain Heinie Berger who operated a sporadic marine charter service from Seward to the Nuka Bay and the Cook Inlet area in the late 1920s. Captain Berger in his vessel *Discoverer* hauled supplies to and from the numerous mining operations on the outer coast. He also occasionally hauled an adventurous tourist to see the sea lions and birds at the Chiswell Islands and spectacular Northwestern Glacier.

At the outer mouth of Berger Bay sits Berger Island, which prominently stands out when sighting up or down Nuka Passage. Vessels transiting through Nuka Passage stay west of the island.

North shore, Berger Bay, Nuka Island.

Kayaking, Camping, and Hiking:

The waters of Berger Bay are well-suited for exploring by a kayak or small boat. The bay's intricate shoreline with numerous nooks and crannies easily arouse curiosity. Several pocket beaches along the shoreline show fragile signs of Sugpiaq habitation in the form of culturally modified trees. The second tiny inlet southeast of the north entrance point has a stream, a wooded valley, and a prominent spit that is perhaps one of the best camping areas in the bay.

Several other camping options are worth mentioning. In the bay's secluded southeast corner, a choice of cobble beaches and tidal ledges lie at the mouth of the shallow inlet. Another camping alternative sits a quarter-mile inside Berger Bay's south entrance point where two pocket beaches stand out along the shoreline. Also, check out the nearby island (see map) where a cleared camping area sits on the island's eastern point.

Anchorage:

To reach the Berger Bay anchorage, steer a course between the wooded islands located midway in the bay. Anchor in 9–14 fathoms, muddy bottom, in the eastern portion of Berger Bay. Expect to collect kelp if anchoring in shallow water. Rocks and mudflats foul the area in the southeastern corner of the bay's head.

Westdahl Cove

Westdahl Cove catches the gulf swell even in good weather. A rock awash at low water lies in Westdahl Cove's outer mouth approximately 1 nm offshore. Submerged rocks, wooded islets, and an extensive shoal stretch westward 0.5 nm from the cove's north entrance point. A reef marked by kelp sits 0.25 nm off the south entrance point, and a series of submerged rocks hide inside the 10-fathom curve along the south shore. Sea otters raft up in the kelp beds around the cove's offshore islets and islands.

Kayaking and Camping:
> Several beach landing options and a mountain stream are located at the cove's head. A secluded camp area lies adjacent to the wooded islet. Another landing beach is located on the north shore of the stream.
> Along the cove's southern shoreline are three pocket beaches and the remains of a Sather fox feeding shed.

Anchorage:
> In light weather, vessels can find suitable anchorage in 5–10 fathoms, southwest of the wooded islet at the cove's head. Strong gulf coast weather can greatly influence sea conditions in the cove.

South Bay

This large, shallow indentation west of Nuka Point presents an unmistakable oceanic feel. Rocky shoals and gnarly reefs lie off the western entrance and along the western shore. Most of South Bay is less than ten-fathoms deep. A long barrier beach, a spacious valley, and a powerful outwash stream dominate the bay's head. The barrier beach is pounded by surf even in light weather. Harbor seals haul out on a secluded gravel shoreline in the bay's northwestern corner.

Camping:
> One of the wildest and most scenic camping areas on Nuka Island is located on a hillside bluff at the eastern head of South Bay. Because of surf, the barrier beach is nearly impossible to access, but a landing beach lies on south shore at the stream's mouth. On the hillside are the remains of several old camps and a flattened shed. Several CMTs hide in the woods waiting to be found. Intriguing hiking terrain lies along the bluff area.

Anchorage:
> With better anchorages located nearby in Westdahl Cove or Berger Bay, the South Bay should only be used as an overnight anchorage in light weather. The bay receives a significant swell from the gulf, and strong winds blast down the valley behind the barrier beach in easterly weather. A vessel can anchor in 3–5 fathoms at the bay's head, west of the surf-ravaged beach.

EAST SHORE, NUKA ISLAND

The eroded eastern shore of Nuka Island is riddled with rocks, islets, and reefs up to 0.5 nm offshore. Nuka Rock, three feet high, lies 0.35 nm south of Nuka Point and is marked by breakers. The irregular bottom, strong Alaska Coastal Current, and water ebbing from Nuka Bay can create tide rips along the island's east shore.

Pinnacle Rock, 68 feet high, stands 0.3 nm offshore. This conspicuous pinnacle marks a large area of islets, submerged rocks, and kelp patches.

Outer Cove

Outer Cove lies near the northeastern tip of Nuka Island. The south-east-facing bight is only a fair-weather anchorage that is used mainly by commercial halibut vessels. A granite islet, 70 feet high, guards the north entrance point. When entering the cove, keep to mid-channel. Rocks, ledges, and islets lie along each shore.

Anchorage:
Large vessels anchor at the mouth in 9 fathoms, 200 yards northwest of the prominent wooded islet along the east shore.
A small boat can continue toward the head by favoring the east shoreline (submerged rocks line the western shoreline, nearly to mid-channel.) The sandy bottom shallows gradually toward the head. Drop anchor in mid-channel before reaching the last point of land on the western shore in 2 fathoms. A wave-ravaged sand-and-gravel beach, eelgrass beds and sand flats occupy the cove's head. Beachcombing is weather dependent.

MAINLAND SHORE, LOWER NUKA PASSAGE

Tonsina Bay

Sea travelers can rest easy once westward of Long Island and tucked safely inside Tonsina Bay. A clutter of islets and rocks, including a rocky shoal, extends north and east of Long Island and partially obstructs the bay's entrance. The main channel into the bay runs between Long Island and the northern shore.

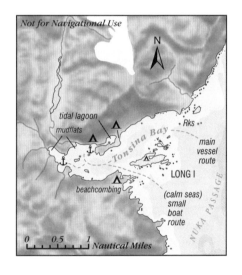

The north entrance channel is deep, but rocks, kelp patches, and shallow water encroach from both the island's shoal and the mainland shore into the channel. In foul weather or during periods of poor visibility, careful navigation is required to safely enter the bay. A pair of rocks, awash at high water and marked by surf and kelp, lie 380 yards south of the distinct wooded islet adjacent the north entrance point. Nearby, 0.25 nm to the west, a rock is located 250 yards offshore, pinching the channel from the north shore.

Extensive tidal flats and sand bars (dry at low water) clog a significant portion of the bay's head and the north shore. The U.S. Coast Pilot #9 mentions that the firm sand flats at the bay's head are suitable for beaching a vessel for repairs.

Landing beach and camping site on the southern entrance point of Tonsina Bay.

The rocky shoal and kelp forest surrounding Long Island provide ideal habitat for sea otters residing in the area. Otter rafts collect in the secluded inlet, tucked into Long Island's north shore.

Kayaking, Camping, and Hiking:

Tonsina Bay is a perfect place to explore by kayak. At the south entrance point adjacent to Long Island are a series of offshore islets. The islets form a barrier, partially buffering the gulf swell on several excellent landing beaches. Make no mistake, this is a special location. At low water, gravel ledges link the off-shore islets to the mainland. Not only is this area great for camping, but also it offers intriguing beachcombing and exploring with desolate offshore views. Several culturally modified trees stand out along the beach berm to remind visitors that hundreds of years ago, the Sugpiaq utilized this area.

Another camping area to consider is on Tonsina Bay's north shore at the top of the pocket beach near the tidal lagoon. This area offers a water source and a chance to explore the lagoon by kayak at slack high water. A prominent, catch-all beach lying east of the lagoon is a treasure trove of trawl buoys and international flotsam.

In calm sea conditions, exploring and camping on Long Island is an inviting alternative. A short but friendly landing (isthmus) beach is located mid-way along Long Island's north shore. This beach has direct access via portage to the sheltered inlet occupying the inner sanctum of Long Island.

Anchorage:

A vessel can find adequate space to anchor in the small north-facing indenta-tion at the head of Tonsina Bay in 9 fathoms, muddy bottom. This is the best and most popular anchorage in Tonsina Bay.

Another anchorage for a small boat lies west of the north shore tidal lagoon, 0.5 nm from the head. To enter the anchorage, pass between the pair of rock islets. Favor the smaller islet and pass west of it. A tidal rock sits off the northeast end of the larger wooded islet. Drop anchor in 10–12 fathoms in the center of the muddy basin. Do not crowd the beach as the water shallows rapidly. From this anchorage, extensive mudflats (dry at low water) stretch westward along the bay's north shore.

Regular visitors include commercial halibut vessels that use the bay for baiting up and as an anchorage when longlining in nearby waters.

Tonsina Bay is also serves as a handy refuge for vessels waiting for satisfactory traveling conditions before proceeding around Gore Point.

Front Point

Front Point is a mountainous headland on the mainland at the south end of Nuka Passage. The shore is rocky and washed by waves. A large reef reveals itself on minus tides 0.5 nm off Front Point. The reef is generally marked by breaking waves. In easterly weather, vessels should give a wide berth to the shoreline around Front Point

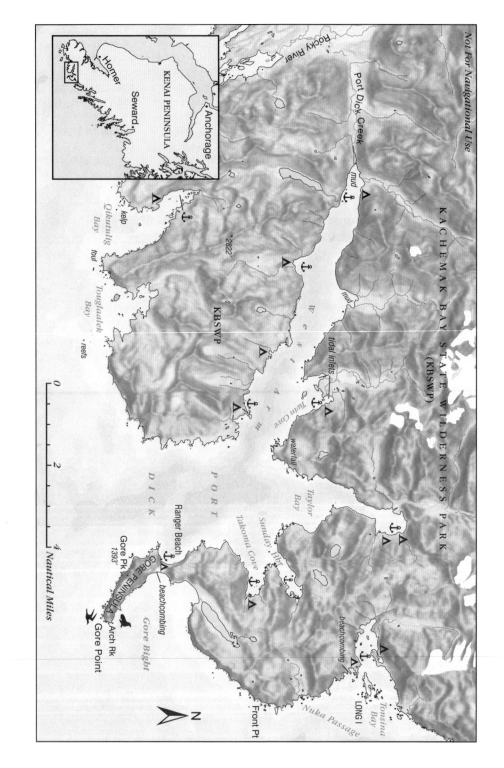

KACHEMAK BAY STATE WILDERNESS PARK (KBSWP)

Rocky River

Port Dick Creek

mud

mud

tidal inlets

Twin Cove

waterfall

KENAI PENINSULA

Anchorage

Homer

Seward

Qikutulig Bay

kelp

foul

Tonglaalek Bay

reefs

2822

KBSWP

W e s t A r m

P O R T

D I C K

Taylor Bay

Takoma Cove

Sunday Hbr

Tonsina Bay

LONG I

beachcombing

Nuka Passage

Front Pt

Gore Bight

GORE PENINSULA

Arch Rk

Gore Point

Gore Pk 1393'

Ranger Beach

beachcombing

0   2   4

Nautical Miles

N

22

Port Dick

GORE POINT TO QIKUTULIG BAY

Wildlife Viewing:

> The waters of the southern Kenai Peninsula were recognized by explorers in the late 1700s for its abundance of marine life, especially whales and sea otters.
>
> During summer months expect to see humpback whales in and around Port Dick, the West Arm, and Taylor Bay. Rafts of sea otter gather to feed throughout the Port Dick area, but they are most abundant at the head of Taylor Bay and the shallow, mud-filled coves of the West Arm.

Kayaking, Camping, and Hiking:

> Only experienced, well-equipped ocean kayakers should attempt paddling around Gore Point. If so, Port Dick is the first, or last, safe haven west of Gore Point. Ranger Beach is a refuge location for kayakers, but accessing the beach is weather dependent. A slew of reliable landing beaches and camping options exist in the West Arm, Taylor Bay, and Takoma Cove.

Anchorages:

> Port Dick has an assortment of optional anchorages located along the south shore of the West Arm and at the head of Taylor Bay. Cruising vessels and fishing boats mostly use Takoma Cove or Sunday Harbor depending which way the wind is blowing.

Port Dick is a multi-arm indentation near the Kenai Peninsula's southern tip. The waters in and around Port Dick are renowned for their intensity, especially during periods of foul weather and spring tides. The area presents a particular challenge to the intrepid small-boat mariner and sea kayaker. Mild weather, good judgment, and patience are helpful when navigating the Gore Point area.

Gore Point

The combination of an irregular bottom, strong tidal currents from Cook Inlet, the westward flowing Alaska Coastal Current, and brisk winds often combine to create turbulent seas around Gore Point. A 5-fathom shoal lies 0.35 nm south of Gore Point. Also, numerous rocks and boulders lie within one-quarter mile of the Gore Peninsula shoreline.

Offshore reef awash on a calm day at Gore Point.

In calm seas, the eastern tip of Gore Point may be worth investigating. Here, around Arch Rock, groups of Steller sea lions cling to the wave-washed rock ledges.

In 1786, Captain Portlock named Gore Point for First Lieutenant John Gore of the *Resolution*. Both Portlock and Gore sailed on Captain Cook's third and last voyage. John Gore assumed command of Cook's *Resolution* after Cook's death in Hawaii in 1778. Lieutenant Gore guided both the *Resolution* and *Discovery* half-way around the world, successfully arriving in England on October 4, 1780, more than a year and a half after taking command. Upon his arrival in England, John Gore was promoted to captain. He died ten years later in 1790.

Before Captain Portlock sailed on his historic round-the-world voyage (1785-1789), Captain John Gore requested that his old shipmate Captain Portlock take along Gore's 11-year old son, also named John. Young John Gore was on board Portlock's *King George* when the ship explored the Alaska coast and bestowed the rocky Kenai Peninsula headland with his father's name.

The young John Gore grew up on board ships of exploration. When he was old enough, both Captain Portlock and the infamous Captain Bligh referred him to the British Naval Academy. The younger Gore spent his entire life in the British Navy until retiring with the rank of a rear admiral. He died in 1853.

Within Port Dick, the shoreline varies with numerous coves, islets, waterfalls, outwash streams, and muddy tidal flats. Some windswept hillsides are wooded while others are scantly vegetated.

Ranger Beach

A prominent, west-facing bight forms the Port Dick side of the Gore Peninsula isthmus. A large, wooded islet, kelp beds, and rocky shoals border the southern shore of the bight. The isthmus is saddle-shaped, one-quarter mile in length and width. The serene west side of the isthmus lies in stark contrast to the turbulent east side.

Kayaking, Camping, and Hiking:
Ranger Beach is a worthwhile landing beach and camping area, but access is weather dependent. Set up camp in the woods behind the beach. In summer, thick patches of salmonberry and blueberry bushes flourish on the isthmus as well as stands of alder, spruce, and hemlock. Hiking across the isthmus is easy — just follow the well-worn game trails that crisscross through the woods, or walk along the edge of the prominent clearing that leads to the eastern shore. Either route takes five to ten minutes. Be prepared to climb over mountains of driftwood upon reaching Isthmus Beach.

Anchorage:
Small boats temporarily anchor midway along the isthmus about 250 yards off the beach in 15–18 fathoms. The sloping bottom is soft and rapidly drops off to deep water. Abandon this anchorage at the first hint of foul weather. An alternative anchorage lies 3 nm to the north in Takoma Cove.

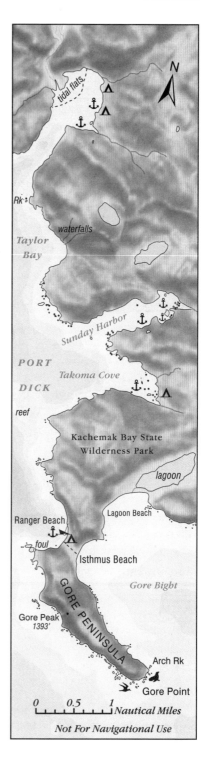

257   RANGER BEACH

Ranger Beach on the Port Dick side of Gore Peninsula isthmus.

Takoma Cove

The recessed, east indentation that holds both Takoma Cove and Sunday Harbor is the most visited destination within Port Dick. Mariners without local knowledge should note that when approaching the area, a perilous reef lurks one-half mile offshore from the south entrance point to the indention.

The inner portion of Takoma Cove is less than 10-fathoms deep and littered with tree-crowned islets and rocks, especially in the northeast corner. Low tide is ideal for observing where submerged rocks lie in wait. Similar to other indentations within Port Dick, extensive mudflats and eelgrass beds occupy the head. Also, the skeletal remains from a fishing boat, uncovers at low water in a small notch at the cove's head.

Kayaking and Camping:

Several landing beaches and potential camping areas lie along the eastern shore of Takoma Cove. Most of these beaches include a water source. Takoma Cove offers a better selection of landing beaches and campsite options than Sunday Harbor.

Anchorage:

A noticeable, tree-crowned islet stands out in the middle of the inner portion of Takoma Cove. Shallow water and covered rocks lie eastward from the islet. A vessel can find room to anchor immediately south of the islet in 6–9 fathoms. Takoma Cove provides protection in east and northeast weather but lies exposed to westerly winds issuing from the West Arm.

Sunday Harbor

A prominent rock islet stands out at the mouth of Sunday Harbor in mid-channel. An assortment of jagged rocks lie just inside the east entrance point. The north shore is steep and rocky. A thickly wooded, V-shaped valley with a fast-moving stream is located at the extreme head of the harbor. Here, mudflats clog a low-lying delta area.

Anchorage:

Vessels can anchor at the head in 6–8 fathoms, mud bottom. An outwash shoal extends off the north shore. Nearby, a tiny alcove affords more protection for a small boat. Drop anchor in the center of the alcove in 6 fathoms, mud bottom.

Sunday Harbor is known to afford better shelter from southeast winds than Takoma Cove. The harbor is more suited for small vessels.

Taylor Bay

Taylor Bay was named by Grant when he first explored Port Dick in 1909. A pair of offshore rocks lie 100 yards off the eastern shore, where the opposing shores narrow midway into Taylor Bay. The oval basin in upper Taylor Bay carries the ravaged look and feel of a heavily glaciated fjord. Although the glacial ice is long gone, the harsh impression remains.

At the head, extensive tidal flats lie along the bay's western shore. A torrent of silty meltwater from streams and waterfalls flow into the valley from the rugged east-facing headwall. A wide swath of dead trees lies helter skelter on the hillside south of the mudflats.

Productive clam and mussel beds grow in the extensive tidal zone. The shellfish serve as a chief food source for the rafts of sea otters that often collect at the head of Taylor Bay.

Kayaking and Camping:

Lower Taylor Bay displays an impressive collection of pocket beaches and towering waterfalls, although the incoming swell from the gulf may discourage beach landings.

The secluded head is likely to be the calmest place in Taylor Bay. An outwash beach and campsite area, with a narrow tidal zone, lies adjacent to the head's northeastern shore. A hillside stream flows nearby. Extensive tidal flats in the upper basin make exploring the western waterfront difficult, especially during low water. Higher stages of the tide are best for exploring beaches by kayak or by foot.

Anchorage:

The muddy basin at the head of Taylor Bay hosts a choice of anchorages dependent on the weather. The north shore has a 7-fathom area with a muddy bottom.

Vessels also can find anchorage along the head's eastern shore, just north of the tidal flats in the basin's southeast corner. Drop anchor in 6 fathoms, muddy bottom.

West Arm

This 7 nm long fjord possesses a series of shallow, muddy coves and inviting pocket beaches. Powerful waterfalls gush from the sea cliffs along the north shore where the mountain peaks are 3,000 feet high. Several hillside areas along West Arm's southern shore show signs of a massive tree die-off.

Port Dick Creek flows down from the valley at the head. The creek's outwash has created extensive tidal flats, providing good waterfowl habitat. The mudflats extend into the arm more than a half-mile from the creek's mouth. A cabin once stood on the southwest side of Port Dick Creek, which burned down many years ago.

Even though Port Dick covers a large portion of the Kachemak Bay State Wilderness Park, no maintained hiking trails exist in the area. It is possible, however, to hike (approximately 4.5 miles) along Port Dick Creek and then bushwhack to the Rocky River trail. GPS mapping recommended.

The Rocky River Trail (formerly the Seldovia-Rocky River Road) is a public easement across Native Corporation lands and other private property. The trail connects to the Seldovia Road at Jakolof Bay but also runs westward, from Rocky River to Picnic Harbor and Windy Bay.

Kayaking, Camping & Hiking:

Several intriguing landing beaches (weather permitting) and potential camp areas lie on the south shore, within a mile of the West Arm's southern entrance point. The area is scenic, with optional places for kayakers to access the shore. Another landing and camp beach, with a water source, lies in the north-facing alcove, 4.5 nm west of the southern entrance point.

On the north shore of the West Arm, Twin Cove rests 1.9 nm west of the north entrance point. Two islands sit in the mouth of this southeast-facing cove, and two tidal inlets form the cove's head. Mud clogs the entire west inlet and the east inlet goes mostly dry at low water. The wooded upland area surrounding Twin Cove presents the best hiking terrain on the northern shore of the West Arm. Several ponds lie in the valley behind the east inlet. Both inlets have suitable pocket beaches at the mouth for camping.

At the West Arm's head, extensive mudflats inhibit easy, low water access to the beach. A gravel spit in the SW corner of Port Dick Creek affords camping.

Anchorage:

The Twin Cove area lies exposed to southeasterly weather, but in mild weather, a vessel can anchor at the mouth of the east inlet. Drop anchor in 5 fathoms, immediately southeast of the prominent islet partially blocking the inlet's mouth.

A good anchorage at the head of the West Arm lies along the south side. Here, two islets stand out along the waterfront. The westernmost islet marks the beginning of the tidal flats that reach all of the way to the head. Drop anchor midway between the two islets in 5 fathoms, muddy bottom. Mariners will discover other anchorages along the south shore that are suitable during light weather.

HEADING WEST FROM PORT DICK

Hazardous offshore rocks and shallow ledges begin at the west entrance point to Port Dick and stretch westward to Rocky Bay. Mariners without local knowledge should stay 2 miles from the coast including Touglaalek and Qikutulig bays. This exposed area is greatly influenced by inshore tidal currents, an irregular bottom, and offshore sea conditions. The area should be avoided when a significant groundswell is present or during periods of low visibility and fog.

Touglaalek Bay

Dangerous rocks and shallow ledges stretch 1.6 nm southward from the east entrance point of Touglaalek Bay. Foul ground exists from Touglaalek Bay to the west entrance of Port Dick. The upper portion of this south-facing bay is less than 4-fathoms deep, sand bottom. Kelp beds with rocks awash surround the islands immediately inside the entrance. Fishing boats sometimes temporarily anchor at the bay's mouth during favorable weather conditions.

Kayaking;
Touglaalek Bay possesses a semi-sheltered inlet and a potential landing beach on the eastern shore tucked inside the entrance point. Accessing the shore is weather dependent.

Qikutulig Bay

Mariners entering the bay should slightly favor the eastern shore to avoid kelp, rocks, and a 2-fathom shoal just inside the western entrance. A string of tree-covered islets occupies the upper head. The area invites a closer look from a kayak or inflatable. The stream at the bay's head flows from a lake located 2.5 miles up the valley.

Kayaking:
The east shore is inaccessible until three-quarters of the way into the bay, where tree-crowned islets partially shelter a south-facing pocket beach from the gulf swell. The beach offers a landing location, weather permitting. A water source flows at the east end of the beach.
Midway into the bay, along the west shore lies a north-facing landing beach with a small lagoon hidden behind the beach berm. This beach is the best landing option on the bay's western shore.

Anchorage:
In mild weather, the anchorage at the bay's head is a convenient overnight location for fishing boats working the inshore waters. Small vessels can drop anchor west of the tree-crowned islets in 15 fathoms or less, muddy bottom. Mariners seeking a more secure anchorage should set a course for Picnic Harbor at the head of Rocky Bay.

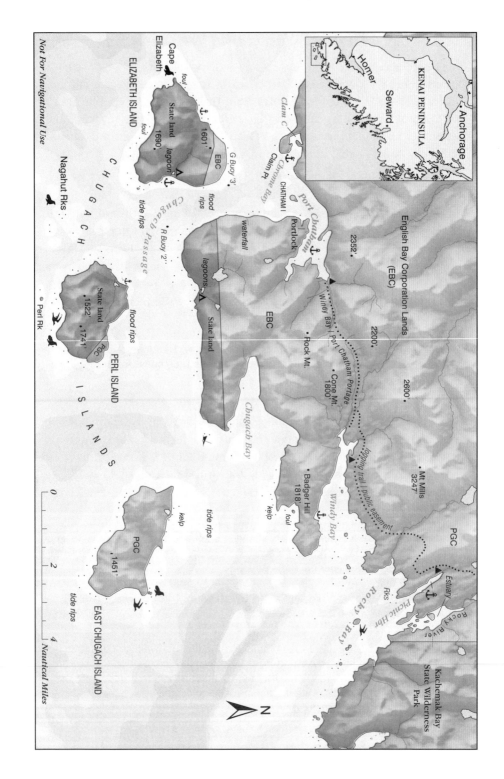

Not For Navigational Use

Nautical Miles
0   2   4

N

Cape
Elizabeth
ELIZABETH ISLAND
Nagahut Rks

CHUGACH

foul
State land
· 1601 ·
· 1690 ·
lagoon
EBC
foul

G Buoy '3'
Clam C.
Chrome Pt.
Chrome Bay
CHATHAM I.
Portlock

Clam Pt.
flood
rips
tide rips

R Buoy '2'

Perl Rk

State land
· 1522 ·
· 1741 ·
PGC
PERL ISLAND

ISLANDS

PASSAGE

flood rips

waterfall

lagoons
State land
EBC

Chugach Bay

Port Chatham

2352 ·

Windy Bay | Port Chatham Portage
Cone Mt.
1800 ·

Rock Mt.

English Bay Corporation Lands
(EBC)

2200 ·

2600 ·

logging trail | public easement

Mt. Millis
3247 ·

PGC

kelp
Badger Hill
1818 ·

kelp
foul

Windy Bay

PGC
· 1451 ·
EAST CHUGACH ISLAND

tide rips

kelp

tide rips

Rocky Bay

Rks
Rocky Hbr.

Picnic Hbr.

Estuary

Rocky River

Kachemak Bay
State Wilderness
Park

KENAI PENINSULA

Homer
Seward ·

· Anchorage

23

Rocky Bay & Port Chatham

ROCKY BAY TO PORT CHATHAM

Special Wildlife Viewing:
  In summer, the southern tip of the Kenai Peninsula is home to high numbers of
  Humpback whales, especially juvenile whales and calves swimming at their
  mother's side.

Kayaking:
  The water between the Chugach Islands and the Kenai mainland is a
  particularly challenging area for sea kayakers. When winds and tidal currents
  oppose each other, tide rips develop. This cannot be emphasized enough when
  dealing with the area. Travel at slack water or when tidal currents are favorable.
  Advanced travel planning is necessary.

Camping and Hiking:
  The upland areas in Rocky Bay, Windy Bay, and Port Chatham are mostly
  private property. The east shore of Rocky Bay (Kachemak Bay State Wilderness
  Park) possesses scores of rarely visited pocket beaches. The tidal beaches
  surrounding Chrome Bay, Port Chatham, and Portlock provide intriguing areas
  to explore. See map for designated public campsite and trail easements.

Anchorages:
  The best mainland anchorages lie within Port Chatham and at the head of
  Rocky Bay in Picnic Harbor. Fishing vessels temporarily anchor in sheltered
  areas around the Chugach Islands and mainland bays. Most anchorages,
  particularly those in the Chugach Islands, are dependent on weather and tidal
  conditions.

The tidal current velocity that flows between the Chugach Islands and the Kenai Peninsula mainland are greater than those found, in most locations along the outer coast. Mariners unfamiliar with the area should note that a flood tide accompanied by a west wind or an ebb tide with an east wind will amplify sea conditions between Port Dick and Port Chatham. Slower boats and sailboats may miss the tide and need to temporarily anchor in one of the mainland bays before continuing their journey. Check tide and current predictions for local corrections.

Strong tide rips regularly arise between the Chugach Islands and the mainland. When traveling west, the tide rips typically begin north of the

Looking southeast down Picnic Harbor.

NW tip of East Chugach Island and can extend northward to within one-mile of the shore of Chugach Bay. Strong tide rips can occur in Chugach Passage off the NW end of Perl Island. Swift flood currents also generate tide rips in upper Chugach Passage, between Elizabeth Island and the mainland.

The strong regional currents and intense mixing of nutrients fuel a rich marine environment abundant with wildlife. Numerous humpback whales can be observed rearing their young at the southern end of the Kenai Peninsula. The whale's attraction to the Kenai coast was recognized by Captain Portlock more than two centuries ago when he identified the southern Kenai Peninsula to be a valuable whale nursery and recommended a whaling station for the region, which never materialized. Other prominent nearshore marine mammals include sea otters, harbor seals, Steller sea lions, and killer whales. The passages and surrounding waters also are rich with salmon, halibut, lingcod, and rockfish.

Rocky Bay

A wooded island, surrounded by islets, rocks and kelp beds, sits in the middle of Rocky Bay. More islets and rocks lie scattered elsewhere about the bay, so care must be taken while navigating, especially along the bay's eastern shoreline where the Rocky River creates a large estuary. From the river mouth, the Rocky Bay seacoast stretches southeastward five-miles. Here, clusters of islets and pocket beaches paint an alluring seascape. For beachcombers, gaining access to these waterfront areas is a rare opportunity.

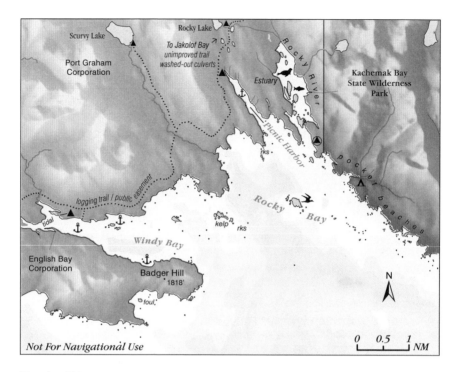

Not For Navigational Use

Rocky River

The Rocky River area offers exceptional wildlife viewing. In summer, harbor seals roam the river delta as hungry flocks of ravens, gulls, and eagles lineup along the waterfront to welcome returning schools of salmon.

The PGC owns the upland area surrounding Rocky River and has extensive holdings westward, including lands north of Windy Bay.

Kayaking:
The Rocky River Estuary invites kayaks and inflatables to access a mile or more of channels meandering northward into the valley. Explore at higher stages of the tide. Scores of beaches are accessible in the delta area, particularly in the river mouth. The terrain eastward from the mouth of Rocky River are included in the Kachemak Bay State Wilderness Park (KBSWP).

Picnic Harbor

Picnic Harbor measures one-mile long and 220–300 yards wide. The waterfront perimeter is low, with trees growing just above high water. The harbor affords the most secure anchorage in the area and provides an excellent base camp for exploring the Rocky River Estuary by kayak or inflatable.

A narrow inlet at the extreme head of Picnic Harbor goes dry at low water. Mud and eelgrass clog the inlet. Several tiny streams enter the inlet to provide a water source, if needed. The nearest access point to the Rocky

River trail lies 150 yards west of the inlet and requires bushwhacking. An unmarked one-acre campsite easement also exists at the harbor's head.

Anchorage:
Vessels can find anchorage near the head of Picnic Harbor in 8–10 fathoms, muddy bottom.

Windy Bay

Wave-washed islets, kelp beds, and rocks lie scattered in the middle of the entrance to Windy Bay. Favor the southern shore when entering the bay. Prevailing westerly winds from Cook Inlet frequently blow through Windy Bay. The bay's easterly exposure also invites winds and seas from the Gulf of Alaska.

Kayaking and Camping:
At the bay's head, a pair of tidal inlets display an intricate shore with potential landing beaches, although access can be hampered by mudflats. Several alternative landing beaches lie along the north shore including a public camp site easement, but beach landings are weather dependent.

Hiking:
The Windy Bay – Port Chatham Portage (public right-of-way) links the two bays. This historical portage is unimproved and unmarked. Adjacent to the north shore of Windy Bay lies a logging road (public easement) that meanders to Rocky Bay. Near Picnic Harbor, the logging road joins the Rocky River trail, which winds to Rocky Lake and Jakolof Bay. The trail is cut by streams and many culverts are washed-out. Topo maps and a GPS are recommended.

Anchorage:
In light weather, vessels can layover in the bay while waiting for a favorable tide to proceed. A recessed area on the south shore, one-mile from the entrance, affords limited protection from the south and southeast. Anchor in 4 fathoms, mud bottom. Alternatively, drop anchor at the bay's head, in 4–6 fathoms on a good-holding mud bottom.

Chugach Bay

Chugach Bay lies exposed to potential unruly seas from the east and southeast. Also, west winds (common in Summer) issuing from the head help define this bay as a tentative anchorage. The north arm is too deep for convenient anchoring. The west arm, 2 miles long, terminates with hillside streams and beaches with driftwood. Kelp beds and navigational hazards range along both the north and south shores of the bay.

In mild weather, beachcombers can land near the outwash beach at the bay's head and explore the rarely visited waterfront.

Anchorage:
Mariners can drop anchor in the west arm, along the south shore of Chugach Bay, one-quarter mile from the head, in 6–10 fathoms, muddy bottom. Beware of the rocks and shallow water hazards that extend off the bay's south shore, three-quarters of a mile from the head.

Elizabeth Island with Claim Pt (right), Chugach Passage.

CHUGACH ISLANDS

The wind-swept Chugach Islands from east to west are named East Chugach Island, Perl Island and Elizabeth Island. The area's nutrient-rich waters are unique in the state. World-renown tides that issue from Cook Inlet converge with oceanic currents flowing through Kennedy Entrance to violently churn the water across the region's irregular bottom. For a century, commercial halibut vessels have longlined the productive southern end of the Kenai Peninsula. Charter and private vessels from Homer also use the area to fish for halibut, silver salmon, lingcod, and rockfish.

A mariner with local knowledge and a fast, seaworthy, vessel can take advantage of the brief periods of slack water when transiting the area. Slow vessels are at a disadvantage. Fishing boats use a variety of anchorages in the Chugach Islands, based on factors including exposure, wind direction, tidal current velocity, and the latest marine weather forecast. Local experience is helpful when using anchorages in the islands.

East Chugach Island

Mariners should note a 4-fathom, kelp-marked shoal, 1.25 nm northward of the island's northwest shore. Tides rips in the vicinity of the shoal sometimes extend to the entrance of Chugach Bay. Also, strong tide rips form off the island's southeast point. The island is owned by the Port Graham Corporation.

Perl Island

Initially named Isla de Arriaga by Don Ignacio Arteaga in 1779, the island was subsequently renamed for Perl D. Blodgett who, in 1894, established the Kenai Peninsula's first fur farm on Perl Island. By 1900, all three Chugach Islands were fur-farmed, with limited success.

The northwest point of Perl Island is privately owned and has several cabins and a landing strip above the beach berm. Fishing vessels occasionally anchor inside the island's northwest point.

Tide rips can occur northward and westward from the northwest shore of Perl Island into Chugach Passage. These tide rips are amplified when a west wind collides with a flood tide or an east wind during an ebb tide.

Elizabeth Island

Cape Elizabeth, on the W tip of Elizabeth Island, was named by Captain Cook, in 1778, when he mistook the island as being part of the mainland.

Kayaking and Camping:
Located midway along the island's east shore is a small bight that affords a landing beach, weather permitting. The area has a lagoon hidden behind the waterfront. A camp area exists near the stream that drains from the lagoon.

Anchorage:
The niche on the island's east side, (mentioned above) is a haven for boats in westerly weather. The anchorage is often used by vessels waiting for a tide change or for sea conditions to improve before proceeding.
Another recessed area located midway along the northwest shore of the island affords temporary anchorage for vessels fishing in lower Cook Inlet.

Chugach Passage

Chugach Passage lies between Perl and Elizabeth Islands and the rounded end of the Kenai Peninsula mainland. The flood current sets north and the ebb sets south, with velocities of 3.1 knots and 1.8 knots, respectively. Tidal velocities increase during episodes of heavy weather. Flood rips occur in upper Chugach Passage between Elizabeth Island and the mainland, especially in westerly winds and during spring tides. Tide rips also spread eastward off the southeast shore of Elizabeth Island.

Mariner should note two lighted buoys mark dangers found in Chugach Passage. At the southeast end a lighted Red "2" buoy, 0.5 nm southwest of the mainland turn, alerts mariners to foul ground off the mainland coast. At the north end, a lighted Green "3" buoy, 0.3 nm off the northeast point of Elizabeth Island, marks a shoal encroaching into the passage from the island's northeast shore.

Kayaking and Camping:
A recessed bight on the passage's north shore (State land) has a beach that fronts a pair of interconnected lagoons. The beach is accessible in light weather and provides unique camping and exploring opportunities.

The west-facing beach at Portlock with Elizabeth Island (background).

Chrome Bay

Chrome Bay indents the mainland coast immediately west of Port Chatham. Avoid the area around the entrance near Claim Point and Kelp Point, where islets, rocks, and kelp-marked shoals extend offshore. Claim Point is the site of an abandoned chromium mine on the hillside. Nearby, another claim known as the Reef Mine worked the rocky islet situated southeast of Claim Point. On the shore of Chrome Bay, a townsite known as Chrome, or Toqakvik, was established in 1917, which provided the mine and Portlock area with workers and supplies. A mine tunnel and discarded pieces of equipment can be found along the bay's waterfront.

Kayaking:

Chrome Bay affords a strategic vantage point for mariners and kayakers to assess sea conditions before proceeding into Chugach Passage.

Anchorage:

Chrome Bay is a popular fair-weather anchorage for fishing boats. Vessels often anchor at the bay's month in 4–6 fathoms or in the center of the bay in 3–4 fathoms, mud bottom.

Clam Cove

On the west shore of Chrome Bay is the entrance to Clam Cove. Eelgrass grows in the cove, which goes mostly dry during low water. A wilderness lodge with several yurts lies partially hidden on the wooded hillside near the cove entrance. The uplands in Clam Cove are private property.

Port Chatham

Chatham Island, surrounded by islets and shoals, rests in the middle of the entrance to Port Chatham. The ship channel lies west of the island, but small boats can use the east entrance by favoring the mainland.

In 1787, Captain Portlock found Port Chatham while surveying lower Cook Inlet, but it was the cartographer and explorer Captain Vancouver who named the bay in 1794 for his armed tender *Chatham*.

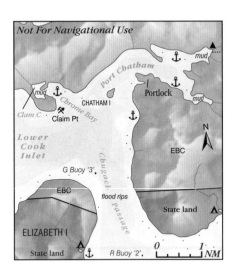

Port Chatham then, as now, affords shelter on a seacoast where safe havens are few and far between. The bay's interior includes northeast and southeast arms, both with extensive mudflats clogging their heads. A prominent quarter-mile-long sandspit protrudes from the north shore, and a spruce-covered peninsula with pocket beaches embraces the south shore. The physical landscape presents various mooring options for small boats in a variety of weather conditions. Toward the head is a Coast Guard mooring buoy with Coast Guard priority use, but in heavy weather, commercial fishing vessels and others tie to the mooring.

Portlock

With help from the Sugpiaq community, Port Chatham became the focal point for pioneering endeavors in the early 20th century. At the time, the main occupations on the Kenai Peninsula involved fishing, logging, and mining, and Port Chatham residents engaged in all three.

In 1915, the construction of a halibut cold storage unit at Portlock, a village on the south shore of Port Chatham, began to boom. Shortly afterward a chromium discovery at Claim Point, in 1917, led to an influx of workers moving from Port Graham to the Port Chatham area. A post office opened at Portlock in 1921.

Between 1920 and 1940, Port Chatham maintained a population of approximately 50 residents. However, after the demise of mining, the cannery's closure, and a series of unexplained events, an already declining population abruptly moved back to Port Graham and Nanwalek in 1949.

Why did all the residents abandoned Portlock? The lack of jobs certainly contributed, but oral testimonies from Port Graham blame Nantiinaq

Low water reveals barnacle-encrusted industrial equipment at Portlock.

(hairy man), a Sasquatch-like creature, for their exodus. The Port Chatham 'Nantiinaq' folklore began in the early 1900s as stories spread about local people and others disappearing in the woods. Other accounts tell of hunters tracking human-like footprints, 18-inches long, as well as an actual Nantiinaq sighting on the beach. The accumulation of events likely fueled the final decision to leave. Today, the mystery of Nantiinaq and the allure of Port Chatham and Portlock remain.

The English Bay Corporation (EBC) owns the upland areas around Port Chatham, Koyuktolik Bay, and Nanwalek. Contact the EBC (907-281-2328) for current permit and access policies.

Kayaking and Camping:
   Crescent-shaped beaches grace the former Portlock townsite. A tidal lagoon on the west side of Portlock is accessible to kayaks and inflatables during high water. On Portlock's north-facing beach lies discarded evidence that civilization once existed here. See map for designated trail and campsite easements.

Anchorage:
   The wind direction and weather forecast determines where most vessels anchor. Mariners can drop anchor off the north-facing beach or east-facing beach at Portlock to go ashore and check out the waterfront.
   In most winds, vessel can take shelter along the bay's north shore, east of the sandspit. Drop anchor in 4–5-fathoms, mud bottom.

Horned puffins, an auk, breed on the sea cliffs of the Kenai Peninsula Outer Coast. Puffins are pelagic seabirds that dive for small fish.

Steller sea lions posture and roar along the outer coast. Sea lions mainly inhabit rocky substrates on points of land and islands. The Pye and Chiswell islands support the highest concentrations of sea lions found on the Kenai Peninsula.

Appendices

- BIRDS OF THE KENAI PENINSULA

- MARINE MAMMALS OF THE KENAI FJORDS

- SELECTED PLANTS OF THE KENAI FJORDS

Devil's Club, a member of the Ginseng Family.

BIRDS OF THE KENAI PENINSULA

Loons

___Red-throated Loon*

___Pacific Loon *

___Common Loon*

___Yellow-billed Loon

Grebes

___Horned Grebe*

___Red-necked Grebe*

Petrels, Cormorants, Herons

___Fork-tailed Storm-Petrel*

___*Leach's Storm-Petrel*

___Double-crested Cormorant*

___Red-Faced Cormorant*

___Pelagic Cormorant*

___Great Blue Heron

Swans, Geese, Ducks

___Tundra Swan

___Trumpeter Swan*

___Greater White-fronted Goose

___*Snow Goose*

___*Emperor Goose*

___Brant

___Canada Goose*

___Green-winged Teal*

___Mallard*

___Northern Pintail*

___*Blue-winged Teal*

___*Cinnamon Teal*

___Northern Shoveler

___*Gadwall*

___*Eurasian Wigeon*

___American Wigeon*

___Canvasback

___*Redhead*

___*Ring-necked Duck**

___Greater Scaup*

___Lesser Scaup

___*Common Eider*

___*King Eider*

___*Steller's Eider*

___Harlequin Duck*

___Long-tailed Duck

___Black Scoter

___Surf Scoter*

___White-winged Scoter*

[1.] Adapted from National Park Service. 1997. Birds of Kenai Fjords National Park, Seward, Alaska. Alaska Natural History Association, National Park Service, Challenge Cost Share Program, with association by Kenai Fjord National Park and Chugach National Forest; J. Andrew, R. McHenry, R. Scher,. D Sonneborn, T. Tobish, 1997. Birds of Seward, Alaska. Seward Chamber of Commerce.; and D. Erikson, M. Davidson, and J. Klein 1983. "Birds of Kachemak Bay". Kachemak Bay, Alaska.

italics = species infrequently observed; * = breeds on the Kenai Peninsula

___Common Goldeneye*
___Barrow's Goldeneye*
___Bufflehead
___Hooded Merganser
___Common Merganser*
___Red-breasted Merganser*

Raptors

___*Osprey**
___Bald Eagle*
___Northern Harrier*
___Sharp-shinned Hawk*
___Northern Goshawk*
___*Swainson's Hawk*
___Red-tailed Hawk
___Rough-legged Hawk*
___Golden Eagle*
___*American Kestrel*
___Merlin
___Peregrine Falcon*
___*Gyrfalcon*

Grouse, Ptarmigan

___*Ruffed Grouse* *
___Spruce Grouse*
___Willow Ptarmigan*
___Rock Ptarmigan*
___*White-tailed Ptarmigan**
___*Sharp-tailed Grouse*

Cranes

___Sandhill Crane*

Plovers, Sandpipers, Shorebirds

___Black-bellied Plover
___Pacific Golden Plover
___Semipalmated Plover*
___*Killdeer*

___Greater Yellowlegs*
___Lesser Yellowlegs*
___Solitary Sandpiper*
___Wandering Tattler*
___*Gray-tailed Tattler*
___Spotted Sandpiper*
___Whimbrel
___*Hudsonian Godwit**
___*Bar-tailed Godwit*
___*Marbled Godwit*
___Ruddy Turnstone
___Black Turnstone
___Surfbird
___*Red Knot*
___*Sanderling*
___Semipalmated Sandpiper
___Western Sandpiper
___Least Sandpiper*
___*Baird's Sandpiper*
___*Pectoral Sandpiper*
___Sharp-tailed Sandpiper
___Rock Sandpiper
___*Dunlin*
___Short-billed Dowitcher
___Long-billed Dowitcher
___Wilson's Snipe*
___Red-necked Phalarope*
___Red Phalarope
___Black Oystercatcher*

Jeagers, Gulls, Terns

___Pomarine Jaeger
___Parasitic Jaeger
___Long-tailed Jaeger
___Sooty Shearwater
___Short-tailed Shearwater
___Northern Fulmer

___Franklin's Gull

___*Black-headed Gull*

___Bonaparte's Gull

___*Sabine's Gull*

___Mew Gull*

___*Ring-billed Gull*

___Herring Gull*

___*Thayer's Gull*

___Glaucous-winged Gull*

___Glaucous Gull

___Black-legged Kittiwake*

___*Red-legged Kittiwake*

___*Caspian Turn*

___Arctic Tern*

___*Aleutian Tern*

Alcids

___Common Murre*

___Thick-billed Murre*

___Pigeon Guillemot*

___Marbled Murrelet*

___*Kittlitz's Murrelet**

___Ancient Murrelet

___*Cassin's Auklet*

___Parakeet Auklet

___*Crested Auklet*

___Rhinoceros Auklet*

___Horned Pufin*

___*Tufted Puffin**

Doves

___*Mourning Dove*

___Rock Doves*

Owls

___Great Horned Owl*

___*Snowy Owl*

___*Northern Hawk-Owl*

___*Great Gray Owl*

___*Short-eared Owl**

___Boreal Owl*

___Northern Saw-whet Owl*

___*Western Screech-Owl*

Hummingbirds, Kingfishers

___Rufous Hummingbird*

___Belted Kingfisher *

Woodpeckers

___*Red-breasted Sapsucker*

___*Downy Woodpecker**

___*Hairy Woodpecker **

___*Three-toed Woodpecker**

___*Black-backed Woodpecker**

___*Northern Flicker**

Flycatchers

___*Olive-sided Flycatcher**

___*Western Wood-Pewee**

___Alder Flycatcher*

___*Say's Pheobe**

Swallows

___Tree Swallow*

___Violet-green Swallow*

___Bank Swallow *

___*Barn Swallow*

___Cliff Swallow *

___*Purple Martin*

Jays, Crows

___Gray Jay*

___Steller's Jay*

___Black-billed Magpie*

___Northwestern Crow*

___Common Raven *

Chickadees

___Black-capped Chickadee*

___Boreal Chickadee*

___Chestnut-backed Chicadee*

Nuthatches, Creepers, Dippers, Wrens

___Red-breasted Nuthatch

___Brown Creeper *

___American Dipper*

___Winter Wren*

Warblers, Thrushes, Kinglets, Pipits

___Golden-crowned Kinglet*

___Ruby-crowned Kinglet*

___*Northern Wheatear*

___*Townsend's Solitaire*

___Gray-cheeked Thrush*

___Swainson's Thrush

___Hermit Thrush*

___American Robin*

___Varied Thrush *

___*Horned Lark**

___Water Pipit *

___*Cedar Waxwing*

___Bohemian Waxwing *

___Northern Shrike*

___Orange-crowned Warbler *

___Yellow Warbler*

___Yellow-rumped Warbler*

___Townsend's Warbler*

___Blackpoll Warbler*

___Northern Waterthrush*

___Wilson's Warbler*

___*European Starling*

Sparrows

___*American Tree Sparrow**

___Savannah Sparrow*

___Fox Sparrow*

___Song Sparrow*

___Lincoln's Sparrow *

___Golden-crowned Sparrow*

___White-crowned Sparrow*

___*White-throated Sparrow*

___*Harris' Sparrow*

Finches, Bunting, & Blackbirds

___Dark-eyed Junco*

___Lapland Longspur

___Snow Buntings*

___*McKay's Bunting*

___Rusty Blackbird*

___*Gray-crowned Rosy-finch**

___Pine Grosbeak*

___*Red Crossbill**

___*White-winged Crossbill**

___Common Redpoll*

___*Hoary Redpoll*

___Pine Siskin*

___*Brambling*

MARINE MAMMALS OF THE KENAI FJORDS

Baleen Whales

Fin Whale (seasonal resident)

Sei Whale (offshore resident)

Minke Whale (seasonal resident)

Humpback Whale (seasonally common)

Gray Whale (seasonally common migrant)

Toothed Whales and Porpoises

Dall's Porpoise (resident)

Harbor Porpoise (resident)

Resident Killer Whale (resident)

Bigg's (transient) Killer Whale (resident)

Offshore Killer Whale (occasional visitor)

Beluga (accidental outside Cook Inlet)

Bering Sea Beaked Whale (rare)

Seals and Sea Lions

Steller Sea Lion (resident)

Northern Fur Seal (uncommonly seen, seasonal migrant)

California Sea Lion (occasional visitor)

Harbor Seal (resident)

Northern Elephant Seal (uncommonly seen, seasonal migrant)

Weasel Family

Sea Otter (resident)

Note: land mammals, including river otters, bears, deer, and moose, may be seen swimming in the fjords.

SELECTED PLANTS OF THE KENAI FJORDS [1]

Lycopodiaceae (Club Moss Family)

Alpine Club Moss *(Lycopodium alpinum)*
Common Club Moss *(Lycopodium clavatum)*
Fir Club Moss *(Huperzia selago)*
Stiff Club Moss *(Lycopodium annotinum)*

Selaginaceae (Spikemoss Family)

Spike Moss *(Selaginella selaginoides)*

Equisetaceae (Horsetail Family)

Common Horsetail *(Equisetim arvense)*
Marsh Horsetail *(Equisetum palustre)*
Water Horsetail *(Equisetum fluviatile)*

Aspleniaceae (Lady Fern Family)

Fragile Fern *(Cystopteris fragilis)*
Lady Fern *(Athyrium filix-femina)*

Pinaceae (Pine Family)

Lutz Spruce *(Picea lutzii)*
Mountain Hemlock *(Tsuga mertensiana)*
Sitka Spruce *(Picea sitchensis)*
Western Hemlock *(Tsuga heterophylla)*

Juncaginaceae (Arrow Grass Family)

Arrowgrass *(Triglochin maritimum)*

Poaceae (Grass Family)

Alpine Sweetgrass *(Hierochloe alpina)*
Beach Rye Grass *(Leymus mollis)*
Bluegrass *(Poa alpina)*
Bluejoint *(Calamagrostis canadensis)*
Mountain Timothy *(Phleum alpinum)*
Red Fescue *(Festuca rubra)*

---

[1] Adapted from J. Pfeiffenberger. 1995. The Complete Guide to Kenai Fjords National Park, Alaska 144 pp; E.C. Murphy and A. A. Hoover. 1983. Research study of the reactions of wildlife to boating activity along the Kenai Fjords coastline. National Park Service Report. 125 pp.; E. Hulten. 1974. Flora of Alaska and Neighboring Territories. Stanford University Press. California. 1008 pp. and United States Department of Agriculture, Natural Resources Conservation Service Plants Database (https://plants.usda.gov)

Cyperaceae (Sedge Family)

    Cotton Grass *(Eriophorum augustifolium)*
    Longawn Sedge *(Carex macrochaeta)*
    Lungbye's Sedge *(Carex lungbyei)*

Araceae (Arum Family)

    Skunk Cabbage *(Lysichiton americanum)*

Juncaceae (Rush Family)

    Drummond's rush *(Juncus drummondii)*

Liliaceae (Lily Family)

    Chocolate Lily *(Fritillaria camschatcensis)*
    False Hellebore *(Veratrum viride)*
    Northern Asphodel *(Tofieldia coccinea)*
    Watermellon Berry *(Streptopus amplexifolius)*
    Wild Chive *(Allium schoenoprasum)*

Iridaceae (Iris Family)

    Blue-Eyed Grass *(Sisyrinchium littorale)*
    Wild Flag *(Iris setosa)*

Orchidaceae (Orchid Family)

    Bog Orchid *(Platanthera dilatata)*
    Heartleaf Twayblade *(Listera cordata)*
    Slender Bog Orchid *(Platanthera stricta)*

Salicaceae (Willow Family)

    Arctic Willow *(Salix arctica)*
    Black Cottonwood *(Populus balsamifera)*
    Feltleaf Willow *(Salix alaxensis)*
    Sitka Willow *(Salix sitchensis)*

Betulaceae (Birch Family)

    Sitka Alder *(Alnus viridis)*

Urticacea (Nettle Family)

    Lyall Nettle *(Urtica lyallii)*
    Stinging Nettle *(Urtica dioica)*

Polygonaceae (Buckwheat Family)

    Mountain Sorrel *(Oxyria digyna)*
    Western Dock *(Rumex aquaticus)*

Chenopodiaceae (Goosefoot Family)

Pigweed *(Chenopodium album)*

Portulaceae (Purslane Family)

Springbeauty *(Claytonia sibirica)*

Caryophyllaceae (Pink Family)

Beach Greens *(Honckenya peploides)*
Canada Sandspurry *(Spergularia canadensis)*
Chickweed *(Stellaria media)*
Moss Campion *(Silene acaulis)*
Sitka Starwort *(Stellaria borealis)*

Nymphaeaceae (Water Lily Family)

Yellow Pond Lily *(Nuphar lutea)*

Ranunculaceae (Crowfoot Family)

Larkspur *(Delphinium glaucum)*
Marsh Marigold *(Caltha palustris)*
Monkshood *(Aconitum delphiniifolium)*
Red Baneberry *(Actaea rubra)*
Western Columbine *(Aquilegia formosa)*

Papaveraceae (Poppy Family)

Alaska Poppy *(Papaver macounii)*
Pale Pink Poppy *(Papaver alboroseum)*

Brassicaceae (Mustard Family)

Rock Cress *(Arabis lyrata)*
Scurvy Grass *(Cochlearia officinalis)*
Winter Cress *(Barbarea orthoceras)*
Yellow Cress *(Rorippa islandica)*

Drosseraceae (Sundew Family)

English Sundew *(Drosera anglica)*
Round Leaf Sundew *(Drosera rotundifolia)*

Crassulaceae (Stonecrop Family)

Roseroot *(Rhodiola integrifolia)*

Saxifragaceae (Saxifrage Family)

Alpine Heuchera *(Heuchera glabra)*
Bog Star *(Parnassia palustris)*
Coast Saxifrage *(Saxifraga ferruginea)*
Lace Flower *(Tiarella trifoliata)*

Northern Black Currant *(Ribes hudsonianum)*
Northern Red Currant *(Ribes triste)*
Red-stemmed Saxifrage *(Saxifraga lyallii)*
Spotted Saxifrage *(Saxifraga bronchialis)*
Trailing Black Currant *(Ribes laxiflorum)*
Tufted Saxifrage *(Saxifraga caespitosa)*

Rosaceae (Rose Family)

Alaska Spirea *(Spiraea beauverdiana)*
Beach Strawberry *(Fragaria chiloensis)*
Bride's Feathers *(Aruncus dioicus)*
Cloudberry *(Rubus chamaemorus)*
Large-Leaf Avens *(Geum macrophyllum)*
Mountain Ash *(Sorbus sitchensis)*
Mountain Avens *(Dryas octopetala)*
Nagoonberry *(Rubus arcticus)*
Oregon Crab Apple *(Malus fusca)*
Partridgefoot *(Luetkea pectinata)*
Salmonberry *(Rubus spectabilis)*
Sitka Burnet *(Sanguisorba canadensis)*
Trailing Raspberry *(Rubus pedatus)*
Yellow Dryas *(Dryas drummondii)*

Leguminosae (Pea Family)

Alsike Clover *(Trifolium hybridum)*
Beach Pea *(Lathyrus japonicus)*
Milk Vetch *(Astragalus alpinus)*
Nootka Lupine *(Lupinus nootkatensis)*

Geraniaceae (Geranium Family)

Wooly Geranium *(Geranium erianthum)*

Violaceae (Violet Family)

Marsh Violet *(Viola epipsila)*

Onagraceae (Evening Primrose Family)

Common Fireweed *(Chamerion angustifolium)*
Dwarf Fireweed *(Chamerion latifolium)*
Enchanter's Nightshade *(Circaea alpina)*
Pimpernel Willow-Herb *(Epilobium anagallidifolium)*
Slender-Fruited Willow Herb *(Epilobium ciliatum)*

Araliaceae (Ginseng Family)

Devil's Club *(Oplopanax horridus)*

Apiaceae(Parsley Family)

    Beach Lovage *(Ligusticum scoticum)*
    Cow Parsnip *(Heracleum maximum)*
    Sweet Cicely *(Osmorhiza purpurea)*
    Wild Celery *(Angelica lucida)*

Cornaceae (Dogwood Family)

    Dogwood *(Cornus canadensis)*

Pyrolacaea (Wintergreen Family)

    Pink Wintergreen *(Pyrola asarifolia)*
    Single Delight *(Moneses uniflora)*

Ericacea (Heath Family)

    Alaska Blueberry *(Vaccinium alaskaense)*
    Alaska Moss Heath *(Cassiope stelleriana)*
    Alpine Azalea *(Loiseleuria procumbens)*
    Blue Huckleberry *(Vaccinium ovalifolium)*
    Bog Blueberry *(Vaccinium uliginosum)*
    Bog Cranberry *(Vaccinium oxycoccos)*
    Bog Rosemary *(Andromeda polifolia)*
    Copper Flower *(Elliottia pyroliflora)*
    Dwarf Blueberry *(Vaccinium caespitosum)*
    Lingonberry *(Vaccinium vitis-idaea)*
    Mountain Heather *(Phyllodoce aleutica)*

Primulaceae (Primrose Family)

    Arctic Starflower *(Trientalis europaea)*
    Shooting Star *(Dodecatheon pulchellum)*

Gentianaceae (Gentian Family)

    Alpine Gentian *(Gentiana platypetala)*
    Glaucous gentian *(Gentiana glauca)*
    Star Gentian *(Swertia perennis)*

Polemoniaceae (Polemonium Family)

    Jacob's Ladder *(Polemonium acutiflorum)*

Boraginaceae (Borage Family)

    Forget-Me-Not *(Myosotis asiatica)*
    Oysterleaf *(Mertensia maritima)*
    Tall Bluebell *(Mertensia paniculata)*

Scrophulariaceae (Figwort Family)

Alaska Indian Paintbrush *(Castelleja unalaschensis)*
Lousewort *(Pedicularis verticillata)*
Yellow Monkey Flower *(Mimulus guttatus)*

Lentibulariacaea (Bladderwort Family)

Butterwort *(Pinguicula vulgaris)*

Plantaginaceae (Plantain Family)

Goosetongue *(Plantago maritima)*

Caprifoliaceae (Honeysuckle Family)

Highbush Cranberry *(Viburnum edule)*
Pacific Red Elder *(Sambucus racemosa)*

Valerianaceae (Valerian Family)

Sitka Valerian *(Valeriana sitchensis)*

Campanulaceae (Bluebell Family)

Harebell, Bluebell *(Campanula rotundifolia)*

Asteraceae (Composite Family)

Beach Grounsel *(Senecio pseudoarnica)*
Coastal Fleabane *(Erigeron peregrinu)*
Douglas Aster *(Symphyotrichum subspicatum)*
Goldenrod *(Solidago multiradiata)*
Hawkweed *(Hieracium triste)*
Pussytoes *(Antennaria monocephala)*
Rattlesnake Root *(Prenanthes alata)*
Siberian Aster *(Eurybia sibirica)*
Sweet Coltsfoot *(Petasites frigidus)*
Yarrow *(Achillea millefolium)*

Bibliography

Andrew, Jon, and R. McHenry, R. Scher. *Birds of Seward, Alaska: Mile 18 Seward Highway, Resurrection Bay, and the Chiswell Islands.* (check list) Seward: Chamber of Commerce. 1997.

Bancroft, Hubert H. *History of Alaska, 1730-1885.* San Francisco: A. L. Bancroft and Company. 1886.

Bailey, Edgar P. *Distribution and Abundance of Marine Birds and Mammals along the South Side of the Kenai Peninsula, Alaska.* The Murrelet. pp 58-72. Winter. 1977.

Barry, Mary J. *A History of Mining on the Kenai Peninsula.* Anchorage: Alaska Northwest Publishing Company. 1973.

Barry, Mary J. *Seward Alaska, A History of the Gateway City. Vol I: Prehistory to 1914.* Anchorage: M. J. P. Barry. 1986.

Boggs, K., S.C. Klein, L. Flagstad, T. Boucher, J. Grunblatt, and B. Koltun. *Landcover classes, ecosystems and plant associations of Kenai Fjords National Park.* Natural Resource Technical Report NPS/KEFJ/NRTR—2008/136. National Park Service, Fort Collins, Colorado. 2008.

Casati, Chris. *Nature Surrounds Fort.* The Seward Phoenix Log. July 3, 1986 pp 8-9.

Capra, Doug. *A Handful of Pebbles: Stories from Seward History.* Seward: A Yankee-Sourdough Publication. 1995.

Chevigny, Hector. *Lord of Alaska: Baranov and the Russian Adventure.* New York: Viking Press. 1943.

Chevigny, Hector. *Russian America: The Great Alaskan Venture 1741-1867.* Portland: Binford & Mort Publishing. 1965.

Cook, Linda and Frank Norris. *A Stern and Rock-Bound Coast: Kenai Fjords National Park Historical Resource Study.* Seattle: Government Printing Office. 1998.

Connor, Cathy and Daniel O'Haire. *Roadside Geology of Alaska.* Missoula: Mountain Press Publishing Company. 1988.

Crowell, Aron L. and D. H. Mann. *Archaeology and Coastal Dynamics of Kenai Fjords National Park, Alaska.* National Park Service, Alaska Region. Research/ Resources Management Report ARRCR/CRR-98/34. Anchorage: Department of Interior, National Park Service. 1998.

De Laguna, Frederica. *The Archaeology of Cook Inlet.* 2nd edition, Anchorage: Alaska Historical Commission. 1975.

De Laguna, Frederica, *Chugach Prehistory.* Seattle: University of Washington. 1956.

Grant, U. S. *The Southeastern Coast of the Kenai Peninsula.* U. S. Geological Survey Bulletin #587. pp 209-38. Washington: General Printing Office. 1915.

Grant, U. S. and D. F. Higgins. *Preliminary Report on the Mineral Resources of the Southern Part of Kenai Peninsula, Alaska.* U. S. Geological Survey Bulletin # 442-D. pp 167-78. Washington: General Printing Office. 1910.

Grant, U. S. and D. F. Higgins. *Glaciers of Prince William Sound and Kenai Peninsula.* U.S. Geological Survey Bulletin #526. Washington: General Printing Office. 1913.

Hart, J. L. *Pacific Fishes of Canada.* Fisheries Research Board of Canada. Bulletin #180. 1973.

Hayes, Derek. *Historical Atlas of the North Pacific Ocean.* Seattle: Sasquatch Books. 2001

Hulten, Eric. *Flora of Alaska and Neighboring Territories.* Stanford. Sanford University Press. 1974.

Isleib, M. E. and B. Kessel. *Birds of the North Gulf Coast.* Biological Paper #14. Fairbanks: University of Alaska. 1973.

Johannsen, Neil and Elizabeth. *Exploring Alaska's Prince William Sound; its fiords, islands, glaciers & wildlife.* Anchorage: Alaska Travel Publications. 1975.

Johnson, John F. C. *Chugach Legends: Stories and Photographs of the Chugach Region.* Anchorage: Chugach Alaska Corporation. 1984.

Kent, Rockwell. *Wilderness: A Journal of Quiet Adventure in Alaska.* (Foreward by Doug Capra). Hanover, NH: Wesleyan UP/UP New England. 1996

Leatherwood, S., R.R. Reeves and L. Foster. *Whales and Dolphins.* San Francisco: Sierra Club Books.

Lethcoe, Jim. *An Observer's Guide to the Geology of Prince William Sound, Alaska.* Valdez: Prince William Sound Books. 1990.

Lethcoe, Jim and Nancy. *Cruising Guide to Prince William Sound, Vol I: Western Part.* Valdez: Prince William Sound Books. 1989.

Lethcoe, Jim and Nancy. *A History of Prince William Sound, Alaska.* Valdez: Prince William Sound Books. 1994.

Long, William E. *Iceberg Production in the Prince William Sound Area.* Public-data File 92-20. Fairbanks: Alaska Department of Natural Resources. 1992.

Matkin, Craig., G. Ellis., E. Saulitis., L. Barnett-Lennard., D. Matkin. *Killer Whales of Southern Alaska.* Homer: North Gulf Oceanic Society. 1999.

McNabb, R.W. and Hock, R. *Alaska tidewater glacier terminus positions, 1948–2012.* Journal of Geophysical Research: Earth Surface, 119(2), pp.153-167. 2014.

Miller, David Wm. *A Guide To Alaska's Kenai Fjords.* 2nd edition. Cordova: Wilderness Images Press. 1987.

Molina, Bruce. *Glaciers of Alaska.* Vol. 28, #2. Anchorage: Alaska Geographic. 2001.

Murphy, E. C. and A. A. Hoover. *Research study of the reactions of wildlife to boating activity along the Kenai Fjords coastline.* Anchorage: National Park Service Report. 1981.

Nagorski, S., E. Hood, G. Eckert, and S. Pyare. *Assessment of coastal water resources and watershed conditions: Kenai Fjords National Park.* Natural Resource Report NPS/NRPC/ WRD/NRR—2010/192. National Park Service, Fort Collins, Colorado. 2010.

National Park Service. *1984 Kenai Fjords National Park, Aialik Bay Field Reports.* Unpublished Reports. U.S. Park Service. Seward, Alaska. 1984.

National Park Service. *1984 Kenai Fjords National Park, Aialik Bay Field Reports.* Unpublished Reports. U.S. Park Service. Seward, Alaska. 1984.

Nelson, Kristel. *Herring Pete Sather: An Alaskan Fishing Legend.* (unpublished manuscript), Seward Library. 1994.

Orth, Donald J. *Dictionary of Alaska Place Names.* Geological Survey Professional Paper #567. Washington: Government Printing Office. 1967.

Petrof, Ivan. *Report on the Population, Industries and Resources of Alaska.* Washington: United States Treasury Department Special Agents Division. 1892.

Pfeiffenberger, Jim. *The Complete Guide to Kenai Fjords National Park, Alaska.* Anchorage: Greatland Graphics. 1995.

Porter, Robert B. *Report on the Population and Resources of Alaska at the Eleventh Census: 1890.* Washington: Government Printing Office. 1893.

Portlock, Nathaniel. *A Voyage Around the World; But more Particularly to the Northwest Coast of America.* New York: Da Capo Press. 1968.

Post, Austin. *Preliminary bathymetry of Northwestern Fjord and neoglacial changes of Northwestern Glacier, Alaska.* U. S. G. S. Open-file report: 80:414. 1979.

Post, Austin. *Preliminary bathymetry of Aialik Bay and neoglacial changes of Aialik Glacier, Alaska.* U.S. Geological Survey. Open-file report: 80:423. 1979.

Post, Austin. *Preliminary bathymetry of McCarty Fjord and neoglacial changes of McCarty Glacier, Alaska.* U.S. Geological Survey. Open-file report: 80:424. 1980.

Pratt, Verna E. *Alaskan Wildflowers.* Anchorage: Alaskarafts Publishing. 1994

Russell, Priscilla N. *English Bay and Port Graham Alutiiq Plantlore.* Anchorage: Chugach Heritage Foundation. 1991.

Sherwood, Morgan. *Cook Inlet Collection.* Anchorage: Alaska Northwest Publishing Company. 1974.

Shalkop, Antoinette (ed.) *Explorations in Alaska.* Anchorage: Cook Inlet Historical Society. 1980.

Sinclair, Jack. *Caines Head: W.W.II history at the mouth of bay.* Seward Phoenix Log, Seward Silver Salmon Derby Issue. 1986.

Solovjova, Katerina G. and Vovnyanko, Aleksandra A. (Translated by Richard Bland and Katya S. Wessels) *The Fur Rush: essays and documents on the history of Alaska at the end of the eighteenth century.* Anchorage: Phoenix Press. 2002.

Sowles, A. L., S. A. Hatch, and G. J. Lensink. *Catalog of Alaskan Seabirds Colonies.* Washington D.C: U.S. Fish and Game Service report. FWS/OBS -78/79. 1978.

Tikhmenev, P.A. *A History of the Russian-American Company.* Seattle: University of Washington Press. 1978.

Teben'kov, Mikhail D. *Atlas of the Northwest Coast of America.* (Translated and edited by Richard A. Pierce and Alton Donnelly). Seattle: University of Washington Press. 1978.

Teben'kov, Mikhail D. *Hydrographic Notes Accompanying the Atlas of the Northwest Coasts of America, the Aleutian Islands and Several Other Places in the North Pacific Ocean.* St. Petersburg. 1852.

U. S. Army Corps of Engineers. *Harbor Defenses of Seward, Alaska. Master Plan.* (drawing). War Department. National Archive, Military Site Aperture Card.

U.S. Department of Commerce, National Ocean Service and Coast and Geodetic Survey. *United States Coast Pilot #9, Pacific and Arctic Coast Alaska: Cape Spencer to Beaufort Sea.* Twelfth Edition. 1985.

U.S. Department of Commerce, NOAA. Alaska Map - Prince William Sound, *Latouche Passage to Whale Bay. #16702.*

U.S. Department of Commerce, NOAA. Alaska Map - Kenai Peninsula, *Point Elrington to Cape Resurrection. #16683.*

U.S. Department of Commerce, NOAA. Alaska Map - Kenai Peninsula, *Cape Resurrection to Two Arm Bay. #16682.*

U.S. Department of Commerce, NOAA. Alaska Map - Kenai Peninsula, *Seal Rocks to Gore Point. #16681.*

U.S. Department of Commerce, NOAA. Alaska Map - Kenai Peninsula, *Gore Point to Anchor Point. #16645.*

Wiles, Gregory C. *Holocene Glacial Fluctuations in the Southern Kenai Mountains, Alaska.* Buffalo: University of New York. 1992.

Wright, E. W. (ed). *Lewis and Dryden's Marine History of the Pacific Northwest.* Seattle: Superior Publishing Company. 1967.

Yerden-Walker, Madelyn. *The People Left Behind, Early Peoples of the Kenai Coast.* Anchorage: Alaska Natural History Association. 1994.

Map data sources

The maps provided in this book are a compilation of data made available by the U.S. Geological Survey, EROS Data Center, Sioux Falls, SD, NOAA, National Ocean Service, Office of Coast Survey, Silver Springs, MD, the National Park Service, Alaska Support Office, Anchorage, AK, Alaska Department of Fish and Game, Anchorage, AK, the Alaska Department of Natural Resources, Land Records Information Section, Anchorage AK, and the Kenai Peninsula Borough, Soldotna, AK. They also include data developed by the Alaska Department of Natural Resources in response to the *Exxon Valdez* Oil Spill that incorporates information from the U.S. Geologic Survey, U.S. Forest Service (Tongass) and the EVOS Trustee Council. These maps have been developed to help clarify the text. They are not intended for navigational purposes and the data providers, author, and publisher do not guarantee their accuracy.

Photo List:

Preface:
Culturally modified spruce tree (CMT) ii
Ogive Glacier at tidewater vi
Taz Basin on Granite Island x
Natoa Island xii
Headwall at Abra Cove xiii

Part I Introduction:
Outwash Beach near Aialik Glacier 1

Chapter 1 Touring Resurrection Bay by Road
Resurrection River Valley & Exit Glacier 4
Waterfront Lowell Point 6
Spring Creek Waterfront 7

Chapter 2 Kenai Fjords Land Ownership
Sea arch in Aialik Bay 10

Chapter 3 Key Vessel Destinations
Ogive Glacier in Northwestern Fjord 14
Salmon trolling, Bear Glacier 16
Bear Glacier Point area, Harding Gateway 19
Taz Basin, Granite Island 20
Sailing vessel in Northwestern Fjord 21
Thunder Bay Anchorage 23

Chapter 4 Kayak Destinations
Upper Northwestern Fjord 24
Sandpsit Lagoon, Fox Island 27
Aialik Glacial Basin 28
Waterfront, Nuka Island 31
Tour vessel near Holgate Glacier 32

Chapter 5 Wildlife in the Fjords
Harbor seal on ice 34
Kittiwake family 36
Steller sea lions on Chiswell Island 37
Sea otter eating lunch 39
Killer whale 42
Mountain goats in fjords 44
Black bear, Aialik Bay 46

Part II History:
PWS Woman (Courtesy of the Alaska State Library PCA 20-249) 48
Lower Northwestern Fjord 49

Chapter 6 Birth of the Fjords
Folded layers of tuff and siltstone, Fox Island.. 50
Basalt formations, Elephant Head Point 52
Upper Northwestern Fjord.. 54
Beach rye grass 55
Recolonization of an emerging glacial environment 56

Chapter 7 Sugpiaq People
PWS Man (Courtesy of the Alaska State Library PCA 20-227)................... 58
Sugpiaq stone tools 60
Culturally modified tree with 2 opposing scars, Nuka Island 61
Seldovia Natives and barabara (Courtesy of the Anchorage Museum
    of History and Art)..63

Chapter 8 Russian Fur Traders
Coal Harbor in 1860, near Port Graham (Courtesy of the Bancroft
    Library)...64
Native fleet at Port Dick (Courtesy of the Anchorage Museum History
    and Art)..67
Teben'kov chart (Detail) #5 (Courtesy of the Alaska State Library PCA
    20-202)..68
Shields drawing of Russian shipyard at Resurrection Bay
    (Courtesy of the University of Alaska, Fairbanks)...............................71

Chapter 9 Charting the Fjords and Marine Disasters
Davidson Map of Kenai outer coast, 1902 (Courtesy of the Bancroft
    Library)...72
Survey steamer McArthur (Courtesy of the NOAA Photo Library) 74
Survey launch Wildcat in Nuka Passage in 1929 (Courtesy: family
    of Rear Admiral Paul A. Smith, C&GS & NOAA Photo Library)...........75
Torrent aground at English Bay 1868   (Courtesy of the Anchorage
    Museum of History and Art..77

Part III Coastal Guide to the Kenai Fjords:
Sailboats rafted together in Thumb Cove.. 79

Chapter 10 Resurrection Bay
Seward boat harbor... 82
Offshore, Lowell Point.. 84
Army Dock at North Beach.. 87
Callisto Head shore with Bear Glacier.. 89
Bear Glacier Point 91
Pillar Point, Harding Gateway... 93
Sport fishing boats, Pony Cove.. 95
Thumb Cove State Marine Park Beach.. 97
Orca Island Cabins, North Arm of Humpy Cove 99
Lower Resurrection Peninsula shoreline... 102
Sandspit lagoon, Fox Island... 104
Eldorado Narrows shoreline 105
View from atop Marys Bay, Rugged Island 106
Army observation bunker, Barwell Island 108

Section 1 Eastward from Resurrection Bay
Vessels anchored near Bainbridge Glacier...111

Chapter 11 Day Harbor
Davidson Point, Driftwood Bay 114
Beach at the head of Driftwood Bay 115
Killer Point, Killer Bay 116
Bootleg Cove waterfront 119
Ellsworth Glacier and the east shore of Day Harbor 120
Ellsworth Glacier 122
Anchor Cove, Day Harbor 124

Chapter 12 Chugach Coast and Puget Bay
Triangle Rocks, east of Fault Point 128
Cabin at head of Whidbey Bay 129
Waterfront, Cape Fairfield 131
Looking west across Little Johnstone Bay 132
Salmon seiner working near Cape Junken 133
Kid Cove, Puget Bay 134
Goat Harbor, Puget Bay 136

Chapter 13 Port Bainbridge
Bainbridge Glacier 141
Looking southward from Puffin Cove 142
Northshore lagoon, Hogg Bay 145
Procession Rocks 147
Isthmus beach at Point Elrington 149

Section 2 Westward from Resurrection Bay
Verdant Cove, Aialik Bay 151

Chapter 14 Aialik Bay
Aialik Cape 154
Rock-bound shoreline, Cliff Bay 155
Bear Cove waterfront 157
Moraine waterfront at Aialik Glacier 160
Harbor seal, Aialik Glacier 161
Abra Falls in Abra Cove 163
Pedersen Lagoon 164
Hiker's overlook, Pedersen Glacier Lake 166
Tour vessels, Holgate Glacier 167
Sandy beach, Quicksand Cove 168
Driftwood and dead snags, McMullen Cove 170
Cobble beach, Verdant Cove 172

Chapter 15 Chiswell & Harbor Islands
Toe Point, Harbor Island 176
Slide Rock, Beehive and Matushka islands 178
Beehive Island 179

Chapter 16 Harris Bay
Western shore, Granite Island 182
Taz Basin 184
Fog invading Granite Passage 185
Granite block shoreline, Granite Passage 186
Cataract Cove 187
Rye grass, Long Beach, Harris Bay 188
Northwestern Glacier moraine 189
Rampart Rock, western Harris Bay 190

Chapter 17 Northwestern Fjord

Northwestern Glacier c. 1980 194
Northwestern Fjord moraine 196
Beachfront, Ribbonfall Cove 198
Erratic Island and Ogive Glacier 199
Southwestern Arm, Northwestern Fjord 200
Northwestern Glacier 202

Chapter 18 McCarty Peninsula

Taroka Lagoon 207
Thunder Bay 208
Chance Lagoon 210
Sea cliffs, Steep Point 211
Square Bay waterfront 212
Beachfront, Delight Creek 216

Chapter 19 Pye Island

Foggy rockbound shore, Wildcat Cove 220
Hoof Bight, Ragged Island 223
Beachcombers at Kitten Pass 225

Chapter 20 Nuka Bay

Gravel pocket beach, Surprise Bay 229
Entrance to Palisade Lagoon 230
Mudflats and eelgrass, Pilot Harbor 233
Ferrum Creek, Nuka River Valley 235

Chapter 21 Nuka Island and Upper Nuka Passage

Islet Basin, upper Nuka Passage 240
Looking across Home Cove 242
Landing beach at the entrance to Pete's Cove 245
Islets at the head of Mike's Bay 247
North shore in Berger Bay 249
Gravel landing beach, Tonsina Bay 252

Chapter 22 Port Dick and Lower Nuka Passage

Offshore reef awash on a calm day at Gore Point 256
Ranger Beach, Port Dick 258

Chapter 23 Rocky Bay to Port Chatham

Looking south down Picnic Harbor 264
Elizabeth Island, Chugach Passage 267
West-facing beach at Portlock 269
North-facing beach at Portlock 271

Appendices

Horned puffin (Fratercula corniculata) 272
Steller sea lions (Eumetopias jubatus) 272
Devil's Club (Echinopanax horridum) 273

Index

Author, Dave Miller 301

Index

A

Abbot, Nicholas 63
Abra Cove xiii, 18, 29, 153, 162-164
Abra Falls 18, 163-164
Addison Glacier 164
Addison Lake 19, 165
Adz Rock 17, 92
Agnes Cove 82, 93-94
Agnes (vessel) 75, 93
Aialik Bay xiii, 1, 10, 18-19, 38, 46,
    62, 75, 94, 151, 153-173, 175-
    176, 234
Aialik Cape 17, 83, 94-95, 153-155
Aialik Glacial Basin 18, 28-29, 153,
    158-162, 165
Aialik Glacier iv, 18, 30, 158-163
Aialik Peninsula xi, 95, 153-154,
    157
Air Defense Station 225
Alaska Coastal Current 22, 176,
    219, 250, 255
Alaska earthquake 51, 148
Alaska Hills Mining Company 233,
    235
Alaska Maritime National Wildlife
    Refuge 9-11, 35, 107, 219
Alaska Natural History Association
    xiii
Alaska Pacific Navigation
    Company 85
Alaska Peninsula 59
Alaska Road Commission 234-235
Alaska SeaLife Center 5, 11, 38, 69
Alaska Steamship Company 171
albedo effect 57
Alert Bay 171
Aleut 66
Aleutian Islands 67, 88, 170
Aligo Point 173, 181
Alma Point 107
Alutiiq 59

Anchor Cove 113, 123-124
Anchor Glacier 201
Anchor Point xiii
ANSCA 17(B) easments 9, 11, 266,
    270
Arch Rock 256
Archimandrite, Joseph 76
Ariadne Cove 228
Ariadne Island 228-229
Arkhimandritov, Illarion 73-74
Army Dock 86-88, 107
Atlas 53, 74, 227
Auk Bay 139-140

B

Babcock Creek 230-231
Babcock, Tom 230
Bainbridge Glacier 18, 111, 139-142,
    144
Bainbridge Island 130, 144-146
Bainbridge Passage 130, 139, 141,
    144
Bair, Dan 101
Bancroft Library 64, 72, 242
Baranov, Alexander 67-71, 76
Barren Islands 23, 36
Barwell Island 17, 36, 81, 102-103,
    107-109
Bear Cove 153-154, 157-158
Bear Glacier 9, 15-17, 19, 29, 81,
    89-92, 94, 105
Bear Glacier Bight 92
Bear Glacier Lake 29, 81
Bear Point 206
Bear Tips 45-47
Beards Hollow 189
Beaufort Sea xiv
Beautiful Isle 228, 231
Beauty Bay 22, 227, 233-235
Beauty Bay Mine 234-235
Beehive Island 35, 178-179
Berger Bay 30, 239, 248-250

Berger, Capt. 248
Berger Island 248
bidarka 60, 66-67
Billings, Capt. Joseph 66, 73, 227
Billings Expedition 73
Black Bay 209
Black Mountain 21, 205, 209
Black Rock Cove 144
Bligh, Capt. 256
Bligh Island 77
Bligh Reef 77
Blodgett, Perl D. 268
Blying Sound 76, 90, 94-95, 101, 103, 115-117, 119, 125, 161
Bootleg Bight 118, 120
Bootleg Cove 28, 113, 118-120
Bootleg Lagoon 28, 113, 118
Boulder Beach 148-149, 209
Bowen Anchorage 113, 123
Bowen, William H. 123
British Columbia 54
Bubnov 73
Bulldog Cove 81, 88, 92
Butts Bay 99

C

Caines, Capt. E.E. 85
Caines Head 6, 13, 26, 55, 81-89, 104
Caines Head Shoreline Trailhead 6
Caines Head State Recreation Area 6, 13, 26, 86-87
Callisto Canyon 13, 86
Callisto Head 17, 88-90
Canal Blyings 95
Cape Fairfield 76, 95, 127, 129-131
Cape Junken 18, 38, 127, 129, 132-134
Cape Mansfield 129
Cape Puget 18, 37, 59, 125, 127, 137, 140
Cape Resurrection xiii, 15, 17-18, 27-28, 36-37, 52, 66, 81, 95-96, 101-103, 107, 113-114, 149
Cape Spencer xiv
Cape Suckling 37
Carol Cove 16, 107
Cataract Cove 20, 181, 186-187
Chamberlain Point 99, 117
Chance Cove 210
Chance Lagoon 205, 210
Chat Cove 153, 155-156
Chat Island 155-156

Cheval Island 94
Cheval Narrows 94
Chicken Pass 155
Chignik Bay 77
Chiklyykhtak Island 103
Chiswell Island 11, 37, 176-179
Chiswell Islands xi, 18, 35, 37, 94, 175-179, 248
Chrome 263, 269
Chrome Bay 263, 269
Chugach Bay 264, 266-267
Chugach Coast 127-137
Chugach Islands xi, 11, 40, 263, 267-268
Chugach Mountains 127, 141
Chugach National Forest 9, 11, 13, 135
Chugach Passage 23, 220, 255, 264, 267-269
Chugachmiut 66
Claim Point 269-270
Clam Cove 269
Cliff Bay 153, 155-156
Cloudy Cape 20, 205, 207
CMT (see Culturally Modified Trees)
Coal Harbor 64, 66
Coleman Bay 18, 153, 158
Cook, Capt. James 65, 256, 268
Cook Inlet 23, 59, 62-63, 65-68, 73-74, 76, 171, 220, 244, 248, 255, 266-268, 270
Cordova 244
Cormorant Rocks 189
Crater Bay 181, 186, 195
Cup Cove 189-190

D

Davidson Family 101
Davidson, George 72, 74
Davidson Point 17, 114-115
Day Harbor 13, 15, 17, 27-28, 38, 43, 62, 88, 96, 99, 101, 103, 113-125, 127-128, 134
Day's Harbor 66, 113
Deegan, Mike 231
Delarov, Evstratii (the Greek) 65-68
Delarov Harbor 66, 68
Delight Creek 11, 214, 216
Delight Lake 215-216
Derby Cove 13, 85-86
Desire Creek 216
Desire Lake 216
Dinglestadt Glacier 217

Discovery (vessel) 67, 132, 256
Disease and Social Change 62-63
Division Island 239-241
Dodge, Alma and Jack 171
Dogfish Bay (see Koyuktolik Bay)
Dora Island 173
Dora Passage 173, 175-176
Dora (vessel) 85, 170-171, 173
Driftwood Bay 13, 17, 27, 101, 113-117

E
Eads, Bob and Mac 5
earthquake 51, 60, 85, 105, 148, 154, 194
East Arm, Nuka Bay (see McCarty Fjord)
East Chugach Island 264, 267
East Lagoon (Puget Bay) 137
Eldorado Narrows xi, 15, 27-28, 81-82, 99-100, 104-105, 113, 115
Eldorado Trail 81, 101, 113, 115
Elephant Head Arch 114
Eleventh United States Census 242
Elizabeth Island 264, 267-269
Ellsworth Glacier 28, 120-122
Ellsworth Valley 28, 113
Elrington Island 139, 147-148
Elrington Passage 139, 147-148
Emerald Cove 15, 99, 101
Endangered Species Act 160
English Bay 11, 63, 66, 76-77, 173, 271
Eocene 52
Erratic Island 196, 199
Evans, Bob 214
Excelsior Glacier 131
Exxon Valdez oil spill xii, 5, 211, 221
Exxon Valdez (vessel) 77

F
Falls Cove 233
Fault Point 123, 125, 127-128
Federal Census Bureau 236
Ferrum Creek 228, 234-235
Fire Cove 184-185, 195
Firth Cove (Resolute Cove) 123
Fish House xiii
Fort Alexander 66
Fort Buckley 107
Fort McGilvray 13, 26, 86, 88
Fourth of July area 6-7, 96

Fourth of July Creek 6-7, 26, 82, 96
Fox Farm 139, 147-148, 243-245
Fox Farm Bay 139, 147-148
Fox Farm Bay isthmus 148
Fox Island 13, 15-16, 26-27, 50-52, 81-82, 103-104
Front Point 22, 253
Frozen Rock 162
fur farm 16, 22, 268
Fur Seal Treaty 40

G
gabbro 52
Goat Harbor 18, 124, 127, 135-136
Godwin Glacier 96, 120
Gore, John 256
Gore Peninsula 22-23, 255, 257-258
Gore Peninsula isthmus 23, 257-258
Gore Point xiii, 11, 22, 37, 67, 220, 253, 255-256
Gos Point 113, 124-125
Goyne, Charles 229
Granite Cape 182, 205
Granite Island x-xi, 19-20, 181-184, 186, 189, 199, 221
Granite Passage 19, 173, 181, 184-185, 195
Grant and Higgins 53, 75, 90, 93, 97, 121, 123, 130-132, 134, 141, 156, 164, 167, 193
Grant, U. S. (see Grant and Higgins)
Grewingk-Yalik Glacial Complex 10, 241
Guard Island 106
Gulf of Alaska 17, 21-22, 25, 36-38, 43, 53, 71, 82, 90, 161, 266

H
Half-mile Beach 142
Halibut Cove 16, 106
hanging valleys 20, 55
Harbor Island xii, 176-177
Harbor Islands 18, 154, 156, 175-177
Harding Gateway xi, 15, 17, 19, 29, 38, 81, 89-90, 93-94, 103
Harding Icefield 4-5, 9, 18, 29, 52-53, 57, 83, 90, 92, 154, 158, 163, 194, 200
Harding Icefield Trail 5
Harding, Pres. Warren G. 89-90
Hardover Point 241
Harrington, Otis 217, 233
Harrington Point 217, 228

Harris Bay 10, 20, 160, 181-191, 193-195, 197, 205
Harris Peninsula 19, 173, 181, 184, 186-187
Harris Point 183, 189-190
Hat Island 99, 103
Hazelwood, Capt. Joseph 77
Head of Day Harbor 28, 121-123
Henderson (vessel) 89-90
Herman Leirer Road 4
Herring Pete (see Sather, Pete)
Higgins, D. F. (see Grant and Higgins)
Hinchinbrook Entrance 68, 76
Hive Island 106
Hogg Bay 18, 139-140, 145-146
Hogg, George 247
Hogg Point 145
Holgate Arm 10, 18, 29, 153, 157, 167-168
Holgate Glacier 18, 32, 157, 167-168
Holgate Head 167-168
Holgate, Thomas Franklin 167
Holocene Retreat 53
Home Cove 30, 239, 242-243, 246
Homer 208, 228, 241, 267
Hoof Bight 219, 222-223
Hoof Point 222-223
Horsehead Bay 13, 128
Horsehead Lagoon 128
Horsehead Point 128
Humpback Bay 98
Humphreys, Henry 67
Humpy Cove 54, 82, 98-99, 103, 117

I

Icy Bay 143-144
Islet Basin 30, 239-240
Isthmus Beach 22, 148, 257
Izmailov, Capt. Grigor'evich 66, 70, 73

J

Jakolof Bay 260, 266
James Lagoon 22, 215
Japanese Current 91
Johnstone Bay 13, 127, 131-133
Johnstone, Lt. James 74, 132
Johnston, Fred 231

K

Kachemak Bay State Park 9, 11, 22, 30, 239, 243
Kachemak Bay State Wilderness Park 11, 260, 265
Kalinin, Danilo 73
Kashevarov, Ivan 73
katabatic winds 25, 57, 92, 94
Kayaker Cove 27, 81-82, 100, 104
Kelp Point 269
Kenai Fjords National Park xi, xiii, 3-4, 9-11, 13, 15-16, 18, 29-30, 46, 90, 92, 158, 166, 227, 231
Kenai Mountains 9, 51, 183, 241
Kenai Peninsula x-xii, xiv-xvi, 9-11, 18-23, 32-44, 51-54, 59-75, 82, 91, 144, 153-155, 175-179, 210-211, 217-227, 236, 242-244, 255-256, 263-270
Kennedy Entrance 267
Kent, Rockwell 16, 106
Kid Cove 18, 134-135
Killer Bay 27, 116
killer whales 19, 36, 42-43, 81, 127, 139, 155, 161, 175, 184, 205, 227, 264
King George (vessel) 256
Kitten Beach 225
Kitten Pass 219, 224-225
Kitten Pass Bight 219
Kodiak 51, 59, 65-70, 76, 241
Kodiak Island 51, 59, 65-70, 76
Kodiak Mission 76
Koniag 66
Koyuktolik Bay 11, 271
Kvasnikoff Falls 30, 233

L

Latouche Passage xiii, 149
Likes Creek 26, 97-98
Likes, S.E. 97
Little Ice Age 53, 74-75, 141, 158, 167, 188, 193, 201, 213, 217
Little Whidbey Bight 130
Lone Rock 179
Lonetree Point 147
Long Beach 168, 182, 187-188, 193, 195, 197
Long Island 251-252
Loussac Library xiv
Lowell, Alfred 85
Lowell, Billy 103
Lowell Island 103
Lowell, Mary 83

Lowell Point 5-6, 13, 25-26, 81-86, 88
Lowell Point Recreation Site 5-6, 13, 83, 86
Lowell Point Road 5-6, 84

M

Mansfield, Lt. Cmdr Henry Buckingham 129
Marine Mammal Protection Act 38, 160
marine mammals 5, 36-44, 59, 77, 149, 161, 179, 184, 255, 264, 278
Maritime Disasters 76-77, 131
Mary's Bay 16, 81-82, 106-107
Mary's Rock 101
Matushka Bight 35, 175, 178-179
Matushka Island 35, 175-176, 178
McArthur Cove 212, 221-222
McArthur Pass 21, 177, 183, 205, 209-211, 217, 220-221, 237
McArthur (vessel) 74, 211
McCarty Fjord 10, 22, 29, 38, 40, 75, 160, 205-247
McCarty Glacier 22, 213-217
McCarty Lagoon 213-216
McCarty Peninsula 221
McMullen, Capt. 170
McMullen Cove 10, 153, 170-171
McMullen Spit 170-171
Middleton Island 53
Midnight Cove 22, 205, 213
Mike's Bay 30, 239, 247
Miller, Anne xvii, 301
Miller, David Wm 301
Miller's Landing 5-6, 83-84, 86, 88
mining 22, 30, 75, 95, 145, 217, 227-228, 230-231, 233-236, 246, 248, 270
Minneapolis Beach 88
Monolith Cove 193, 198
Monolith Point 197-198
Montague Island 68-71, 76, 95
Moonlight Bay 205, 213, 216
Moore, Capt. Hugh 68-69
moraine bar 18-19, 22, 29, 158, 163, 182, 187-189, 193-197, 213, 216-217
Morning Cove 211, 221
Murphy's Bight 124-125

N

Nantiinaq 270-271
Nanwalek 11, 63, 66, 173, 236, 270-271

Nash Road 6-7
National Marine Fisheries Service 21, 37-38, 223
Natoa Island xii, 177
No Name Island 95
North Beach 13, 26, 83, 86-88, 92, 104, 190
North Gulf Coast 19, 62, 66-67, 71, 76-77, 82, 131, 147, 193
North Twin Bay 139, 148
Northeast Trading Company 65, 67, 69
Northeastern Bight 193, 201-202
Northeastern Glacier 201
Northern Eagle (vessel) 69, 76
Northwest Bight 120
Northwest Passage 182, 188-189, 193-196
Northwestern Fjord xi,10, 14, 19-21, 29, 38, 40, 49, 54-55, 75, 182, 187-188, 193-203
Northwestern Glacier 24, 54, 182, 188-189, 193-194, 202-203, 248
Northwestern Lagoon 189, 193, 196-197
Northwestern University 167
Nuchek 66, 68
Nuka Bay 9-10, 21-22, 30, 38, 40, 62, 66, 210, 212, 215, 217, 219-220, 227-237, 240, 245-246, 248, 251
Nuka Bay Comet (vessel) 215
Nuka Bay Mining Company 234
Nuka Island 11, 22, 30, 38, 62, 177, 215, 239, 241, 243-251
Nuka Passage 11, 13, 22, 30, 62, 75, 210, 237, 239-242, 245, 248, 251-253
Nuka Point 239, 250
Nuka River 22, 30, 228, 233-235
Nuka River delta 30, 234
Nuka Rock 250
Nukalaska Mine 236

O

Ogive Glacier vi, 14, 199, 201
Okhotsk 69-70, 76
Oleg (vessel) 70
Ophiolite 51-52
Orel (see Northern Eagle)
Otter Cove 29, 188, 193, 196-197
Outer Cove 123, 251
Outer Island 21, 37, 219, 223-225

P

Paguna Arm 11, 191, 206-207
Paguna Glacier 206
Palisade Lagoon 227, 230-231
Palisade Peak 229
Paradise Cove 153, 156
Passage Canal 66
Patsy Point 107
Patterson (vessel) 129
Pedersen Bight 162, 166
Pedersen Glacier 19, 29, 33, 158, 161, 164-166
Pedersen Glacier Lake 19, 29, 33, 161, 164
Pedersen Lagoon 11, 18-19, 29, 33, 153, 158, 164-166
Pedersen Spit 164-166
Pegas (vessel) 70
Perl Island 264, 267-268
Pete's Cove 239, 243-247
Pete's Pass 177
Petrof Bight 22, 241-242
Petrof Glacier 241
Petrof, Ivan 63, 236, 241-242
Petrof Lake 13, 241-242
Petrof Point 22, 241
Petrof Valley 241
PGC land 11, 189-190, 228, 260
Phoenix (vessel) 68-71, 76
Picnic Harbor 23, 260-261, 263-266
Pillar Point 17, 92-93
Pillow basalt (lava) 15, 52, 81, 100-101, 115, 149
Pillow Rock 101, 115
Pilot Harbor 227, 232-233
Pilot Rock 90, 94, 103, 155
Pinnacle Rock, Cape Fairfield 76-77, 131
Pinnacle Rock, Nuka Island 250
Pocket Bight 232
Point Adam 35
Point Barwell 66, 102
Point Elrington xiii, 37, 139, 148-149
Point Pyke 139, 146
Point Waters 144
Polished Passage 201-202
Pony Cove 82, 94-95
Pony Point 17, 94-95
Porcupine Cove 81, 92-93
Porcupine Glacier 13, 98

Port Andrews 66
Port Bainbridge xiii, 9, 13, 18, 40, 111, 127, 130, 137, 139-149
Port Chatham, 9, 11, 23, 62, 263, 266, 269-271
Port Dick 11, 23, 40, 62, 67, 255-261, 263
Port Dick Creek 260
Port Etches 66, 68-69
Port Graham Corporation (PGC) 11, 162, 165-166, 188-190, 197, 206, 208-209, 216, 228, 231-232, 236-237, 260, 265, 267
Port Townsend 170
Porter, Robert 241
Portlock 23, 66, 73, 102, 113, 179, 220, 256, 263-264, 269-271
Portlock, Capt. Nathaniel 66, 73, 102, 113, 179, 220, 256, 264, 270
Post, Austin 75, 199
Pribilof Islands 65
Prince of Wales Passage 147
Prince William Sound xiv, 18, 44, 48, 51, 53, 58-59, 62, 65-68, 70, 73-77, 96, 123-124, 127, 130, 132, 139-140, 143-144, 147, 149, 242
Procession Rocks 38, 139, 146-147
Prospect Glacier 97
Public campsite easements 216
Public trail easements 11, 227
Public Use Cabins (PUC) 10, 13, 86, 98, 163
Puffin Cove 18, 139-140, 142-144
Puget Bay 11, 13, 18, 127, 134-137
Puget Glacier 18, 134
Puget, Lt. Peter 137
Pye Islands 21, 37, 66, 183, 210-211, 219-225, 237
Pye Reef 224

Q

Qikutulig Bay 261
Quartz Bay 227-228, 231-232
Quicksand Cove 168-169

R

Rabbit Cove 224
Rabbit Island 223-224
Ragged Island 21, 211, 219-221, 223
Rampart Beach 181, 188-189, 197
Rampart Rock 188-190
Ranger Beach 255, 257-258
Rasmuson Library xiv
Raven's Knob 105

Redstone Beach 193, 203
Redstone Glacier 203
Reef Mine 269
Renard Island (see Fox Island)
Repose Cove 205, 213
Resolute Cove (See Firth Cove)
Resolution (vessel) 256
Resurrection Bay 3, 6-7, 9, 11 13,
    15-17, 25-26, 29, 35, 40, 43,
    50-51, 53-54, 57, 66, 68-71, 73,
    76, 79, 81-109, 113-117, 120, 123,
    171, 177
Resurrection Bay Islands 16,
    81-83, 90, 102-107
Resurrection Bay shipyard 70
Resurrection River 4-6
Resurrection River Valley 4-5
Ribbonfall Cove 193, 196-198
Ripple Cove 185-186
Roaring Cove 221-222
Rocky Bay 23, 62, 261, 263-264
Rocky Point 86, 88-89
Rocky River 23, 260, 264-266
Rocky River trail 23, 260, 264-266
Rolfh III (vessel) 246
Rorqual whales 41
Round Island 103
Rugged Island 16, 37, 87-88, 90,
    106-107
Russian-American Company
    64-65, 71
Russian Ekaterinburg Field
    Battalion 69
Russian fur traders xiii, 60, 65-66,
    70, 73
Russian Orthodox Church 70
Russian Shipyard (Resurrection
    Bay) 71

S

Safety Cove 13, 27-28, 99, 113,
    116-117
Saint Paul Harbor 69
Sandspit bight 105
Sandspit lagoon 104
Sandspit Point 13, 15-16, 26-27, 81,
    99-101, 103-105
Sandy Bay 190-191
San Francisco Bay 162
Sargent Icefield 121, 127, 140-141
Sarychev, Lt. Gavrila 66, 73, 227
Sather, Josephine 22, 215, 243, 247
Sather, Pete 177, 237, 243

Sea Lion Rocks 15, 101
Seal Rocks xiii, 37, 179, 195
Seldovia 59, 63, 260, 266
Seldovia Road 260, 266
Seldovia-Rocky River Road 260
Severovostochnyi Orel (see *Northern
    Eagle*)
Seward xiii-xvi, 3-7, 11, 13, 18, 20-22,
    26, 29, 35-36, 40, 77, 81-83, 85-86,
    90, 94, 96-98, 101-104,106, 113, 118,
    123, 127, 164, 173, 177, 215, 219, 231,
    233-234,244, 246, 248
Seward boat harbor 3, 40, 82, 102
Seward Chamber of Commerce 3
Seward Highway 3-6
Sheep Creek 217
Shelikhov, Grigorii 65
Shelter Cove 22, 227, 233, 235-236
Shields, James 69-71, 73, 76
Shuyak Island 76
Siberia 53, 67, 70, 76
Silver Salmon Derby 96, 246
Simeon (vessel) 70
Sitka 43-44, 56-57, 70-71, 76, 87, 98, 212
Slate Island 46, 162
Slava Rossiy (vessel) 66
Slide Rock 178
smallpox 62
Smokehouse Mike 247
Sonny Fox Mine 230
South Bay 239, 250
South Beach 26, 81, 86, 88-89, 92
South Beach Bight 88-89
South Twin Bay 148
Southwestern Arm 193, 199-201
Southwestern Glacier 193, 200-201
Spire Cove 92-93
Split Glacier 233
Spoon Glacier 97
Spring Creek 7, 26, 81, 96
Spring Creek Campground 7, 96
Spring Creek Maximum Security
    Prison 7, 96
Spruce Creek 83-84
Squab Island 30, 162
Square Bay 205, 211-212
State Marine Parks (SMP) 13, 16-17,
    26-27, 81
State of Alaska xiv, 9, 11, 13, 105, 121,
    135, 241, 268
Steep Point 205, 211
Storm Mountain 228, 234
Striation Island 14, 201-202

Sugar Loaf Island 106
Sugpiaq xiii, 59-62, 66, 103, 154, 157, 173, 177, 179, 206-207, 211, 227, 236, 249, 252, 270
Sunday Harbor 255, 258-259
Sunlight Glacier 197
Sunny Cove 13, 16, 81-82, 105
Surok Point 20, 191, 205-207
Surprise Bay 227, 229-231
Surveyor (vessel) 123
Swanson Bay 146
Swanson Point 145-146

T

Takoma Cove 23, 255, 257-259
Talin, Capt. 76
Talus Bay 117-118
Talus Point 117
Taroka Arm 207
Taroka Lagoon 207
Taylor Bay 23, 255, 259
Taz Basin x,19-20, 181, 183-184, 190
Teben'kov, M. D. 53, 68, 74-75, 91
Tertiary Period 181
Three Hole Bay 156, 177
Three Hole Point 153, 156
Three Saints Bay 66-67
Thumb Cove 13, 15, 17, 26, 52, 55, 79, 81-82, 96-98, 104
Thunder Bay xi, 21, 23, 205, 208
tidewater glaciers xi-xii, 20, 29-30, 54-55, 60, 74-75, 154, 201
Tiger Glacier 143
Tlingit Indians 69
Toe Point 176-177
Tonsina Bay 11, 22, 239, 251-253
Tonsina Creek 85
Tonsina Point 6, 26, 81, 83-86
Tooth Cove 157-158
Topeka Point 99, 117
Toqakvik 269
Torrent (vessel) 76-77
Touglaalek Bay 261
Tourist Information 3
Triangle Rocks 128
Tuerck, Ed 244
Twin Cove 260
Twin Falls Grotto 187
Twin Islands 173
Twin Rocks 88
Two Arm Bay xiii,10, 20, 205-207

U

Unimak Pass 171
Union Army 241
United States Geological Survey 75, 90, 101, 199
University of Alaska xiv, 71, 76, 243, 247
upper Nuka Passage 11, 239-240

V

Valdez xii, 5, 77, 173, 211, 221
Valdez Arm 77
Vancouver, Capt. George 67, 73-74, 130, 132, 137, 171, 179, 270
Vancouver Island 171
Vasil'evich, Kanilik 73
Verdant Cove 151, 153, 171-173, 175, 177
Verdant Island 171
Vietti, Domonic 145
Visitor Center (Kenai Fjords National Park) xiii, 3

W

Waterfall Bight 15, 101
West Arm, Nuka Bay 217, 227-228, 237
West Arm, Port Dick 255, 260, 266
Westdahl Cove 239, 249-250
Whale Bay xiii, 143
Whidbey Bay 13, 127, 129-130
Whidbey, Lt. Joseph 74, 130, 132, 137
Wildcat Cove 220, 222
Wildcat Pass 224, 246
Wildcat (vessel) 75
Wilderness: A Quiet Adventure in Alaska 106
Windy Bay 260, 265-266
Windy Bay Port Chatham Portage, 266
Wisconsin 53
Woelker's Bight 122
Woody Cape 97
Woody Island 70
World War I 214
World War II 13, 16, 86, 88, 99, 107, 117, 225, 228, 230, 235

Y

Yakutat Bay 66
Yalik Bay 22, 62-63, 66, 227, 236-237, 246
Yalik Glacier 22, 237, 241
Yalik Point 9, 237
Yalik Valley 241
Yukon (vessel) 76, 131

The author, Dave Miller homesteaded in Day Harbor on the Kenai Peninsula outer coast after serving in the Vietnam War. He has extensively explored the Kenai Peninsula seacoast by small boat and kayak. The coastal guide material and travel tips in this book were compiled from his journals, travel logs, commercial fishing records, and recollections from more than 45 years of exploring, beachcombing, and photographing wild and remote places in the Kenai Fjords, Cook Inlet, Prince William Sound and Southeast Alaska. His articles and photographs have appeared in *Alaska Magazine*, *Alaska Geographic*, *Wilderness*, and other publications.

Dave lives with his wife Anne, a marine biologist in Seward, Alaska. They also fish commercially for halibut and spend time at their homestead in Day Harbor.

Dave and Anne